BEHIND THE SCENES
IN WARRING GERMANY

LECTOR HOUSE PUBLIC DOMAIN WORKS

This book is a result of an effort made by Lector House towards making a contribution to the preservation and repair of original classic literature. The original text is in the public domain in the United States of America, and possibly other countries depending upon their specific copyright laws.

In an attempt to preserve, improve and recreate the original content, certain conventional norms with regard to typographical mistakes, hyphenations, punctuations and/or other related subject matters, have been corrected upon our consideration. However, few such imperfections might not have been rectified as they were inherited and preserved from the original content to maintain the authenticity and construct, relevant to the work. The work might contain a few prior copyright references as well as page references which have been retained, wherever considered relevant to the part of the construct. We believe that this work holds historical, cultural and/or intellectual importance in the literary works community, therefore despite the oddities, we accounted the work for print as a part of our continuing effort towards preservation of literary work and our contribution towards the development of the society as a whole, driven by our beliefs.

We are grateful to our readers for putting their faith in us and accepting our imperfections with regard to preservation of the historical content. We shall strive hard to meet up to the expectations to improve further to provide an enriching reading experience.

Though, we conduct extensive research in ascertaining the status of copyright before redeveloping a version of the content, in rare cases, a classic work might be incorrectly marked as not-in-copyright. In such cases, if you are the copyright holder, then kindly contact us or write to us, and we shall get back to you with an immediate course of action.

HAPPY READING!

BEHIND THE SCENES IN WARRING GERMANY

EDWARD LYELL FOX

ISBN: 978-93-90314-16-4

Published: 1915

© 2020
LECTOR HOUSE LLP

LECTOR HOUSE LLP
E-MAIL: lectorpublishing@gmail.com

CAPT. TZSCHIRNER AND THE AUTHOR
Captain Tzschirner of Hindenburg's staff and Edward Lyell Fox in Eydtkuhnen after the battle.

BEHIND THE SCENES IN WARRING GERMANY

BY

EDWARD LYELL FOX

Special Correspondent with the Kaiser's Armies
and in Berlin

1915

**TO
E. W. F.**

CONTENTS

Chapter	Page
I. THE THRESHOLD OF WAR	1
II. "THE BELOVED KING"	14
III. TO THE WEST FRONT	21
IV. ON THE BACK OF THE BIRD OF WAR	29
V. BEHIND THE BATTLELINE	38
VI. A NIGHT BEFORE YPRES	52
VII. IN THE TRENCHES	64
VIII. CAPTURED BELGIUM AND ITS GOVERNOR GENERAL	80
IX. PRISONERS OF WAR	85
X. ON THE HEELS OF THE RUSSIAN RETREAT	98
XI. THE BATTLE OF AUGUSTOWO WALD	113
XII. THE WAR ON THE RUSSIAN FRONTIER	129
XIII. THE HERO OF ALL GERMANY	139
XIV. WITH THE AMERICAN RED CROSS ON THE RUSSIAN FRONTIER	147
XV. THE SECRET BOOKS OF ENGLAND'S GENERAL STAFF	158
XVI. THE FUTURE—PEACE OR WAR	168

LIST OF ILLUSTRATIONS

Page

I. Capt. Tzschirner And The Author iv
II. Notifications From The German Foreign Office 16
III. Court Filled With Drilling Soldiers 42
IV. Ober-lieutenant Herrmann 42
V. With French Prisoners At Zossen. 92
VI. Burying Russians on the East Prussian frontier. 99
VII. Reinforcements following our motor into Russia. 100
VIII. Photographs of alleged British staff books 159
IX. Aviator's guide book 162
X. Aviator's key map 165

BEHIND THE SCENES IN WARRING GERMANY

CHAPTER I

THE THRESHOLD OF WAR

In the lingering twilight, the Baltic's choppy swells turned dark and over the bow I saw a vague gray strip of land—Germany! I was at the gateway of war.

For two hours the railway ferry had plowed between the mines that strew the way to Denmark with potential death, and as slowly the houses of Warnemunde appeared in shadow against the darkening day, some one touched my arm.

"Safe now."

He was the courier. He had traveled with me from New York to Copenhagen, a bland, reserved young man, with a caution beyond his years. I had come to know he was making the trip as a German courier, and he was an American with no Teutonic blood in his veins! Knowing the ropes, he had suggested that he see me through to Berlin.

"It's good we came over the Baltic," he remarked, "instead of making that long trip through Jutland. We save eight hours."

"Yes," I agreed, "nothing like slipping in the back door."

And being new to it then, and being very conscious of certain letters I carried, and of the power implied in the documents which I knew he carried, I wondered what the frontier guard would do. During the two hours we ferried from the Danish shore the passengers talked in a troubled way of the military search given every one at Warnemunde and I smiled to myself in a reassuring way. Yes, they would be searched, poor devils!... But the courier and I? I wondered if the German Lieutenant at Warnemunde would ask us to take coffee with him. I even took out my watch. No, it could hardly be done, for by the time the soldiers had finished searching all these passengers the train would be leaving. Too bad! Coffee and a chat with some other lieutenant, then.

"Yes," the courier was saying as the ferry docked and we caught, under the glint of the sentries' rifles, a glimpse of the *Landwehr* red and blue, "it will be so easy here—just a formality, whereas if we had taken the other route it no doubt would have been harder. You see," he explained, "when a train crosses the Kiel canal a soldier is posted in every compartment, the window shades are pulled down and the passengers are warned not to look out on penalty of instant death. Of course that is necessary for military reasons. Naturally the whole inspection at that frontier is more severe because of the Kiel canal."

By this time the big boat had been made fast to a long railroad pier and as we crossed the gang plank we made out in the bluish haze of an arc lamp, a line of soldiers who seemed to be herding the passengers into what appeared to be a long wooden shed newly built. Crowds are the same the world over, so no one held back, all pushing, luggage and passports in hand, into the frame structure built, I realized, for purposes of military inspection.

Sluggishly the mass moved forward. Presently I saw it divide halfway down the room, to pause before two openings at which six soldiers waited, like ticket takers in a circus. I was near enough now to observe the lantern light dimly shining upon two crude desk tops, slanting down from the wall which gave entrance through a doorway to a larger room beyond; and everywhere gleamed the glint of gun barrels, the red and blue or gray of military hats, while an increasing flow of German, punctuated with *"Donnerwetter!"* and *"Das ist genug,"* was heard above the shuffle of feet and the thumping of trunks and bags on the counters in the room beyond. I wondered what two men in civilian clothes were doing among the soldiers; I saw them dart about, notebooks in hand. Later I learned more of these men who seemed to have it in their power to make the passengers they challenged either comfortable or uncomfortable.

And then it was my turn. Having seen the passenger in front throw both hands over his head, unconsciously inviting the kind of search given a criminal, I decided such submissiveness a blunder. As I expected, the soldier was a perfectly sane human being who did not begin punching a revolver against me—which certain printed words I had read in New York implied was the usual prelude to a German searching party—rather this soldier most courteously asked to see my wallet. I gave it to him. I would have given him anything. Our cooperation was perfect. There was no need for me to bring my exhaustive knowledge of the German language into play. Talking fluently with my hands, now and then uttering *"danke,"* I tried to assist his search, meanwhile hopelessly looking about for the courier. I was depending not only upon his fluent German but also upon his superior knowledge of the situation to help me to pass serenely through this ordeal. Alas, the crowd hid him.

Suddenly my soldier grunted something. Until now we had been getting along splendidly and I could not conceal my surprise when he took from my wallet a handful of letters and stared at them in bewilderment. The more he stared the more his regard for me seemed to vanish. Although he could not understand English he could recognize a proper name, for the letters bore the addresses of decidedly influential men in Germany. They challenged his suspicion. Thoroughly puzzled he opened the letters and tried to read them. When he compared my passport with a letter I saw his face light up. I realized that he had recognized my name in the contents. Whereupon, greatly relieved, assured now that everything was all right, I held out my hand for both letters and wallet. Not yet. A rumble of words and the soldier called one of those busy civilians with the notebooks.

This person spoke a little English. The letters interested him. Where had I found them?... My spine began to feel cold. I replied that they had been given me in New York and remembering that I had the courier to rely on, I suggested that they have a word with him. It was then that I heard an excited deluge of words and, glancing over my shoulder, I observed that the courier was thoroughly flanked and surrounded by five *Landwehr* who apparently were much in earnest about something. Concluding that some cog had slipped I racked my wits to make the best of what was rapidly becoming a difficult situation.

The soldier having turned me over to the civilian I noticed several suspicious glances in my direction, and blessed the luck that had impelled me to go to the American Legation and the German Consulate in Copenhagen for visés. That the civilian who was taking such an interest in me belonged to the secret service, I was certain. I appealed to his sense of discretion.

"Your passport seems all right," he thoughtfully observed, and opened a little book. "Where are you going?"

I told him to Hamburg but could not tell him where I would stay, for the excellent reason that not the name of a single Hamburg hotel was known to me.

"Only for a few days, though," I said, adding hopefully; "after that I go to Berlin to Hotel Adlon."

As fast as his pencil could move he wrote the address in his book.

"These letters," he said reluctantly, tapping them on his hand, "I must take now. If everything is all right, they will be sent to you in Berlin."

"But it is important that I have them," I protested, "they are my introductions. You cannot tell me how long I may have to wait for them? You can see from them that I am a responsible person known to your people."

"I know," he replied, "but they are written in English, and to bring letters written in English into Germany is forbidden. I am sorry."

He was thus politely relieving me of all my credentials when I happened to think that in my inner waistcoat pocket lay a letter I had yet to show them—a communication so important to me that I had kept it separate from the others. Moreover I remembered it was sealed and that properly used it might save the day. It was worth a trial.

Realizing that the thing had to be staged I impressively drew the police spy aside and employing the familiar "stage business" of side glances and exaggerated caution I slowly took the note—it was a mere letter of introduction to the Foreign Office—from my waistcoat. If the soldier's eyes had opened wide at the other addresses, the police agent's now fairly bulged. Handing him the envelope I pointed to what was typed in the upper left hand corner—*Kaiserliche Deutsche Botschaft, Washington, D. C.*—and simply said *"Verstehen sie?"*

He *verstehened*. Being an underling he understood so well that after a few moments he returned all the letters he had appropriated and instantly changing his manner, he facilitated the rest of the inspection. After my baggage was examined by more soldiers (and those soldiers did their duty, even going through the pockets of clothes in my trunks) I was told I might go.

"*Gute reise*," the police agent called—"Good journey."

Although treated with all courtesy I was afraid somebody might change his mind, so hurrying out of the last room of the long wooden shed I proceeded down the platform to the train at a pace that must have shown signs of breaking into a run. There in my compartment the thoughts that came to me were in this order:

There must be reason for such a rigid inspection; no doubt spies must have been caught recently trying to enter Germany at Warnemunde.

If I hadn't lost the courier in the crowd there would have been plain sailing.

The minutes passed. It was nearly time for the train to start. Where was the courier? Presently, rather pale, nervous in speech, but as reserved and cool as ever he limply entered the compartment and threw himself on the cushions.

"They took everything," he announced. "All they left me was a pair of pajamas."

"What! You mean they have your papers?"

"All of them," he smiled. "Likewise a trunk full of letters and a valise. Oh, well, they'll send them on. They took my address. Gad, they stripped me through!"

I began laughing. The courier could see no mirth in the situation.

"You," I gasped, "you, who by all rights should have paraded through, from you they take everything while they let me pass."

"Do you mean to say," he exclaimed, "that they didn't take your letters."

"Not one," I grinned.

"Well, I'll be damned!" he said.

Locked in the compartment we nervously watched the door, half expecting that the police spy would come back for us. We could not have been delayed more than a few minutes, but it seemed hours, before, with German regard for comfort, the train glided out of the shed. It must have been trying on my companion's good humor, but the absurdity of stripping a courier of everything he carried, was irresistible. Perhaps it was our continued laughter that brought the knock on the door.

Pushing aside the curtains we saw outside—for it was one of the new German wagons with a passageway running the entire length of one side of the car—a tall, broad-shouldered, lean man with features and expression both typical and unmistakable.

"An Englishman!"

We saw him smile and shake his head. I hesitatingly let fall the curtain and looked at the courier.

"Let him in," he said. "He's got the brand of an English university boy all over him. We'll have a chat with him. You don't mind, do you?"

THE THRESHOLD OF WAR

"Mind!" In my eagerness I banged back the compartment doors with a crash that brought down the conductor. I saw my companion hastily corrupt that official whose murmured "*Bitteschon*" implied an un-Teutonic disregard for the fact that he had done something *verboten* by admitting a second class passenger into a first class coupé; and the stranger entered.

We were gazing upon a strikingly handsome fair-haired man not yet thirty. His eyes twinkled when he said that he supposed we were Americans. His manner and intonation made me stare at him.

"And you?" we finally asked.

"I'm going first to Berlin, then to Petrograd," he said, perhaps avoiding our question. "Business trip."

We chatted on, the obvious thought obsessing me. Of course the man was an English spy. But how absurd! If his face did not give him away to any one who knew—and my word for it, those police spies do know!—he would be betrayed by his mannerisms. His accent would instantly cry out the English in him. Of what could Downing Street be thinking? It was sending this man to certain death. One began to feel sorry for him.

Feeling the intimacy brought by the common experience at Warnemunde, I presently said:

"You certainly have your nerve with you, traveling in Germany with *your* accent."

"Why?" he laughed. "A neutral is safe."

Expecting he would follow this up by saying he was an American I looked inquiring and when he sought to turn the subject I asked:

"Neutral? What country?"

"Denmark," he smiled.

"But your accent?" I persisted.

"I do talk a bit English, do I not? I had quite a go at it, though; lived in London a few years, you know."

Nerve? I marveled at it. Stark foolhardy courage, or did a secret commission from Downing Street make this the merest commonplace of duty? Charming company, he hurried along the time with well told anecdotes of the Russian capital and Paris, in both of which places he said he had been since the war began. As we drew near Lübeck, where a thirty-five minute stop was allowed for dinner in the station, and the stranger showed no signs of going back to his own compartment, I could see that the courier was becoming annoyed. Relapsing into silence he only broke it to reply to the "Dane" in monosyllables; finally, to my surprise, the courier became downright rude. As the stranger, from the start, had been extremely courteous, this rudeness surprised me, more so, as it seemed deliberate. Bludgeoned by obvious hints the stranger excused himself, and as soon as he was gone my companion leaned towards me.

"You were surprised at my rudeness," he said, and then in an undertone; "it was deliberate."

"I saw that. But why?"

"Because," he explained, "seeing we are Americans that fellow wanted to travel with us all the way through. He must have known that American company is the best to be seen in over here these days. He might have made trouble for us."

"Then you also think he's English?"

"Think! Why they must have let him through at Warnemunde for a reason. He has a Danish passport right enough. I saw it in the inspection room. But I'll bet you anything there's a police spy in this train, undoubtedly in the same compartment with him."

One felt uncomfortable. One thought that those police spies must dislike one even more now.

"That means we may be suspected as being confederates," I gloomily suggested.

Whether he was getting back for my having guyed him about losing his papers I do not know, but the courier said we probably were suspected. Whereupon the book I tried to read became a senseless jumble of words and our compartment door became vastly more interesting. When would it open to admit the police spy?... Confound the luck! Everything breaking wrong.

But at Lübeck nothing happened—nothing to us. A train load of wounded had just come in and our hearts jumped at the sight of the men in the gray-green coats of the firing line, slowly climbing the long iron steps from the train platforms. Hurrying, we saw them go clumping down a long airy waiting room and as they approached the street their hobbling steps suddenly quickened to the sharper staccato of the canes upon which they leaned. Hurrying too, we saw there a vague mass of pallid faces in a dense crowd; some one waved a flag;—it stuck up conspicuously above that throng;—some one darted forth;—"*Vater!*"—"*Liebes Mütterchen!*"

Past the burly Landsturm, who was trying his utmost to frown his jolly face into threatening lines that would keep back the crowd, a woman was scurrying. One of the big gray-green wounded men caught her in his arm—the other arm hung in a black sling—and she clung to him as though some one might take him away, and because she was a woman, she wept in her moment of happiness. Her *Mann* had come home....

Forgetting the dinner we were to have eaten in the Lübeck station, we finally heeded a trainman's warning and turned back to our car. There remained etched in my mind the line of pallid, apprehensive faces, the tiny waving flags, the little woman and the big man. It was my first sight of war.

From Lübeck to Hamburg the ride was uneventful. The hour was not late and beyond remarking that the towns through which we passed were not as brilliantly lighted as usual, the courier could from the car window observe no difference between the Germany of peace and of war. Here and there we noticed bridges and trestles patroled by *Landwehr* and outside our compartment we read the handbill requesting every passenger to aid the government in preventing spies throwing explosives from the car windows. From the conductor we learned that there had been such attempts to delay the passage of troop trains. Whereupon we congratulated ourselves upon buying the conductor, as we had the compartment to ourselves. One thought of what would have happened had there been an excitable German in with us and while the train was crossing a bridge, we had innocently opened a window for air!

It was almost ten when the close, clustered lights of Hamburg closed in against the trackside and we caught our first glimpse of the swarming *Bahnhof*. Soldiers everywhere. The blue of the Reservists, the gray-green of the Regulars—a shifting tide of color swept the length of the long platforms, rising against the black slopes of countless staircases, overrunning the vast halls above, increasing, as car after car emptied its load. And then, as at Lübeck, we saw white bandages coming down under cloth-covered helmets and caps, or arms slung in black slings; the slightly wounded were coming in from the western front.

All this time we had forgotten the Englishman, and it was with a start that we recalled him.

"If he spots us," advised my companion, "we've got to hand him the cold shoulder. Mark my words, he'll try to trail along to the same hotel and stick like a leech."

Again he was right. At the baggage room the Englishman overtook us, suggesting that we make a party of it—he knew a gay café—first going to the hotel. He suggested the *Atlantic*. Bluntly he was informed we were visiting friends, but nothing would do then but we must agree to meet him in, say, an hour. Not until he found it an impossibility did he give us up and finally, with marvelous good nature, he said good night. The last I saw of him was his broad back disappearing through a door into a street.

The courier nudged me.

"Quick," he whispered, "look,—the man going out the next door."

Before I could turn I knew whom he meant. I saw only the man's profile before he too disappeared into the street; but it was a face difficult to forget, for it had been close to me at Warnemunde; it was the face of the police spy.

"I told you they purposely let him get through," continued my friend. "That police fellow must have come down on the train from Warnemunde. I tell you it's best not to pick up with any one these days. Suppose we had fallen for that Englishman and gone to a café with him to-night—a nice mess!"

It was in a restaurant a few hours later that I saw my first Iron Cross, black against a gray-green coat and dangling from a button. In *Bieber's*, a typical better class café of the new German type, luxurious with its marble walls and floors, and with little soft rugs underfoot and colored wicker tables and chairs, one felt the new spirit of this miracle of nations. On the broad landing of a wide marble staircase an orchestra played soldier songs and above the musicians, looking down on his people, loomed a bust of Wilhelm II, *Von Gottes Gnaden, Kaiser von Deutschland*. About him, between the flags of Austria-Hungary and Turkey, blazed the black, white and red, and there where all might read, hung the proclamation of August to the German people. We had read it through to the last line: *"Forward with God who will be with us as he was with our Fathers!"* — when we heard an excited inflection in the murmurings from the many tables — *"Das Eiserne Kreuz!"* And we saw the officer from whose coat dangled the black maltese cross, outlined in silver. His cheeks flushed, proud of a limping, shot-riddled leg, proud of his Emperor's decoration, but prouder still that he was a German; he must have forgotten all of battle and suffering during that brief walk between the tables. Cheers rang out, then a song, and when finally the place quieted everybody stared at that little cross of black as though held by some hypnotic power.

So! We were Americans, he said when we finally were presented. That was good. We — that is — I had come to write of the war as seen from the German side. Good, *sehr gut*! He had heard the Allies, especially the English, — *Verfluchte Englanderschwein!* — were telling many lies in the American newspapers. How could any intelligent man believe them?

In his zeal for the German cause his Iron Cross, his one shattered leg, the consciousness that he was a hero, all were forgotten. Of course I wanted to hear his story — the story of that little piece of metal hanging from the black and white ribbon on his coat — but tenaciously he refused. That surprised me until I knew Prussian officers.

So we left the man with the Iron Cross, marveling not at his modesty but that it embodied the spirit of the German army; whereas I thought I knew that spirit. But not until the next night, when I left Hamburg behind, where every one was pretending to be busy and the nursemaids and visitors were still tossing tiny fish to the wintering gulls in the upper lake; not until the train was bringing me to Berlin did I understand what it meant. At the stations I went out and walked with the passengers and watched the crowds; I talked with a big business man of Hamburg — bound for Berlin because he had nothing to do in Hamburg; then it was I faintly began to grasp the tremendous emotional upheaval rumbling in every Germanic soul.

My first impression of Berlin was the long cement platform gliding by, a dazzling brilliance of great arc lamps and a rumbling chorus of song. Pulling down the compartment window I caught the words *"Wir kämpfen Mann für Mann, für Kaiser und Reich!"* And leaning out I could see down at the other end of the Friederichstrasse Station a regiment going to the front.

Flowers bloomed from the long black tubes from which lead was soon to pour; wreaths and garlands hung from cloth covered helmets; cartridge belts and knapsacks were festooned with ferns. The soldiers were all smoking; cigars and cigarettes had been showered upon them with prodigal hand. Most of them held their guns in one hand and packages of delicacies in the other; and they were climbing into the compartments or hanging out of the windows singing, always singing, in the terrific German way. Later I was to learn that they went into battle with the

"Wacht am Rhein" on their lips and a wonderful trust in God in their hearts.

I felt that trust now. I saw it in the confident face of the young private who hung far out of the compartment in order to hold his wife's hand. It was not the way a conscript looks. This soldier's blue eyes sparkled as with a holy cause, and as I watched this man and wife I marveled at their sunny cheer. I saw that each was wonderfully proud of the other and that this farewell was but an incident in the sudden complexity of their lives. The Fatherland had been attacked: her man must be a hero. It was all so easy, so brimming with confidence. Of course he would come back to her.... You believed in the Infinite ordering of things that he would.

Walking on down the platform I saw another young man. They were all young, strapping fellows in their new uniforms of field gray. He was standing beside the train; he seemed to want to put off entering the car until the last minute. He was holding a bundle of something white in his arms, something that he hugged to his face and kissed, while the woman in the cheap furs wept, and I wondered if it was because of the baby she cried, while that other childless young wife had smiled.

Back in the crowd I saw a little woman with white hair; she was too feeble to push her way near the train. She was dabbing her eyes and waving to a big, mustached man who filled a compartment door and who shouted jokes to her. And almost before they all could realize it, the train was slipping down the tracks; the car windows filled with singing men, the long gray platform suddenly shuffling to the patter of men's feet, as though they would all run after the train as far as they could go. But the last car slipped away and the last waving hand fell weakly against a woman's side. They seemed suddenly old, even the young wife, as they slowly walked away. Theirs was not the easiest part to play in the days of awful waiting while the young blood of the nation poured out to turn a hostile country red.

I thought I had caught the German spirit at Lübeck and at the café in Hamburg when the hero of the Iron Cross had declined to tell me his tale; but this sensation that had come with my setting foot on the Berlin station—this was something different. Fifteen hundred men going off to what?—God only knows!—fifteen hundred virile types of this nation of virility; and they had laughed and they had sung, and they had kissed their wives and brothers and babies as though these helpless ones should only be proud that their little household was helping their Fatherland and their Emperor. Self? It was utterly submerged. On that station platform I realized that there is but one self in all Germany to-day and that is the soul of the nation. Nothing else matters; a sacrifice is commonplace. Wonderful? Yes. But then we Americans fought that way at Lexington; any nation can fight that way when it is a thing of the heart; and this war is all of the heart in Germany. As we walked through the station gates I understood why three million Socialists who had fought their Emperor in and out of the Reichstag, suddenly rallied to his side, agreeing "I know no parties, only Germans." I felt as I thought of the young faces of the soldiers, cheerfully starting down into the unknown hell of war, that undoubtedly among their number were Socialists. In this national crisis partizan allegiance counted for nothing, they had ceased dealing with the Fatherland in terms of the mind and gave to it only the heart.

Even in Berlin I realized that war stalks down strange by-paths. It forever makes one feel the incongruous. It disorders life in a monstrous way. I have seen it in an instant make pictures that the greatest artist would have given his life to have done. It likes to deal in contrasts; it is jolting....

With General von Loebell I walked across the Doeberitz camp, which is near Berlin. At Doeberitz new troops were being drilled for the front. We walked towards a dense grove of pines above which loomed the sky, threateningly gray. Between the trees I saw the flash of yellow flags; a signal squad was drilling. Skirting the edge of the woods we came to a huge, cleared indentation where twenty dejected English prisoners were leveling the field for a parade ground. On the left I saw an opening in the trees; a wagon trail wound away between the pines. And then above the rattling of the prisoners' rakes I heard the distant strains of a marching song that brought a lump to my throat. Back there in the woods somewhere, some one had started a song; and countless voices took up the chorus; and through the trees I saw a moving line of gray-green and down the road tramped a company of soldiers. They were all singing and their boyish voices blended with forceful beauty. "In the Heimat! In the Heimat!" It was the favorite medley of the German army.

The prisoners stopped work; unconsciously some of those dispirited figures in British khaki stiffened. And issuing from the woods in squads of fours, all singing, tramped the young German reserves, swinging along not fifteen feet from the prison gang in olive drab—"In the Heimat!" And out across the Doeberitz plains they swung, big and snappy.

"They're ready," remarked General von Loebell. "They've just received their field uniforms."

And then there tramped out of the woods another company, and another, two whole regiments, the last thundering "Die Wacht am Rhein," and we went near enough to see the pride in their faces, the excitement in their eyes; near enough to see the Englishmen, young lads, too, who gazed after the swinging column with a soldier's understanding, but being prisoners and not allowed to talk, they gave no expression to their emotions and began to scrape their rakes over the hard ground....

I stood on the Dorotheenstrasse looking up at the old red brick building which before the second of August in this year of the world war was the War Academy. I had heard that when tourists come to Berlin they like to watch the gay uniformed officers ascending and descending the long flights of gray steps; for there the cleverest of German military youths are schooled for the General Staff. Like the tourists, I stood across the street to-day and watched the old building and the people ascending or descending the long flights of gray steps. Only I saw civilians, men alone and in groups, women with shawls wrapped around their heads, women with yellow topped boots, whose motors waited beside the curb, and children, clinging to the hands of women, all entering or leaving by the gray gate; some of the faces were happy and others were wet with tears, and still others stumbled along with heavy steps. For this old building on Dorotheenstrasse is no longer the

War Academy; it is a place where day after day hundreds assemble to learn the fate of husband, kin or lover. For inside the gray gate sits the Information Bureau of the War Ministry, ready to tell the truth about every soldier in the German army! I, too, went to learn the truth.

I climbed a creaking staircase and went down a creaking hall. I met the Count von Schwerin, who is in charge. I found myself in a big, high-ceilinged room the walls of which were hung with heroic portraits of military dignitaries. My first impression was of a wide arc of desks that circling from wall to wall seemed to be a barrier between a number of gentle spoken elderly gentlemen and a vague mass of people that pressed forward. The anxious faces of all these people reminded me of another crowd that I had seen—the crowd outside the White Star offices in New York when the *Titanic* went down. And I became conscious that the decorations of this room which, the Count was explaining, was the Assembly Hall of the War Academy, were singularly appropriate—the pillars and walls of gray marble, oppressively conveying a sense of coldness, insistent cold, like a tomb, and all around you the subtle presence of death, the death of hopes. It was the Hall of Awful Doubt.

And as I walked behind the circle of desks I learned that these men of tact and sympathy, too old for active service, were doing their part in the war by helping to soften with kindly offices the blow of fate. I stood behind them for some few moments and watched, although I felt like one trespassing upon the privacy of grief. I saw in a segment of the line a fat, plain-looking woman, with a greasy child clinging to her dress, a white haired man with a black muffler wrapped around his neck, a veiled woman, who from time to time begged one of the elderly clerks to hurry the news of her husband, and then a wisp of a girl in a cheap, rose-colored coat, on whose cheeks two dabs of rouge burned like coals.

Soldiers from the Berlin garrison were used there as runners. At the bidding of the gentle old men they hastened off with the inquiry to one of the many filing rooms and returned with the news. This day there was a new soldier on duty; he was new to the Hall of Awful Doubt.

"I cannot imagine what is keeping him so long," I heard an elderly clerk tell the woman with the veil. "He'll come any minute.... There he is now. Excuse me, please."

And the elderly clerk hurried to meet the soldier, wanting to intercept the news, if it were bad, and break it gently. But as he caught sight of the clerk I saw the soldier click his heels and, as if he were delivering a message to an officer, his voice boomed out: "*Tot!*" ... Dead!

And the woman with the veil gave a little gasp, a long, low moan, and they carried her to another room; and as I left the gray room, with the drawn, anxious faces pushing forward for their turns at the black-covered desks, I realized the heartrending sacrifice of the women of France, Belgium, Russia, England, Servia, and Austria, who, like these German mothers, wives, and sweethearts, had been stricken down in the moment of hope.

That night I went to the Jägerstrasse, to Maxim's. The place is everything the name suggests; one of those Berlin cafés that open when the theaters are coming out and close when the last girl has smiled and gone off with the last man. I sat in a white and gold room with a cynical German surgeon, listening to his comments.

"It is the best in town now," he explained. "All the Palais de Danse girls come here. Don't be in a hurry. I know what you want for your articles. You'll see it soon."

Maxim's, like most places of the sort, was methodically banal. But one by one officers strolled in and soon a piano struck up the notes of a patriotic song. When the music began the girls left the little tables where they had been waiting for some man to smile, and swarmed around the piano, singing one martial song upon another, while officers applauded, drank their healths, and asked them to sing again.

Time passed and the girls sang on, flushed and savage as the music crashed to the cadenzas of war. What were the real emotions of these subjects of Germany; had the war genuine thrills for them? I had talked with decent women of all classes about the war; what of the women whose hectic lives had destroyed real values?

"Get one of those girls over here," I told the surgeon, "and ask her what she thinks of the war."

"Do you really mean it?" he said with a cynical smile.

"Surely. This singing interests me. I wonder what's back of it?"

He called one of them. "Why not sing?" Hilda said with a shrug. "What else? There are few men here now and there are fewer every night. What do I think of this war? My officer's gone to the front without leaving me enough to keep up the apartment. *Krieg? Krieg ist schrecklich!* War is terrible!"

My German friend was laughing.

"War?" he smiled. "And you thought it was going to change that kind."

But I was thinking of the woman with the veil whom I had seen in the Hall of Awful Doubt; and outside the night air felt cool and clean....

But my symbol of Berlin is not these things—not bustling streets filled with motors, swarming with able-bodied men whom apparently the army did not yet need. Its summation is best expressed by the varied sights and emotions of an afternoon in mid-December.

Lódz has fallen; again Hindenburg has swept back the Russian hordes. Black-shawled women call the extras. Berlin rises out of its calmness and goes mad. Magically the cafés fill.... I am walking down a side street. I see people swarming toward a faded yellow brick church. They seem fired with a zealot's praise. I go in after them and see them fall on their knees.... They are thanking Him for the Russian rout.... Wondering I go out. I come to another church. Its aisles are black with bowed backs; the murmur of prayer drones like bees; a robed minister is intoning:

"Oh, Almighty Father, we thank Thee that Thou art with us in our fight for the right; we thank Thee that—"

It is very quiet in there. War seems a thing incredibly far away. The sincerity of these people grips your heart. I feel as I never felt in church before. Something mysteriously big and reverent stirs all around.... Then outside in the street drums rattle, feet thump. A regiment is going to the front! I hurry to see it go by, but back in the church the bowed forms pray on.

CHAPTER II
"THE BELOVED KING"

Being impressions gained during my talk with His Majesty King Ludwig of Bavaria

Knowing what was in the wind when the summons came that night, I hurried down Unter den Linden and through Wilhelmstrasse to the Foreign Office. Several days before, Excellence Freiherr von Mumm had discussed the possibilities with me and as the old-fashioned portal of the Foreign Office swung back to admit me, I wondered if the news would be good or bad. Without delay I was ushered into the office of Dr. Roediger. He was just laying the telephone aside.

"It has been arranged," he said. "I was just talking with München. You are to leave Berlin to-night on the 10.40 train. Upon your arrival in München in the morning, you will go to the Hotel Vierjahrzeiten. At ten in the morning present yourself to Excellence Baron von Schön at the Prussian Embassy in München. He will inform you as to the details. At twelve o'clock His Majesty, the King of Bayern, will be pleased to receive you.... Adieu and good luck."

Thanking Dr. Roediger for the arrangement—with true German thoroughness they had laid out a perfect schedule for me, even to the hotel at which I was to stop in München—I had a race of it to get packed and catch the train. But once in the compartment, with the train whirling away from Berlin, I had a chance to collect my thoughts. So, His Majesty would no doubt talk with me upon some subject of interest to Americans. I ran over half a dozen of these in my mind, but King Ludwig's personality kept obtruding. What sort of a man was he? I had seen an excellent colored photograph of him in a gallery in Unter den Linden. It was one of those pictures which make you wonder at the reality and in this case made me anticipate the meeting with unrestrained keenness. I remembered that he had waited long for the throne, that it had not descended to him until September of 1913, that he had been crowned King of his beloved Bayern at the regal age of sixty-eight. I recalled that his house, the house of Wittelsbacher, was the oldest in Germany, the line going back to the year 907. King Ludwig, ruler of that southern German land where so many Americans like to go, his home in Munich, which every American sooner or later comes to admire for its famous galleries and golden brown Münchener beer; King Ludwig, what would be his message to the United States?

Ten o'clock the following morning found me shaking hands with Baron von Schön, the Prussian Ambassador to Bavaria. It was the Baron who was Germany's

Ambassador to France at the outbreak of war, and how I regretted that obligations of his diplomatic position forbade a discussion of those frantic nights and days in Paris before the war. We could talk of other things, however, and as there were two hours before the appointed time of my presentation to King Ludwig, Baron von Schön helped me to get my bearings. To my consternation I learned that the King spoke only a little English. I informed the Baron that I spoke only a little German. Whereupon immediately the Geheimrat's office in the Embassy began to ring with one telephone call after another, for an interpreter had to be secured, a man whom His Majesty would be pleased to receive with me. And finally such a man was found in Counselor of Legation von Stockhammern.

After motoring down a long avenue, lined with pretty residences, the car turned in, approaching a rather old, unpretentious but severely dignified building of faded yellow brick, suggesting Windsor. This was the Wittelsbacher Palast, the home of King Ludwig. I remembered having seen that morning on my way to the Embassy, a far more imposing looking palace, the Residence, and contrasting its ornateness with the simplicity of the building which we were approaching, I wondered at royalty living there. It was typical of the democratic King I came to know.

As our motor rolled up, I saw two blue and white striped sentry boxes marking the entrance and through an arched driveway I had a glimpse of an inner court paved with stones, where an official automobile waited. Then I was escorted through the entrance to the right wing of the palace. Here Staatsrat (Secretary of the Royal Cabinet) von Dandl, a tall, soldierly looking man in uniform, greeted us, after which I was taken to an antechamber, where Counselor of Legation von Stockhammern, my interpreter, was waiting. There appeared a young Bavarian officer in full dress uniform, whom I was told was the Adjutantour to the King. Upon being introduced he left as quickly as he had come. It lacked a quarter hour of the time of reception, and Von Stockhammern and I were talking about München, when the young Adjutantour as quickly returned and said that His Majesty would receive me.

I climbed with Von Stockhammern several flights of a wooden staircase; the tan and red bordered corded runaway reminded you of a church, as did the bare white walls, and you felt a solemn silence, accentuated by the jangling of the sword; and then turning with a last flight of steps, I saw above two guards in the uniform of the Hartschier Regiment, two white coated, blue trousered, plumed statues standing beside a wide entrance door. The click of presenting arms and the statues came to life, and passing between them we found ourselves in what was evidently an antechamber of the Audience Saal, a comfortably furnished room; the walls covered with small oil paintings. I remember a silk-stockinged, stooping doorman who wore black satin breeches, like a character that I had seen sometime in a French romantic play. He was standing with his hand upon the knob of two brown oaken doors as if awaiting a signal. Apparently it came, although I heard nothing, for suddenly the brown doors swung back, and I found myself gazing into the long high-ceilinged room, the Audience Saal, and in the middle of this room stood an elderly man, in the dress uniform of an officer in the Second Bavarian Infantry. The uniform was blue and red and braided with gold, and the man had a white beard and a wonderfully kind face. It was His Majesty King Ludwig of Bavaria.

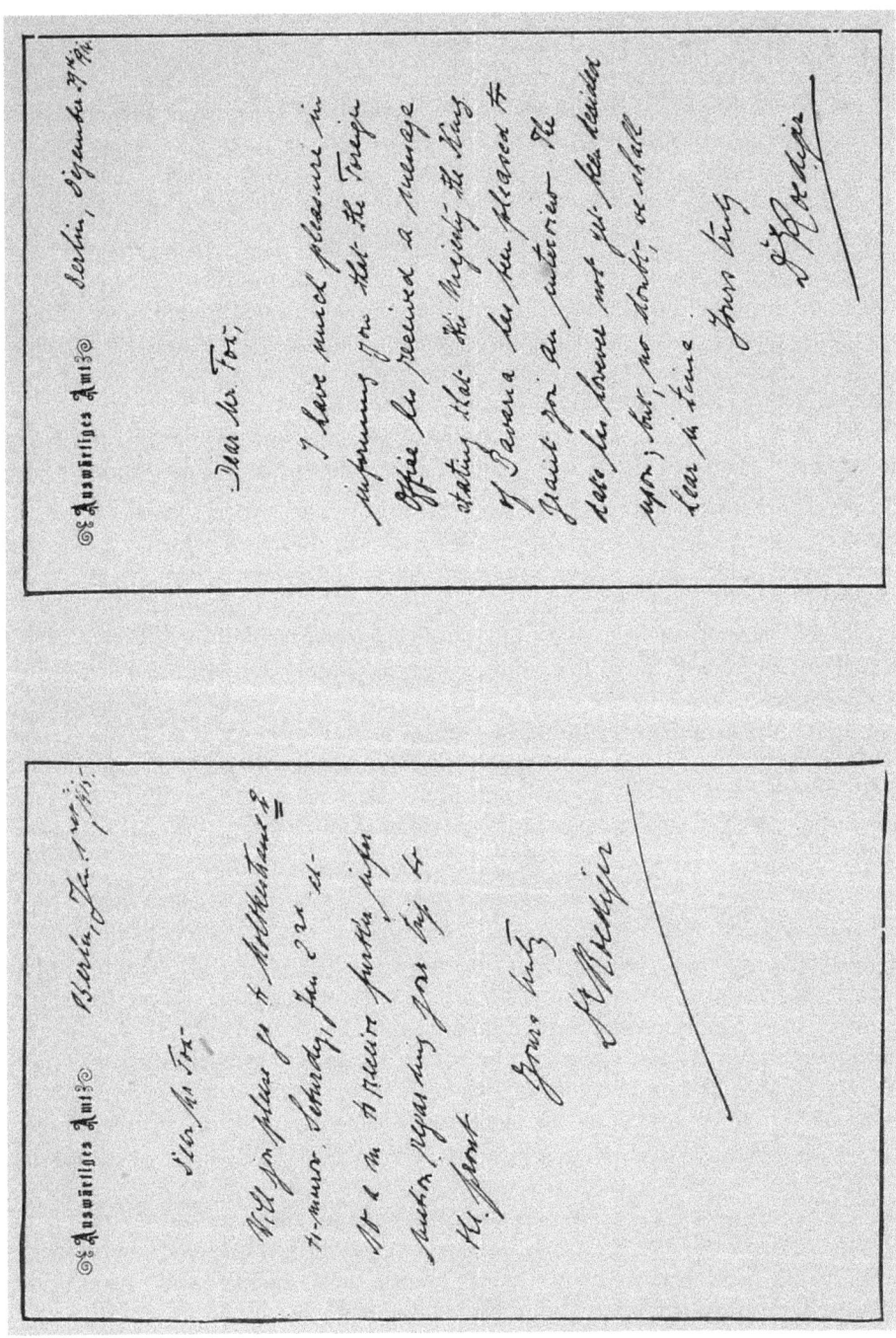

NOTIFICATIONS FROM THE GERMAN FOREIGN OFFICE

Reproduction of the author's notifications from the German Foreign Office.

My first thought, as I walked towards him, was of how closely he resembled the picture I had seen of him in the gallery on Unter den Linden. But as I drew nearer, I saw that the picture had not caught the man. You were conscious of kind eyes smiling a welcome through silver spectacles. You instantly felt that kindness seemed to be a dominant note of his character, and you realized the intellectual power behind that wide, thoughtful forehead; and you saw a firm mouth and chin suggesting determination, kindness, brains, force, every inch a king! But somehow, had I not known he was a king, the military regimentals which he wore might have been a little incongruous; he impressed me as being the kind of man you might expect to see in the black coated garb of a professor; a man of great, grave and forceful dignity and learning, and utterly foreign to the popular American conception of a monarch.

This impression was borne out a moment later, when as Staatsrat von Dandl came forward to present me, King Ludwig showed me a delightful courtesy. Casting court etiquette aside, he welcomed me in true American fashion, his hand outstretched.

There began then the usual preliminaries to a conversation and while we exchanged greetings, I noticed that His Majesty was wearing a great number of minor orders, strung in a bright ribboned line across his chest, and beneath them, on the left side, the Iron Cross, the Star of St. Hubertus, and the Order of the Crown. Presently, in a pleasantly modulated voice, King Ludwig told me that through his people he had long felt a great friendship for America.

"All Germany has been deeply touched by the many kindnesses of your country since the beginning of the war. You have been so thoughtful," he said. "You have sent us your wonderful Red Cross doctors and nurses. Throughout the empire we have heard expressions of good will from your visiting countrymen. We have felt the spirit that prompted the gifts of the American children which came through your Mr. O'Loughlin to the children of Germany. Especially have we been touched here in München, where your wonderful hospital is, and where we have so many Americans. Between Germany and the United States there exists a strong bond through commercial relations, but between your country and Bavaria there is something more intimate. It is because so many of your countrymen come here. They like the Wagner-festspiel, they are so fond of German music and our Bavarian art. They like to spend their summers among us. They get to know us and we them. You have no idea how many Americans live here in München. And they find here the high regard in which your country is held. They find that two of the best artists of their own nation, Miss Fay and Miss Walker, both Americans, are regarded as the best artists in the München Opera, and our people hold them in great esteem. They are received in court society, and are very well seen."

The subject of America made the King enthusiastic and the sincere ring of his voice and the warmth of his smile increased as he spoke. So I took the opportunity of asking His Majesty a question so many of my countrymen are thinking. What of America and war?

"America need fear no war," he replied quickly, adding, "No war on your own soil. Geographically you are safe. You have only two neighbors, Canada and Mexico." And the King smiled. "We, on the other hand, are surrounded by enemies who are powerful. You have the Pacific between you and your adversaries."

King Ludwig's omission of the Atlantic Ocean struck me as being significant. He seemed to take it for granted that we could have but one adversary—that yellow octopus of the Far East. Whereupon I mentioned something which had come to me in Berlin concerning certain islands in the Pacific. For a moment King Ludwig looked grave, and then he said slowly: "America needs no large army; if she should need one she can make it quickly. She has already shown that. To attack her on her home soil is not practical, but she should have a large navy. I have heard many compliments of your American navy, of its equipment, discipline and gunnery; but it must be kept large."

"So you think, Your Majesty, that we are safe from war?"

"On your home soil, yes," he repeated, "but your navy must be strong. When war will come, you can never tell. But you must never fear war. We knew over here that this war was coming. We have long known it. We have always wanted peace. For forty-one years I myself have been working for peace, but we have always been surrounded by jealous neighbors. Last January I spoke at a dinner given in honor of the anniversary of the birthday of His Majesty Emperor Wilhelm II. I said then that we do not wish a war, but that the German people have always shown that they do not fear war."

I reflected what there was in the European situation of January, 1913, to make King Ludwig talk of that time, in a way which suggested the close proximity of this war. And I asked him concerning that situation.

"Yes, we knew war was coming," he admitted gravely. "Last winter the great debates were going on in the French parliament over the question of changing the term of military service from two to three years. We could not understand that. The extra years would increase the annual strength of the French army fully fifty per cent. It was ominous. Then we knew that Russia had nine hundred thousand men under arms whose term of service had expired and who had every right to return to their homes. Why were they not sent? Yes, we knew it was coming, but we did not fear it, and Germany will fight to the last drop of blood. You have but to see the spirit of our troops and the spirit of the recruits, disappointed because their offers to serve in the army are rejected. We do not need every recruit now, and as we do take new men, there are hundreds of thousands more, ready to serve the Fatherland—to the end."

"And when will the end be?" I asked His Majesty. When would peace be declared? The King smiled, but it was a smile of reluctance.

"Who can say?" Then that Imperial chin suddenly seemed made of stone, and there was fire in his eyes. He declared: "There will be no end to this war until we have peace conditions which we shall judge to be worthy of our nation and worthy of our sacrifice. This war was forced upon us. We shall go through with it. We do not finish until we have an uncontestable victory. The heart and soul of the whole country is in this fight. Between all the German kings and confederated princes, there is absolute unswerving unity. We are one idea, one hope, one ideal, one wish."

Instantly I thought of the Socialists. We had heard in America there could be no war. We had been told that the German Socialists would not let their country go to war.

The King smiled, for it was obviously inconceivable to him. "We Germans," he explained, "quarrel between ourselves in peaceful times, but when we are surrounded by enemies, we are one. And the Socialists know that war was as much against our plans as it was against theirs. In times of stress, Germany is always a united nation. Beside the Fatherland, dogmas are trivial. We Germans like to talk. We are great philosophers. We go deep into things, but it is against our racial instincts to let our own individualism come before the welfare of the State. It is because we have deep national pride that we are one people to-day."

"And, Your Majesty, after the war?" I asked, "what then? Is it to be the last war of the world, so terrible that humanity will not tolerate another?"

"This is for each nation to say," he replied gravely. "Our hands are clean. For more than forty years we have worked for the peace of Europe, and there have been times when, had our policy been such, it might have been to our advantage to go to war. Our hands are clean," he repeated. "They brought this upon us. We did not want it. After it is over, we shall rebuild. I foresee an era of great prosperity for our country. We shall not be impoverished. Many of our industries are working day and night now. Until last August they were busy with the products of peace; now it is with the products of war. So many skilled workmen are needed to-day that we cannot take them from the shops to send them to the front, even though their regiments go. And after the war the factories will all go on as before, manufacturing the things of peace, and those other industries which are closed now will be doubly busy. War, no matter how severe it may be, cannot check the commercial growth of a country like Germany."

When King Ludwig spoke of the industrial future, it was the voice of one who had given deep study to everything of vital importance to his country.

Baron von Schön had told me that all his life King Ludwig had been a hard worker, that political economy, agriculture, industry, waterways, were all subjects which fascinated him, that most of His Majesty's evenings were spent attending conferences, given by the specialized learned men in every branch of a nation's prosperity.

I mentioned the wonderful spirit of the Bavarian troops I had seen, and His Majesty's face grew bright.

"I have two sons at the front," he said proudly. "Prince Francis, commander of a brigade. He was wounded in Flanders, but he will be back before the war is over; and as you know, Crown Prince Rupprecht is also fighting in the West."

And I thought that an expression of longing crossed that kindly face, as though the King wished he could be there too.

"I also am wounded," he said with a smile, "but that was long ago—1866."

The conversation changed; it became more personal. Like most Americans, King Ludwig showed himself to be thoroughly fond of sport. He told me that he liked all forms of outdoor sports and admired America for its almost national participation in them. He spoke of his fondness for sailing, and horses, of yacht races on the Sternberger See. He mentioned with enjoyment his great stables, where personally he concerns himself with the breeding of his own horses, taking a great pride in them whenever they race. He told me of his farm, Leutstetten, near München, where he likes to spend the summers, living an outdoor life.

Further expressing again his warm feeling of friendship—a friendship deeper than that dictated by the rules of mere international courtesy, for it has come from the Americans who have lived from time to time in Bavaria—King Ludwig concluded our talk with the message of German's deep and sincere friendship to the people of the United States.

We shook hands again; it was an American farewell. The dapper Adjutant came into the room, and I bid His Majesty "Adieu." My last impression was of his straight uniformed figure standing in the center of the room, across his breast the Iron Cross and the Order of St. Hubertus; then the oaken doors closed. Back into the little antechamber with the countless oil paintings, back through the austere reception hall, past the white coated, white plumed Hartschier guards, down the great staircase, and with Legation Counselor von Stockhammern, I was escorted into a motor. As we drove down to the Promenade Platz, where I was to call at the Foreign Ministry of Bavaria, I asked the Counselor about the Wittelsbacher Palast.

"It is the palace," he said, "where the King has lived all his life, and which he does not like at all to leave. When he became King two years ago, he did not change in his tastes. Only on the occasion of great ceremony is he to be seen in the Residence, where lived the former King of Bavaria."

And I understood now what I had heard before, that King Ludwig was fond only of a simple life, and that he loved only work, and family happiness; and I thought that here was no case of mere birth making a man high in the land, for Ludwig of Wittelsbacher would have made his way if he had been born outside the purple; and I thought of something I had heard, how a Bavarian Socialist had once said that though his party might battle against the Government, they could never battle against King Ludwig.

"Everybody in Bayern supports King Ludwig with all their heart," Von Stockhammern was saying.

"I know now why you Bavarians love him," I replied.

CHAPTER III
TO THE WEST FRONT

A note from Dr. Roediger of the Foreign Office directed me to report early in January at ten o'clock at that building on Moltkestrasse and Königsplatz, where lives and works that marvelous central organization of the German army, the Great General Staff. There I found waiting Dawson, the photographer who had accompanied me from America, and a plump, smiling, philosophical Austrian, Theyer, a Cino-operator who was to go along with Dawson and make "movies" of the front.

Climbing endless wooden stairways in the old building, I was finally shown into a room that only lacked wax flowers under glass to recall the Rutherford B. Hayes period of interior decorating. Presently the door opened to admit an officer whom I liked at the first glimpse, and in his careful, groping English Ober-Lieutenant Herrmann of the Grosser General Stab introduced himself. He explained that he would accompany us on our trip to the front and bring us back to Berlin; whereupon I blessed the Staff for giving me an officer with merry eyes and delightful personality. He would do everything in his power—not small as I later learned—to have me shown the things I wanted to see in that forbidden city, the army front.

That afternoon I bought a dunnage bag such as navy men the world over use, and remembering Ober-Lieutenant Herrmann's advice to carry as little as possible, I packed only a change of boots, socks, under-clothing, and flannel shirts. Come to think of it, an elaborate series of cloth maps, each a minutely described small district of the whole Western front, took up as much room as anything else. And as I had heard officers say that a hypodermic with a shot of morphine was good to carry in case one was hit, that went in, too. During our conversation at the General Staff, Ober-Lieutenant Herrmann had emphasized the point that it must be understood that this trip I was about to make was entirely upon my own responsibility. A suit of army gray green was desirable and a hat or gloves of a similar neutral color, prevented me from being a conspicuous mark.

I think I was at Anhalter Bahnhof the next night half an hour before the gate opened for the Metz train. There were no sleeping compartments available, so securing a day compartment to themselves, Dawson and Theyer withdrew to concoct a series of movie narratives, while the Ober-Lieutenant induced the conductor to lock me up with him in a nearby compartment meant for four, After the train had pulled out we discussed the war between the United States and Japan, which all well informed people whom I have met in Germany, diplomatic, naval, and army, believe must soon come. For the first time I noticed that the Ober-Lieutenant's uniform was different from any of the thousands of uniforms that I had seen in Germany; trimmed with blue of a shade that I had never before noticed, and across his left chest I observed an order, and that was also as totally different, a bar about four inches long and one inch high, wound with the black and white of the iron cross and yellow and red. Pinned to it were two golden bars, bearing strange words: *Heroland,* and some outlandish word that I have forgotten.

"You're puzzled at my uniform," smiled the Ober-Lieutenant. "It does not surprise me. There are but two others in Germany. My uniform is that of the regiment of German Southwest Africa. The Emperor created it a special regiment after our campaign there." And I found myself looking at the tiny golden bars, and wondering what deeds of daring this merry-eyed man had performed there. His medals bore now the names of battles in Africa. "My regiment," he explained, "is still in Africa. Since August I have been with the General Staff in Berlin."

We talked long that night, while the train rushed towards the Southwest. He told me of his experiences in German Southwest Africa, and of the ways of the natives there. We slept that night, each sprawled out on a compartment seat, and I awoke with a huge arc lamp glaring through the window. My watch showed seven and when I drowsily heard the Ober-Lieutenant say that we were in Frankfort, and that the train stopped half an hour, and would I like to get out for coffee?

I rubbed open my eyes. We passed the photographers' compartment, to find them both asleep, but then photographers in warring Germany can have nothing but easy consciences; they see so little.

Long after day had broken—with the photographers still sleeping—we passed the brown mountains of the Rhine, and at Bingen, where we saw the old robber's castle clinging to the cliffs, with the watch tower on an islet below, the train stopped. Opening one of the wide car windows we saw a commotion under a shed of new boards, and there swarmed forth the women of Bingen, with pails of smoking coffee and trays of sandwiches. We saw them crowding past, and then by stretching our necks we were able to see, three cars down, one after another helmeted head and gray-green pair of shoulders pop forth, while the women smiled happily and passed up the coffee and bread.

"I think a car full of soldiers for the front was joined on during the night," observed Herrmann.

Our train passed through Lorraine which those who generalize like to tell us was the cause of this war, forgetting Lombard Street and Honest John Bull. I had heard how they hated the Germans, these people of Lorraine, but at every station there were the women and girls with the cans of coffee and the plates of *Butterbrot.* One saw no poverty there, only neat, clean little houses—no squalor. Germany is wise in the provisions made for the contentment of her working classes.

We drew near Metz, cupped by the distant blue ring of the fortified Vosges where last August the army of the Crown Prince smashed the French invasion. I saw beside a road four graves and four wooden crosses and wondered if on one of those broiling summer days, a gray motor of the Red Cross had not stopped there to bury the wounded. A field flew by, serried with trenches that rotated like the spokes of a great wheel; but the trenches were empty and the road that followed the wire fence close by the tracks, was bare of soldiers. There was no need longer for trenches, or that barbed entanglement of rusted wire, for the guns rumbled now far beyond the guardian hills.

The shadows of a domed station fell over the train, likewise the shadows of supervision, for I was to see none of the fortifications of Metz. Historic Metz that guards the gate to Germany by the south, was not for a foreigner's eyes. For only ten minutes was I in Metz and, although it was the natural thing to do to spend them waiting on the station platform, I had a feeling, though, that had I wished otherwise and attempted to go out into the city, a soldier would have barred the way. Never, not even in the captured French and Belgium cities that I later saw, did I gain the impression of such intense watchfulness as prevailed at Metz.

"We are going to the Great Headquarters now," said Ober-Lieutenant Herrmann, explaining for the first time our destination. Whereupon, I forgot my disappointment at not seeing Metz, and wondered if he had not deliberately withheld this as a surprise for me. The Great Headquarters! You thought of it as the place of mystery. In Berlin you remembered hearing it spoken of only vaguely, its location never named. You had heard it kept in darkness, that all lighted windows were covered, lest French flyers seek it by night. You knew that from the Great Headquarters three hundred miles of battle line were directed; that it was the birthplace of stratagems; the council table around which sat the Falkenheim, Chief of the General Staff, Tirpitz, ruler of the Navy. Perhaps the Emperor was there!

I think I must have turned over in my mind for half an hour a certain question, before deciding that it was not a breach of military etiquette to put it to Ober-Lieutenant Herrmann.

"Where," I finally asked, "is the Great Headquarters located?"

"At Charleville," he promptly answered. "We shall not arrive there until evening." And then, getting out a number of those marvelous maps of the General Staff that show every tree, fence and brook, in the desired district, he traced for me the route the train was following. "We cross the Frontier into France, just beyond Fentsch and then go diagonally northwest through Longuion, Montmédy and Sedan to Charleville. We are going behind the battle line, out of artillery range, of course, but still the French flyers watch this line," and Herrmann bent down to glance towards the sky. "We may get some excitement."

There is something discomfortingly casual in the way these Prussian officers talk of danger, and from the moment I saw the frontier post, with its barber-pole stripings, slip by unguarded, and realized that frontier guards were a thing of the past and that I was now with the invaders in France, I could not help but feel that an aeroplane bomb was the thing to be expected.

We passed, on a siding, a troop train filled with new troops from Bavaria. One of the compartment doors was open and I saw that the floor was strewn with straw. The soldiers grinned and waved to us and pointed to the blue and white streamers so that we might know from what part of Germany they came.

When we were approaching Audun le Roman, which is just across the frontier on the road to Pierrepont, I saw on a hill not a quarter of a mile from the train a row of gray plastered houses. Through them, the gray sky showed in ragged, circular patches, framed by the holes in their walls. Sunken roofs, shattered floors, heaps of black débris, the charred walls gaping with shell holes; beside one house, a garden surprisingly green for so early in the year, serenely impassive to the story of the ruined walls—that row of little houses was as a guidepost. At last we followed the road to war.

I saw in the next field a black swarm of birds pecking at the plowed ground. Plow furrows? One wondered.... For a mile we did not see a living thing, only the black birds, that feed on death.

"This place," observed Ober-Lieutenant Herrmann, whose face seemed to have lost some of the former indifference to war, "was apparently under heavy artillery fire when the Crown Prince invaded towards Longwy."

At Pierrepont I saw the first formal sign of the German occupation. Near the railroad station in a little square, where you could not miss it, loomed a large wooden sign, that began with *"nichts"* and ended with *"verboten."* Then the train passed over a trestle and across the dirty little road that ran beneath. I saw a German soldier hurrying towards a squatty peasant house. I could see the door open and a blue-smocked old man appear on the threshold. Why had the soldier hurried towards him; what was the old man saying? Stories? You felt them to be in every little house.

The train crept on. I saw a French inn with a German flag painted over the red signboard. The tracks ran between fields scarred on either side with the brown, muddy craters of shells. At the Longuion Station I watched a German soldier standing on a ladder, painting out all French words within the sweep of his brush. Further on I saw a two-wheeled cart in a deserted farmhouse yard; its shafts were tilted up, and a load of bags rotted on the ground, as though the owner, unhitching the horse, had fled.

Almost stopping, so slowly did the train move, it approached a tunnel that the retreating French had blown up. Inky darkness closed in, and the Ober-Lieutenant was saying that the Germans were digging the tunnel out, when a yellow torch flared against the window. I sprang to open it and saw the ghostly forms of soldiers standing along the rails.

"Zeitung! Zeitung!" they cried, and in answer we tossed out to them all the newspapers in the compartment. You had a feeling that the tunnel was dangerous, for the shaky, temporary wooden trestle was yielding to the train's weight. The tunnel marked the beginning of a destroyed railroad and, as we proceeded, I found myself looking into a house flush against the track. It was like a room on the stage, the fourth wall removed. All the intimate possessions of the owner were before me; the pink wall paper was hideous in its flamboyant bad taste. Herrmann came to my rescue.

"The tracks from now are either repaired or laid new by our engineers. As they retreated, the French blew up everything. In some cases we had to run our line through houses."

The engineers had cut away the half of the house which was in their way and left the remainder to be boarded up.

A gray castle, that crowned a hill, had been the vortex of the terrific fighting that raged around Montmédy. It seemed tranquil enough now. I saw the front door open, and down the terrace there shuffled a squad of baggy red-trousered French prisoners with their watchful guards.

When we passed through Sedan it was almost dark, swarming with the Germans as in 1870. One after another we tarried at the stations of these captured towns. Finally we pulled up to a larger station where the shadowy forms of houses were closer together. I was awakened from my speculations by the Ober-Lieutenant saying: "We are in Charleville, the Great Headquarters."

As I left the train I felt a thrill of anticipation that grew apace during the long explanation that Herrmann was giving the station guards. Outside loomed the vague tops of trees, and the whiteness of a house accentuated against the dark night. Here and there a solitary light burned, but Charleville was a place of darkness.

Herrmann had expected an automobile to be waiting, but when to the saluting click of sentries' heels, we had gone the length of the station front, he said to me: "You please get Mr. Dawson and Mr. Theyer and wait in the dining-room. I shall walk to Headquarters and see what we are to do."

Of course, I suggested going with him. There might be a chance of seeing Falkenheim, who now is responsible for the movements of more than a million men on the West front; perhaps I might even see the Emperor. Perhaps Herrmann guessed why I insisted so strongly on keeping him company on his walk to the Great Headquarters.

"The roads are muddy," he said, in a way that blended consideration with decision. "Remain in there," and he pointed to the door of the station dining-room, "until I return."

Then he showed us into a typical way station restaurant that would have reminded you of any dirty American railroad lunchroom, had not the principal object of furniture been a large buffet, shining with bottled French wines and liqueurs. As I sat down at one of the marble-topped tables, I realized that we were the only civilians in the room, except the three men with white aprons and the pretty low-class French girl who was waiting to take our order.

"*Diner*," I said briefly, not attempting to remember French after struggling for weeks with German, and fell to studying the room. It apparently was an officers' mess of the General Staff. The clean field-green jackets and the dashing gray capes gave a touch of romance to that dingy dining-room.

We lingered long over the coffee and Theyer, the Austrian, was telling how he had been with Jack London, taking movies for Pathé in the South Sea Islands, when Ober-Lieutenant Herrmann finally returned.

"We must go at once to the hotel," he said, "and go to bed. We shall have to be up by five, and on our way to Lille."

So it was Lille! There was real fighting in that northern section of France.

"How long do we remain in Lille?" I asked, disappointed at being rushed away from the Great Headquarters.

"Five days," he replied, setting my fears at rest. "We shall use Lille as a base and go out to different points on the front."

I knew then why he had been so long in returning; clearly he had been receiving his instructions at the Great Headquarters, and the slight distrust I had come to feel at being rushed away from Metz and now from Charleville was entirely dissipated. After all, they meant business; Lille proved that; and five days at the front!

If ever I return to Charleville and want to go to the Hotel de Commerce, it will be impossible without a guide. I remember going the length of a long street of shady trees, crossing a wide square, and then turning off into a narrow alley where ancient lanterns, well masked, hung over from grilled wall brackets. I remember flashing my electric pocket lamp down on the cobbled street, for just an instant, when Herrmann dropped his gloves. We stumbled down a blind alley that called to mind the habitation of François Villon in "The Lodging for a Night." Then Herrmann was rattling the knocker on the huge oaken doors of a two story flat-roofed house that looked a century old. The door groaned back and I found myself gazing into the blinking eyes of an old portier who held a candle and who would have demanded what we wanted had he not suddenly spied the military gray of Herrmann's cape and at once asked us to come in.

The few hours I slept that night were in a venerable, four-posted bed, in a low-ceilinged, high-casemented room such as you sometimes see on the stage in a romantic play. I remember hearing a rapping on the door, almost as soon, it seemed, as I had closed my eyes.

Five o'clock! And I heard the portier shuffling down the hall and then the hollow, rapping sound of another early morning call on the Ober-Lieutenant's door. Below in the alley panted one of the gray-green army motors waiting to bring us to the station. Cold sprouts, coffee, and a roll, and we had climbed into a compartment of the train for Lille. From now on, soldiers with fixed bayonets composed the train crew. We crossed a wooden trestle built by German pioneers high above a green swirl of water between pretty trees, and on the left we saw the ruins of a stone bridge dynamited by the French. We rushed out at St. Vincennes to eat at an officers' mess, and as the train moved on I saw at a siding a long line of cars, their sides and roofs marked with the Red Cross; and even as we passed I saw two stretchers being borne along the track and lifted with their wounded through the open windows of one of the cars. I saw a white bandaged leg as the stretcher tilted and then the attendants inside the car covered it from sight. Hourly the front drew nearer.

Trenches appeared. The train suddenly slid into a station and stopped. We were in Lille. While two soldiers were loading the luggage, photograph apparatus and all, upon a small truck, Herrmann suddenly plucked my arm. "Look," he exclaimed, pointing up at the huge glass-domed roof. I saw there a big hole, edged with splintered glass, and a fragment of blue sky beyond. "That's the hole made by a French aeroplane bomb. The Staff told me to look for it when we came to Lille. The bomb never exploded and was picked up on the tracks over there."

Not the most reassuring thought in the world, that French fliers had marked this place for destruction. In the waiting-rooms I saw nothing but soldiers—fresh troops with clean uniforms, unshaven men whose clothes were brownish with the mud of the trenches. By that time I had become used to being saluted, and to enjoy the click of a sentry's heels. While Ober-Lieutenant Herrmann was telephoning for a military automobile I noticed one of the *Landwehr* guards begin to eye suspiciously the photographers and their formidable luggage. I saw him call another of the dark-coated *Landwehr*, and they were obviously on the point of making a possible arrest when the Ober-Lieutenant returned, averting the situation.

We were, the Ober-Lieutenant informed us, to wait in the Café de Paris,—which was just across the square from the station,—until he returned.

"The telephones have all been cut," he explained with a smile. "I shall have to walk to Headquarters and bring back a motor for us. I may be gone half an hour, or an hour, but please remain in the café. Remember Lille is a captured city."

So we crossed the square, Dawson, Theyer and I, while the wind brought us the grumbling of heavy cannon from the West where, not fifteen miles away, the Germans were making their terrific drive on that segment of the Allies' line, extending out from the Channel shore. Boo-omm, Boo-omm, Boo-omm, with the last syllable prolonged like a low note on the piano. Army transports rattled over the cobbled square; one of the gray motors with its muffler cut out, snorted past; and then the eye began to take in its surroundings.

There on my left, as I went away from the station, I saw a place of destruction, an entire block of ruined buildings, their shattered sides rearing with hideous ugliness against the perspective of untouched houses beyond. Blackened walls, gaping holes, roofless skeletons of houses; and within, a chaos of plaster and falling floors, one house after another, some almost razed to the ground, others with only their tops shot off, but all desolation and ruin. It was not the destruction that made me stop in the square and stare about me, for I had become sated with shelled houses, all the way from Charleville to Lille; it was amazement at the artillery fire that could lay low an entire block and not even drop a shell. The undisturbed cobbles in the square confirmed this conclusion. What deadly accuracy! How, if something be marked for destruction in this war, can it escape? I stood in the square for several minutes and counted thirty-eight soldiers and sixty civilians walk past the ruins and no one so much as turned his head to glance even indifferently upon them.

"How long," I asked the fatherly, white-haired Frenchman who brought us our coffee in the Café de Paris, "is it, since those buildings over there were destroyed?"

"A month, sir," he said, and in a moment he added wearily, "Our city has been captured and recaptured three times."

And it was easy then to know why they had all walked by without the slightest interest in the ruins beside them; think of people becoming bored with destruction! A typical French café with its big window, the Paris gave a view of the sidewalk. I saw a beautiful, dark-eyed French boy, dirtily clad, selling post cards of Lille to a good natured German infantryman. The soldier went away and then, what appeared to be the other members of the firm, a bigger and a smaller boy, darted from a doorway to divide the spoils with the dark-eyed youngster who had closed the deal. I saw five different parties of German soldiers come into the Café de Paris, and I heard not even a loud word or jest against the French; and three black-bearded Frenchmen played dominoes nearby. The soldiers ordered their coffee, or wine, paid for it, and minded their own business, just as they would at home, perhaps even more scrupulously so.

Ober-Lieutenant Herrmann was an hour longer than he expected, but he had good news for me.

"I have a car outside," he said hurriedly. "We shall bring Mr. Dawson and Mr. Theyer to the Staff and then I shall take you to an aeroplane base not far from here. It has been arranged for you to go up—if you wish."

Hmm! The battle line could not be more than forty kilometers away, and a French flyer had almost wrecked the Lille station.

"A fine day for flying," observed the Ober-Lieutenant. "You can see much," and he smiled. "A fine day also for the French fliers."

"*Schön*," I said, but refused to believe that a German aeroplane was ever hit. "Let's go."

CHAPTER IV
ON THE BACK OF THE BIRD OF WAR

Two hours after the crawling military train had set us down in what used to be the Gare du Nord in Lille, but which is now the Nord Bahnhof, I was hurriedly getting into a fur-lined military undercoat in the Hotel d'Europe. About to go up in one of Germany's war planes, I was determined to be comfortable, if not mentally, physically. Ober-Lieutenant Herrmann laughed when he saw me appear, as bulky with clothing as a polar explorer, and said: "We shall have to hurry if we are to reach the aviation base before dark." We hurried.

I have ridden with Robertson, Strang, and other race drivers. I have had my blood turned to ice when they skidded their cars around hairpin turns. But I never rode before with a chauffeur of the German army who was in a hurry; nor shall I again—if I can help it. Bound for a place near Lens, so small that it appears only on the wonderful *Automobilkartes* that the Germans have made of all Europe, the brown leather-coated soldier-chauffeur began to distance everything on the road. It was one of those long, rakish motors, painted field gray green, that the Benz Company manufactures only for the army, cabalistic black letters and numerals marking its hood. As, with the muffler cut out, we roared through the streets of Lille, I saw the civilians pause to watch us pass with sullen eyes. Poor Herrmann had his arm working like a restless semaphore, returning salutes, and as we thundered through the silenced business streets at mile a minute speed, military trumpetings warned the poor bewildered citizens of Lille of our approach. The car began its mad dance through the outskirts of the city and down between the sentinel poplars toward Lens. Not two months before I had been riding down Fifth Avenue on the roof of a slumbering bus; to-day I was speeding in a German car through captured France.

Ahead we saw the gray canvas tops of a transport train. The trumpet blared, but those mud-splashed, creaking wagons had the right of way. What if the two lancers who rode as a rear guard did recognize the officer in our car? After all, he was only an officer, and they were bringing ammunition for the entrenched battle line. So our soldier-chauffeur swore, but indifferent to his "*Donnerwetters*," the drivers astride the transport horses stolidly held their course as, with an angry rasping of the tires, we skidded over to the side of the road, and rushed on in a splatter of mud. I looked at Ober-Lieutenant Herrmann and shouted: "They knew their business, those fellows back there."

"Certainly," he replied, "their work is most important. They were entirely right in not turning off the road for an officer's automobile. Everything depends on the transports, you know."

Whereupon I began to have a greater respect for the light, rattling supply wagons that we passed by the dozen on the road to Lens, and found myself thinking how unjustly those men might be regarded. "What did you do in the war?" ... "I drove a supply cart." ... How unheroic it sounds. Yet the Ober-Lieutenant told me that those men astride the bulky, unpicturesque dray horses were often put to the severest tests of courage.

"During our drive on Paris," he said, "the French would often succeed in covering a segment of road with their long range artillery, and continually drop shells upon it. They knew, of course, that our infantry, by making a detour through the fields, could avoid this death zone, but they shelled on, knowing that our transport trains would have to go by the road. So the transports would make a rush for it, and of course many were killed."

Another mile passed without our seeing any more of the gray wagon trains, and now the distant artillery grumbled louder. Two Uhlans cantered by, scanning us, and further on we passed another patrol. A corral of the familiar gray-topped wagons beside red brick farm buildings showed the location of a base of supplies, and in front of the house we saw a naked soldier unconcernedly scrubbing himself in a tub of water. And always the sullen roaring guns grew steadier and more disconcertingly clear.

"On this section of the line," Ober-Lieutenant explained, "the Staff told me that the French generally begin their heaviest firing every day at half past three."

I asked him why that was—it was like the curtain going up in a theater at a certain time. But he did not know, and could not even guess. I was wondering how much further we were going to rush towards that unearthly booming when at a muddy crossroad, patrolled by a Uhlan, as motionless as Remington might have painted him, we made a quick turn and plowed away. Apparently we were bound for a weather-beaten house and barn, half hidden by a leafless clump of willows, apparently shorn by shrapnel, for the broken branches hung down dead in a perfect arc as though the projectile had burst, perhaps right there above the tiny moss-banked stream, and sprayed its leaden shower.

As our motor, which had been heavily crawling along the farmhouse lane, finally sogged in the mud, refusing to go further, I followed Ober-Lieutenant Herrmann out of the machine, across the yard to where a sentry stood before the barn door. They exchanged words and then the barn door slid back a trifle, a youngish man, wearing the black leather helmet and coat of the aviation corps, appearing in the aperture. Excusing himself, Herrmann drew him aside and now and then I heard their voices raised in assent; they were evidently discussing my proposed flight. I guessed that Herrmann wanted to know exactly how much danger there would be. Conjecturing that he was apparently satisfied that the risk was a minimum, and that the aviator had been instructed to bring me nowhere near the firing line, I waited for their conference to break up.

Their talk evidently finished to the satisfaction of both, introductions were in order. Then the aviator, Hals, shouted a command into the barn and instantly there issued from the gloom within, four soldiers. I watched them roll back the creaking door and then, as though it were a fragile thing, they began slowly to push out the aeroplane—a monoplane I judged, as its long, tapering fuselage protruded into the farm yard, and then I saw with a start that the wings were a biplane's—a strange craft.

Events passed with bewildering rapidity. Half in a daze I saw the tall, solemn-looking aviator survey my warm clothing with an approving nod. The next instant I was buckling on a steel head protector, and when I noticed the machine again, it had been wheeled out into the flat, neighboring field. A level place I observed, packed hard with shale and dirt, made into a landing place for the planes. I caught a glimpse, at the extreme end of the field near the house, of two soldiers, fitting two wooden objects, painted the drab green of the field, into two pairs of prepared holes, one thirty feet behind the other. They were stout hoops, supported by posts, and rimmed with electric light bulbs. I noticed that the rear was perhaps two feet less in diameter than the other, and that when you stood directly in front of them, they gave the effect of concentric circles, their circumference but a foot apart.

"What is that for?" I asked Hals, and he explained that if it grew dark, the lights were lit, and if from above the aviator saw two fiery circles concentric, he knew that he could fly straight for them and alight in safety.

"But I hope," he added, "that nothing will prevent us from landing in daylight."

I did not like that "nothing will prevent us." I found myself wondering what could prevent us, deciding finally that it was only the usual jocular way of the aviator to frighten his passenger unduly before the flight begins. Had I but known!

I was hurrying across the field towards the aeroplane, its fish-like tail bearing the black inscription "B 604/14," which I later came to know meant biplane number 604 of the year 1914. Ober-Lieutenant Herrmann was wishing me luck and in the same breath whispering admonitions to the grave aviator. I climbed up into the observer's compartment and found myself staring, first at the brown propeller blades only the length of the wagon in front of me, then at the brass petrol tank overhead, and the thick, curving celluloid shield behind, through which I could see the black sleeved arms of the aviator, moving towards the levers. I glanced down at Herrmann, who looked a little nervous I thought. Two soldiers were grasping the brown wings on my left. The brown propeller began to spin, lazily at first, then faster, while the engine that I could have reached forward and touched, began its roaring. A quick comparison between the observer's compartment of this machine, and the one in which I had sat at the Doeberitz Flugplatz near Berlin came to me—that one had the tiny, brass, bomb-dropping levers, two on each side of the rail; these were all in one line and on the left; that one had a writing shelf that fell out from the front wall of the tiny tonneau, so had this, and I touched the lever that brought the shelf sloping down towards my knees; the floor of that machine had seemed solid, though perhaps not, for this was cut to admit the insertion of an observing device which, protruding up between my knees, offered a lens on which the eyes might be cupped by a shield as on a Graflex camera. I was wondering if four bombs dangled from the four releasing hooks below, when the engine started, smiting my ears with a mad roaring, and driving cold air against my face. I remembered to pull down my goggles and the next moment I felt a shudder run the length of the machine as it lurched forward, running over the field, to rise slightly, bump gently on its rubbered wheels, and then gliding upward on a gradual slant, sail towards the willows, dead sentinels grotesquely standing at the far end of the field with their shrapnel-torn branches dangling against the gray-ringed dreariness of sky.

One or two little spasms of fear and, as the aeroplane climbed towards a wood, I began to want to recognize instantly all the objects on the earth. They spread out, unrolling as on a huge panorama, a patchwork of many shaded woods and fields; there the brownish ribbon of a road losing itself like a thread in the gray distance, here little groups of absurdly small brick houses, off to the right a church steeple and beside it the uneven blackened walls of a shell-riddled building. The motor had settled now into an ever-increasing clamor, in which, if you caught one false beat, you would have cause for alarm. No longer visible, the propeller blades had lost their individuality in a grayish blur out there in front, shadowy scimiters whirling too fast for the eye to see. You thought of the engine and the blades but a moment, and then they seemed to become a part of you, and I wonder now if my heart did not try to synchronize its beat with theirs.

We climbed higher and higher. Although minutes ago, objects had ceased to seem strange by their magical tininess, you could sense the growing height now by the development of color; you never knew that the drab winter earth could have so many hues and wondrous shades of brown, gray, green, ochre, and purple; they separated each into fantastic tintings, as though earth's beauties were not for those who dwelt upon it. The long army transport that we had passed on the road, was just a gray worm, crawling along in its brown dirt. And over there by the village, in that field where the thin bluish smoke wraiths were crawling, must be the field kitchens ... and that multitude of specks, a regiment off duty, back from the trenches, waiting to be fed.

A gust felt cold on my cheek. The machine was turning. Now faintly, almost lost in the roaring of our motor, I imagined I heard once more that other sound, the grumbling of the guns, and now I thought of it as the hungry growls of some monster, already sated with the puny living things in that other world beneath us, but which ever grumbled for more. And then suddenly I saw a white cloud appear in the gray sky, and then the white cloud was gone and there came a second, a third, a fourth white cloud, then no more for a minute it seemed, and then four more again. And you knew that over there the enemy's shrapnel was bursting. Fascinated, I watched the pure ringing, billowing beauty of the smoke, celestial, white roses that bloomed out of nothing, dropped death from their petals, and died themselves in the gray sepulcher of sky. We banked away; we saw the white clouds no more.

I was conjecturing in a feverish sort of way how far we had been from the trenches and if that shrapnel line had been bursting over them, or if the enemy, spotting a base of some kind, had begun to shell it, when growing out of the air there approached a sound. Scarcely audible at first, like the faint whining of the wind, gathering its frenzy, now whistling, screaming, shrieking, I heard somewhere near in the void, the song of a shell. And when writing on the observer's table, I was trying to jot down how it felt, I heard another, nearer it seemed, and the pencil fell from my fingers, rolling down until it stopped by the ledge while I sat staring at it and trying not to think what might have occurred had we been a few seconds faster or the shell a few seconds slower. And then I felt myself slide forward in the seat and I knew that the machine was diving down. There was no danger, I felt; of course the aviator was all right, No shrapnel had burst near us but then, we might have been within rifle range. No! Absurd! Yet I quickly glanced over my shoulder and felt centuries younger when I saw the smile on Hals' solemn face. And then, as unexpectedly as it had begun, the downward bolt ceased. Hals was rattling the celluloid screen. It dawned on me that he wanted to tell me something. I leaned back and he leaned forward. I could hear him but faintly although he shouted. "Those shells were on the same elevation as we, or we could not have heard them. So I dove." And there they were screaming their death song overhead now, although I could no longer hear them.

We flew towards a yellow château and then once more began to climb. Of course we were out of the path of the shells, but Hals had not then known that we were in the line of howitzers. The minutes passed, and slowly I admitted that the danger was over. A stinging pain, moreover, was settling above my eyes, and what I might have put down to the quick breathing of excitement, I realized now to be the gasping of the lungs in a rarified atmosphere. High indeed we were climbing, for the earth seemed to shrink and its many colors to blend themselves in a vague tinting suffusion of purple and gold, the veil of a dream.

Heaven only knows what the officers must think who sit in the observing compartment as did I, though they know that this upward climb has a purpose, a purpose of war, as I was soon to see. More faint, then befogged, became the diaphanously veiled earth. Clouds interspersed, graying the vision, clouds and a drifting, wet mist that settled in beads on the glass of my goggles so that I was continually rubbing away with my gloved fingers. We were hidden now, from the earth, and the earth from us. Marching gray gloom all around, ghostly wet wisps that straggled past, caressing one's face. In that Nomad's void, in which even the voice of the engine seemed hesitant and more subdued, I began to feel as if I was making some awful intrusion—into what I did not know, but one felt the guilt of an appalling, defying presumption.

And then I realized that we had been slowly descending through the clouds, for suddenly to the left I saw a patch of the purplish dream veil, and in a moment we were gliding down through the clouds and running just beneath them. Hals was shouting and pointing down. And I saw the battlefield.

At first you thought of a cotton field, of white blown buds and then, as your vision shook off the spell of the bursting shells, you discerned down there a purplish, grayish patch of the earth, of which you were no longer a part, so remote, that only by peering down between your knees into the graflex-like observing glass set in the bottom of the car, could you distinguish even vaguely a single object in that colorous haze of distance. And then gradually there took shape in the glass, as in a crystal ball, accented lines and dabs of color, and there grew before you the black, zigzagging scars of the trenches—although you knew them to be brown with wet clay—and behind them more black lines, only straighter—and you guessed those to be reserve pits—and behind them, approaching at right angles, more black lines, only fewer and further apart—and these you judged the approach trenches. As you stared with the glass your eye never ranged the whole battle line, always the white puffing smoke obscured the view in tiny, white, swift-dispelling clouds, that rose from the area between the zigzagging lines. You wondered which were the French and which were the German trenches. Now a white spot suddenly appeared, exactly upon one of the black lines, and in fancy you heard the explosion of a shell and the groans of men, and you wondered if observers had seen officers coming up and if that shell had been particularly well aimed. A patch of earth, purplish gray in that hastening dusk, and illimitable lines of black stretching away, puffing white smoke quickly coming, quickly going; that was the battlefield as I saw it below the clouds.

Possibly my eyes were accustoming themselves to the great height, for in the glass between my feet objects were becoming clearer. From the thinnest thread the black lines had thickened perceptibly and now as it grew darker, I began to see innumerable, tiny, yellow-red tongues that had a way of darting out from the black lines and as suddenly withdrawing, and I began to think I heard a faint sound like the broken rolling of a drum, and somewhere very far off some one seemed to be beating a bass drum with less frequent but perfectly timed strokes, and there came up to me the booming of the battle—or did I imagine it? Observers tell me it is next to impossible to hear.

Even clearer became the battlefield, clearer though it was ever darkening, and it dawned upon me that we were descending; approaching that patch of black-lined land where the pygmies played with death. It was with a weird trembling fascination that you saw the picture in the glass become more and more distinct. It looked like a relief map now, with objects coming out of the purplish gray haze, and you wondered at the geometrical precision of it all. By staring steadily at the black scarred lines you slowly discerned another color and there at intervals, which gave that same impression of mathematical exactness, you made out darker colored dots. "The soldiers!" Involuntarily the words escaped me. And then the black lines seemed to march across the glass and were gone and you saw now only the parallels of the approach trenches, one at one extreme of the lines, the other but half visible on the outer edge.

You knew then that you were flying away from the battle firing line, but even as you looked, what seemed to be a row of broken boxes, moved across the glass, hesitated and paused there as the aeroplane hovered above them; and in that moment a yellowish box which seemed to stand apart from the others, and which you guessed to be the great house of the village, was blotted out by the spewing gray white smoke of a *grenat* and when the glass cleared you saw that the yellow box had changed to a jagged shape, red with flames. Fascinated, you watched the burning house, and then you realized that the celluloid shield behind you was rattling from violent rapping. Hals was shouting something; finally I guessed what it was—"Want to go down?" I shook my head no. As he bent to the levers, I think he chuckled.

I wondered if what immediately followed had anything to do with that mirth. My muscles were cramped from bending over the glass. I tried now the naked eye, but the gray dusk was blackening and the fringe of flame on the trenches becoming redder and more vivid. But this flame, which should have been even more lurid, began to grow dim and to wane away, like a thousand guttering candles, and I knew then that we were climbing once more; why, only the man behind me knew.

The flickering trenches slid by and away; below us the earth had become calm, luminous blue, pricked here and there with yellow pin points of light; but still I thought I heard that measured, muffled beating as of a great drum, only presently it became harsher as though the drummer was wielding his stick with sudden fury, an insanely growing fury; and you felt a wind on your face, then it was gone, and you felt it again, for the aeroplane had begun to swing round in a slow circle, a nightbird you thought, seeking something below. And then again came the roars, two, one almost upon the other; they seemed ahead on our right somewhere; and again I felt the wind on my cheek, but not again; we were flying straight now.

By this time I thought I knew what Hals had planned. Those pausing, slow, swinging circles had been made in order to get the exact source of the sound, and now Hals was flying towards it—his object the location of one of the enemy's batteries, a new battery, I judged as yet unknown to the Germans, possibly the one that had dropped the shell on the yellow house. Now, had Hals known that the shell was from a battery just getting into action? Because they are men of air as well as of earth, have these soldier-fliers strange powers?

I noticed that the tiny lights from what must be a farmhouse down there, had a way of increasing and as suddenly decreasing from two to four to two; and always the vanishing lights would be patches, not pinpricks, more vivid, too, as though they were not shone through glass, but came from doors that opened into illuminated rooms. And I was wondering why these doors always kept opening and closing. The place must be a brigade headquarters or something equally important. That was it! Soldiers were constantly coming and going. And as regularly appearing, these patches of light grew more lurid, and the guns raged on, I thought with a smile that the firing might well be the slamming of those farmhouse doors, for just then the two had perfectly synchronized—the sudden flaring lights, the faint sound of guns. And then it happened again, one upon the other, and I must have risen to my feet for it dawned upon me—There's the battery over there! Those lights that I thought were part of the farmhouse! Our motor seemed to thunder unnaturally loud then, again they flashed down there, again the faint boom tore up to us. "*Kollosal!*" Hals had spotted the French guns.

Of the race back through the night, I have only the most feverish recollections. I knew we were flying faster than ever before, for the fuselage was throbbing madly and you had a feeling that to escape an awful strain put upon it, the engine was trying to tear itself loose. And then you thought of the need for this speed. Had I been careless with the electric torch? Had we been seen? Might not even now the enemy be after us? Perhaps a telephone call from the battery down to the trenches where the muzzle of an aeroplane gun was tilted to the sky. Or had they telephoned their own aeroplanes to put up after us? Why the speed that Hals evidently deemed necessary?

You knew, too, that somewhere down there, shells from the German batteries were whining towards the enemy's positions. You knew, too, that to reach the earth, you would have to bolt down through this battle-filled sky. The chances were one in five thousand that we would be in the line of our own shell fire. You did not like to think of that one chance. The machine had ceased to shake. I imagined that Hals was looking down on all sides. The wind, certain signal of a turn, struck my cheek. The slow swinging circles began as before. And then, just upon sighting the French battery, Hals suddenly drove the machine forward. Off to the left, what had seemed an unnaturally bright point of light grew incredibly fast into a circle of light and beside it a smaller circle, and their circumferences seemed to be restlessly moving, intersecting here and there with exasperating frequency, although gradually becoming steadier and finally becoming almost concentric, intersecting not at all, the smaller though seeming to have moved in front of the larger, shifting from side to side, although never touching the outer fiery rim. And suddenly I remembered the two circular frameworks, fitted with the electric bulbs, in the field by the shrapnel-scarred willows and I recalled the explanation of them, that they were guide posts for an aviator at night, and that once he had them concentric, he knew that he was flying true to his landing field.

So we were almost home now—home!—the thought made you grimace—miles away! And in a moment now we must drop, begin that bolt down through that zone, through which the shells of our own batteries were flying. And I heard that most disconcerting of all sounds that you hear in the air, the shutting off of the motor—an instant, and as we slid forward, I felt for the brass handles to brace myself, and no longer sped round by the motor's power, the propeller blades became as the strings of a monstrous harp through which the rushing wind wailed a weird song; and we bolted down.... If a shell passed I did not hear it. Gaining in violence, the wind shrieked through the slowly spinning blades, shrieked as though the very air had gone mad; and just when you had begun to doubt that it was beyond human skill to bring an aeroplane to earth through the night like this, you felt a sudden forward horizontal glide, and the next moment the rubber tired wheels were bouncing over the hardened field, and the shadowy forms of soldiers seemed to spring out of the earth, laying hold of the wings as though to make it captive, and the concentric lights were gleaming just in front; and a voice you knew to be Ober-Lieutenant Herrmann's was calling, with a trace of relief, you thought: "Well, how was it?"

Laboriously climbing down from the fuselage, I looked for the aviator, Hals.

"He ran off to telephone," a soldier said.

"The French battery," I said aloud.

As we motored back to Lille, I heard a German howitzer open fire.

CHAPTER V
BEHIND THE BATTLELINE

The service was as good as you get at the Waldorf. Moving with deft skill round the long table, as if their training in the array had consisted of passing platters of food, the soldiers in field gray silently importuned you to have at least another helping of cheese. In a detached way I was gazing at the big canvas hanging on the brocaded wall, the lower part of the picture half hidden by the smart jackets and shaven heads of the Prussian officers, sitting opposite; then I saw a soldier opening one of the stained glass windows, and muttering along the wet wind, I heard the muffled grumbling of the guns.

"An excellent canvas, is it not?" the staff officer at my right was saying, a slender man with one of those young mustaches; he wore a monocle, and the Iron Cross. "The Marquis, you know, has one of the best collections in France. He has several Rubens, I believe, but I have never seen them," he added hastily. "The gallery is on the second floor, and the Marchioness has a perfect terror of our going in there—we barbarians," he laughed.

Through the opened window I could see the green tops of the winter trees, enveloping each in a separate silvery haze, as the unceasing rains that have turned these Western battle lines into quagmires drizzled down. The sullen monotone of the guns made you glance around at Commander von Arnim, the rather frail, reserved, iron-grayed aristocrat who leads the Fourth Army Corps. Finding no trace of emotion there, you scanned the line of his staff, whose faces, thoughtful, mature, or as young and dapper as musical comedy ever staged its "Lieutenant of the Huzzars," all seemed as unconcerned as though they were lunching in a Berlin café. And, when the noise of the guns obsessed you, your ear caught the incongruity of the tinkle of coffee cups and you wanted to laugh, although you did not know why.

The Lieutenant who had spoken of the Marquis's paintings was saying that he had been in New York last winter—and asked where one went there after the restaurants closed at one o'clock? Just then I saw that Ober-Lieutenant Herrmann, who had been talking with Commander von Arnim, wanted to speak to me. I had learned that the Ober-Lieutenant generally had something keenly interesting to say, especially after conversing with a Corps Commander.

"We must go now," said Ober-Lieutenant Herrmann.

"Back to Lille?" I asked in dismay.

BEHIND THE BATTLELINE

"Not until the evening when we go to the Second Bavarian Corps Staff for dinner. Meanwhile we see something behind the battle line."

Assured that they were not hurrying me away because at three o'clock—so they all had said—the French artillery invariably began heavy firing, I said good-by to the officers and climbed into one of the fast army motors, painted the same gray green as the uniforms, unable to shake off the feeling that it was not war at all, but that this buff-walled château in the beautiful iron-fenced park, had not been commandeered as an army headquarters, but that it was simply the home of one of these young men who had invited all his brother officers from a nearby garrison to a luncheon; and that now we were leaving to catch a train. But as the motor lurched soggily from the soaked driveway I took a last glance at the château; a wisp of blackish smoke beaten low by the rain, was creeping along the brick chimney, and an old servant was sweeping away the mud that our boots had left on the stoop; but as the motor swung past the little square-paned library windows I saw that they were pierced with tiny holes, through which passed the thin tendrils of six wires, caught against a great tree and leading off through the park; and in the window I saw a soldier telephoning, while another at a table seemed to be writing down what the man in the window was calling off. Ahead a tranquil driveway tunneled through the trees....

The army chauffeur, ignoring the insane skidding of the car, was racing through a desolated country. It is the contrast that always catches you in this war, and in the sugar beet fields that came up to the road I began to see an increasing number of mounds, some four, some thirty feet long, incongruously protruding from the flat ground. And I began to see little wooden crosses, turned the deeper yellow that new wood turns in the rain, and some of the crosses loosened by the downpours, leaned over, their arms resting in the mud, and on one a helmet hung. On either side the unharvested fields of sugar beets had become the harvested fields of the dead....

Where I saw the white sides of a farmhouse, no smoke mounted from the gaunt, gray chimney; and in the yard beyond, no human thing moved, for we were passing through a countryside where the armies had passed. We drove on, but we could not leave the long, sinister mounds behind, and I began to think: What an awful thing it is not to be able to go a hundred yards without seeing a grave. I noticed that Ober-Lieutenant Herrmann no longer sat hunched with the blue collar of his cape turned up to his ears and staring straight ahead; restlessly he seemed ever glancing from left to right. I wondered what he, a soldier, who had been decorated for bravery in German Southwest Africa, thought of these things that he so restlessly saw.

"A great battle was fought here early in October," he said, after a time. "Sixty thousand men were engaged." He paused. "There were six thousand dead. Every day for five days a hundred were wounded for each mile of a forty-mile line."

That was all, but his eyes roved from grave to grave. For two miles we followed the avenue of wooden crosses and then, still in the open country, the car stopped. I saw that the car ahead with the staff officers had stopped too, and that they were getting out.

"Over to the right there," said a captain, pointing towards a clump of trees through which the ruins of cottages loomed dismally in the rain, "is a village which we had to shell because the French had a position there. Then they took up positions in the cemetery," and, with a wave of his hand, the Captain indicated an ancient brick wall that had seemed to enclose a grove of tall cassia at the end of the sugar beet field. "It took us three days of hard fighting to capture the cemetery," he continued, as we waded through the mud.

"Three days and how many lives?" I thought, as we approached the brick wall, "and now it is not considered of enough importance to have a single soldier on guard"; which is one of the false impressions that always comes to you after hearing that a certain point was taken at such sacrifice, and then to find that point abandoned. For the moment you seem to think of it as being typically futile of war; and then its place in the vast strategical contemplation of a battle line three hundred miles long emerges from your temporarily befogged vision. It is the military point of view to think that too much peace makes a nation soft, and you become angry at the feeling that has whispered that war is futile and forthwith you place war where the idealists forget that it belongs, not beside barbarism, but with civilization.

We entered by the rusted iron gate and stood among the place of desecrated graves. But as I walked among them, their white monuments chipped with rifle balls, the leafless boughs of the great trees overspreading above splintered with shrapnel, the red wall torn open here and there to admit the shells that must have burst in that rain-filled crater by the iron-railed shaft; as I saw a clutter of rifle butts, smashed off against a tombstone, perhaps, so that the metal parts could be taken back to an ordnance factory to be molded again, I was thinking of the men who had fought here, and whether they had lived. I was wondering how many of those thick, white, bullet-chipped tombstones had shielded men from death. I was wondering how many more of them would have been killed had they fought in the open field; and as I examined the shattered granite slabs, I thought of the protection they had given.

One of the staff officers was speaking to me. "Will you return to headquarters with us for tea?" he was saying, and he gave a slight shudder. Perhaps it was from the cold rain.

As we motored into Vis en Artois, the sun broke through the gray-ringed dreariness of sky. Up a narrow hill street with the powerful car waking the echoes among the low white stone houses, two or three peasants in wooden shoes flattening themselves against the walls to escape the muddy spray from our tires, and we stopped in what seemed to be the village center. Down the street I could see the last hooped roof of a transport caravan, and from a stealthy creaking in the house across the street, I had an idea that shutters were being slowly pushed open and that there were frightened, bewildered eyes behind.

With Ober-Lieutenant Herrmann, whose French is better than mine, I crossed the street to read the proclamation—*Avis!*—pasted to the wall of a church. Worded by the Germans and signed by the French Burgomaster of Vis en Artois, it told the inhabitants what to do if they would keep out of trouble.

From the church we walked to a tall, gray stone, square-turreted building that loomed above everything in the village and passing through a wide archway we came into a court filled with drilling soldiers. I wondered what it could have been before the war, for the stacks of hay and the manure piles were wholly incongruous. Clearly, it now was being utilized as a transport station, for at the end of the court I saw four empty, gray, canvas-covered wagons. Turning to the soldiers, you were instantly struck by the fact that they were smaller than any you had ever seen in uniforms. All of the same size divided into squads, each in the hands of a drill sergeant. I watched them doing the "goose steps," to the proud clapping of their boots on the cobbled court, while others marched by briskly in twos, saluting. It was the barest rudimentary training that they were being put through—but it was stiffening them for the firing line—and as they drilled these raw troops, I could hear in the distance the drumming of the guns. It seemed to electrify these stocky little fellows in the new uniforms, for their feet stamped the louder, and their saluting hands snapped up like automatons; and I wondered if it were hard to content yourself with harmless drilling in a manure-strewn yard, with the music of war playing for you to march; or if behind any of those stupid, utterly peasant faces there lurked a craven thought that they were glad to be there and not where those shells were bursting. But as I watched them and felt the eagerness with which they went about the drill, I found myself thinking of the craving I had seen the Jews of New York's Ghetto show for education and that these stolid peasants were just as eager to learn that they might go to war. And I wondered if after all it might not be a lark for the youth in them, better than giving themselves day after day to an industrialism that made them old before their time. Was it not better than trudging off in the morning to the blowing of a whistle? I asked Ober-Lieutenant Herrmann where they came from.

"They are all Saxonians," he explained; and I remembered what a German Socialist had told me, that the low laboring class of Saxony is notoriously poor and short-lived, their years taken by work in the mines. No wonder they had pranced at the roll of the guns! They were thinking of it as a deliverance.... Into what?

We walked under the gray arch and across the muddy street into a paved school yard, where evergreen hedges bloomed in pretty red tubs. The sun, as if to make up to those rain-soaked men who crouched in the trenches but six kilometers away, streamed down, as in a glory before its setting, and as the school yard rung to the fall of our heavy boots, it seemed for a moment as if the brown door must open and children come pouring forth.

We entered the school house and turning into the classroom on the left, I saw twelve cots made of rough boards and twelve wan, unshaven men who lay there as men dead, although, at the sound of our approach, their eyes turned in a disinterested stare. I observed a German, who seemed to tremble under the covers, and as I walked beside his bed, I saw that the sweat was standing out on his face.

COURT FILLED WITH DRILLING SOLDIERS
"We came to a court filled with drilling soldiers."

OBER-LIEUTENANT HERRMANN
Ober-Lieutenant Herrmann, detailed by the General Staff to accompany Mr. Fox along the Western front.

"How high is his fever?" I asked the surgeon.

"He has no fever. He is sweating with pain."

I turned to go out. I think the surgeon was offended that I did not make the rounds with him, for, with true German consideration and thoroughness, it was doubtless his plan to show me every detail of his little hospital.

"Eight weeks ago," he was saying, as I walked back towards the door, "we had two hundred wounded in here—but now," and his tone was almost apologetic.

I asked him how far the wounded had to be transported from here before they could be placed in a hospital train.

"Thirty-five kilometers," he said; "that is to Cambrai," and he was explaining something about his interesting cases, and doubtless wondering why I did not write them down in the memorandum that stuck from my pocket. Two weeks before I would have done so, but as you come to see the wounded in this war, you feel—rightly or wrongly; I do not know—that it is the grossest banalism to draw a notebook before the eyes of the wounded and write of their sufferings. Unthinking, I did it once in the hospital at Gleiwitz, and I shall never forget the look in a dying Austrian's eyes.

Close by the door, I noticed a black-bearded Frenchman, his leg heavily bandaged, and over his head on the schoolroom wall hung a cheap copy of an etching of Friedland with the victorious French cuirassiers galloping by. What a world of sadness looked out from that wounded Frenchman's eyes. As we walked out into the court, you could hear the cannon more plainly, a steady crashing seeming ever to grow in violence as though one new battery after another was being unlimbered to make work for the surgeons in little school houses the countryside round. In great indignation, the surgeon drew a fragment of metal from his pocket and explained that two days ago an English aviator had dropped the bomb of which that was a part, only eighty meters from the hospital. But I scarcely heard him. From the manure-strewn courtyard across the street floated a cheer. Had the Saxonians been told they were to be sent to the trenches? And I wondered if this was to be their deliverance—the beds of unpainted wood, where I had seen a man sweat with pain.

That evening, after a successful dinner, Herrmann took the edge off our pleasure by announcing that we must get up at five o'clock next morning. "You will be taken to the trenches with Captain Kliewer's party (another group of correspondents had come to Lille). We will all meet in Commines for luncheon and in the afternoon you may see a field battery in action. Of course, it is expected that you will not want to go, and it is understood that those who wish to remain in Lille may do so with the full approval of the staff."

Rotkohl was approved; so was the Dutch general. Rotkohl said something about his grandmother, who lived on the Christiania Fjord, and the general—well, he said there were more pretty girls to be seen in Lille than along those muddy roads; besides it might rain, and suppose his patent umbrella did not work. In three motors, one for Ober-Lieutenant Herrmann and I, and the others for Captain

Kliewer's party, we raced through Lille long before dawn, to get into the trenches before daylight would reveal our approach to the French. We lunched with the Second Bavarian Army Corps at Commines as the guests of General von Stettin and we told every officer in the room that we wanted to see the trenches by night, and, being Bavarians, they thought it a tremendous joke, and roared with laughter.

Bidding the Bavarian staff good-by, we went out to our motors. With Ober-Lieutenant Herrmann and the photographers, I was supposed to go to a battery already in action. Hauptmann Kliewer's party were going to see their battery later. Telling myself that this early start—the heavy artillery firing never begins around Commines until four in the afternoon—was being made so that the photographers could photograph the battery, and that at this time of day there would be little doing there, I explained the situation to Ober-Lieutenant Herrmann. With the utmost good nature—I knew from his smile that I had guessed right—he spoke to Hauptmann Kliewer, who courteously granted my request. So, with Poole, Reed and Dunn, I rode away from Commines, Hauptmann Kliewer following with an officer in another car. Poole was telling us that the Major who sat beside him at luncheon said that last night the English had dropped four shells into Commines, evidently taking a long chance on hitting headquarters; and Reed came back with another officer's story of how the enemy's observers had seen a motor leaving Commines and had put three *grenaten* in the field beside the road not forty yards away. And as the gray-green army auto car soughed down the heavy roads and you saw the puddled fields beginning to mirror a suddenly sunlit sky, you wondered if the enemy's observers could see your car too, and you caught yourself, every now and then, watching the sky, as though to spy the shell they had picked out for you. Nothing happened in that ride, but from the moment of leaving Commines we thrilled to innumerable paradoxical motions too laboriously complex to describe, that always come when you are approaching the firing line and the novelty has not worn off. Growing heavier with the sound, until it became almost the slow roll of huge drums, the sky filled itself with the echoes of the guns, crashing and crashing as though the heavens were a vault of blue steel. And always, out of that growing grumble towards which we rode, we heard more distinctly the explosions of the shells, each in a separate disconcerting violence, and always louder, nearer.

Two Uhlans, their mortar board helmets covered with cloth, galloped by; we overtook a transport train, the light, springy wagons moving easily through the mud, the drivers posting in their stirrups, which somehow seemed like an exhibition of beautiful riding that should have been done in a park. We turned out, our wheels spinning in mud up to the hubs, to let one of the big gray motor ambulances painted with huge red crosses, rumble by, with its red load for the field hospital in Commines. We passed two rosy-cheeked peasant girls, who carried food in baskets, and then the clank and jangle of a string of caissons, going at a canter, as though a battery needed shells. Perhaps the very battery we sought.

Somewhere on that road we must have crossed the Belgian frontier, for after passing through silent, shelled Maraid we drove into Houthem, Commando of the Second Bavarian Corps. We had been following a road that ran parallel to the firing line only a mile on our left. Shells from the German batteries had been flying overhead, but the muffler cut-out had drowned their wicked whine. We were in Houthem, and across the muddy fields there was that row of trenches where the German line seems to come to a point, and where there was a colonel of whom we had heard in Commines, Oberst Meyer of the Seventeenth Bavarians, who had pushed forward as far as he dared go, lest he be enfiladed, was waiting now for his supports to come up—hence the point that you may have seen on your newspaper maps of January of the lines near Ypres.

I looked out from under the dirt-colored top of our motor to find that we had stopped before a little yellow-brown building over the door of which was nailed a black and white letter shingle, saying that here were the headquarters of an artillery regiment. Seeing Hauptmann Kliewer and the Corps Staff officer from Commines get out of their car and enter the house, I concluded they were arranging for our visit to the battery, and climbed out with the others to look around. We stood at the intersection of one narrow, muddy road with another that seemed to lead off at right angles towards the trenches. I looked up the village street, at the end of which a red brick church laid its high white steeple against the blue sky. I could see the shell holes in the church walls, but the steeple appeared untouched. Poor marksmanship! I saw what had been a row of houses. All that was standing now was their walls, and in the ruins of one I saw soldiers picking up the heavy roof tiles; they would use them to floor their dugouts in the trenches.

A group of soldiers, evidently off duty, had been watching us, and one of them came over. "I'm a German-American," he said, introducing himself. "I lived in Brooklyn. I worked in an exporting house on Hanover Square."

"You're not a German-American," I replied. "There's no such thing. You're a German. That's why you came over to fight, isn't it?"

"Sure," he grinned; and then he put to me that everlasting question: "What do Americans think now? Are they more friendly than when I left?" (That was in August, and he had stowed away on an Italian steamer.)

I told him that I thought they were; whereupon, apparently greatly relieved, he told me something about the street upon which we stood.

"You see those houses over there?" and he pointed to the row of ruins. "Well, when we first came here, Artillery Headquarters were in the last house. Then a shell hit it when the officers were out—*Gott sei Dank!*—so they moved next door. A shell bursting on the street here"—and he indicated where the road was filled in—"smashed up that house so that it caught fire. Then the Colonel moved down to the yellow house there. I wonder when he'll have to move again."

I wondered too, and began to feel uncomfortable. Over in front of the yellow house—the first floor had evidently been a store—I saw a group of soldiers looking in the window. They were closely inspecting and talking about the photographic reproductions that have evidently been hung there by orders, there where all the soldiers, back from the trenches on their relief, might see. For I noticed that there were pictures of captured Russian guns, of General Hindenburg, of the victorious German troops entering Lódz. And I thought that here was but another instance of the marvelous system which is carrying on this war against nearly all Europe.

Pictures of triumph from the Eastern lines posted where the soldiers in the West can see and be thrilled with national pride.

I began to notice these soldiers who, back from the trenches and cleaned up, were strolling around Houthem as on holiday, shaved, their uniforms made as clean as possible, smoking cigars, they reminded me of the workmen you see stopping before the windows of the cheap shop in a factory town on pay-envelope afternoon. In a field close by I saw a swarm of them, gathered round one of the yellow and black *Liebesgaben* wagons that bring gifts from home to the soldiers free of charge. Presently, his back bending under the weight of a bulky white bag, I saw one of the soldiers come away from the wagon and slowly shuffle down the street. You guessed he had been the one chosen to get the gifts sent to the men of his company, and as he plodded on past the shelled houses, I heard him whistling. There came, a few minutes later, from behind a gray shed where a transport had been delivering lumber, two other soldiers, and on their shoulders they carried a long box made of new wood—a coffin. And in confusion I thought it must be for some officer, and I thought of the man with the *Liebesgaben* pack and of the homes that had sent the gifts it contained, and that when he would read off the names, that there would be names of the dead....

The yard in front of the white-steepled church of the Annunciation of Mary the Virgin was filled with the familiar little wooden crosses, fitted in, it seemed, between the old tombstones of the Belgian inhabitants. As Hauptmann Kliewer swung back the heavy door, I was amazed to see that the church swarmed with soldiers. A confusing clash between the instincts of religion and military necessity, and I walked among the soldiers. They were recruits receiving a last drill in the use of arms, stiffening them before they went down into the trenches. You told yourself that you were glad all the benches had been torn from this church so that these men might be drilled here without being exposed to the shelling that their detected massed presence anywhere around Houthem would of a certainty bring on. I know had it not been war, instincts of my upbringing would have revolted against this, that the thoughtless like to speak of as desecration. But the more you see of war, the more you come to measure the things of war time solely in terms of life and death. It is not the spilling of Holy Water that matters, only blood.

Almost in a daze, I stared up at the gaping holes that the shells had made in the roof. Broken slates stuck down from out the smashed plaster ceiling, and you thought of them as of bones, and the brown tatters of hanging plaster as wounded flesh, for you came to think of this place as being a stricken personality, call it a stricken religion, if you like. But was it not written that He suffered so that a world might be saved? Surely, then, what could mean a few shell holes in one of His houses, if most of those who hid there might still be spared.

I walked between the lines of young recruits, some loading, others learning the sights, others emptying their magazines, and I came at last to a shrine of the Virgin built in a recess in the wall. Above it I could see a patch of the blue sky, framed in the hole of a shell; but it was not the shrine that held me; it was the soldiers before it. They were down on one knee, and I wondered if they were Catholics worshiping there while the others drilled. *"Feuer!"* And each man whom I had thought on reverent knee, snapped a gun to his shoulder; I heard the hammers click. They had been learning to shoot kneeling. I wondered if any of them thought of the Virgin.... "Damn dumbheads!" cried an officer. "Faster!"

Explaining that the enemy had left an observation post in the steeple and that the Germans were using it for the same purpose now, Hauptmann Kliewer led us into a circular staircase of wood that coiled away into the darkness of the narrow tower. Did we wish to climb up to it? The Hauptmann explained that it was dangerous, for "knowing we had observers in the steeple, the French artillery would, sooner or later, open fire." But arguing with yourself that the French had evidently tried to hit the steeple before but had only succeeded in putting a few shell holes in the church roof, you became convinced of the comparative safety of it, and began to climb the spiral stairs. The higher you got, the more rotten the boards became, and I was wondering if there wasn't more danger from my two hundred odd pounds being brought down on a rotten step than there was of a shell crashing through the brick cylinder. After climbing up a series of shaky vertical ladders we stepped out on the observing platform. To put us at our ease, Hauptmann Kliewer warned us all about not gathering around the observing window, a hole, a foot square, cut in the wall, adding that the platform was not strong. So, two at a time, we stood at the window and looked out.

I saw the country laid out as it is from a low-flying aeroplane, the soggy fields exaggerating the squareness that the gray fences gave; beyond the flat red-roofed houses I saw a dark green fringe of trees, and then above that a tiny puff of white smoke appeared, then another, until I counted four, all billowing out in the thinnest of fleecy clouds, until thinning all in a white blur, they vanished.

"That's shrapnel," Hauptmann Kliewer was saying. "Our trenches are right by the woods there."

And it came to me, the wondrous glory of the little white clouds; if that was so the soldiers might look upon beauty before death. The wind was blowing towards us, and we heard the shrapnel's peculiar whistling burst and then the heavy shaking roar of *grenaten* and over to the right, just at the edge of the wood, I saw rising the blackish smoke of heavy shells. About a mile away, exactly opposite, I saw a brown tower between the trees.

"Our artillery observers are in there," explained Hauptmann Kliewer, "and the French must know it, for they've had a cross fire on it from right and left all day."

I watched the steeple with a new fascination. Shrapnel framed it in a soft billow of clouds, and lower, where *grenaten* struck the ground, I saw the dissolving blackish smoke. Would they hit it?

"They have fired a hundred shells at the tower since morning," laughed the Hauptmann. "They're not shooting very well to-day."

I forgot everything but the brown tower. I felt that any moment it must sway and topple over, but when we were told to leave, it was still standing. I wonder if it is there now. As we left the church and plowed through the mud to our motors,

I saw a battalion of artillerymen drawn up before the little yellow headquarters, receiving their instructions. I caught one admonition not to be careless with ammunition, and then we were told that we were going to a battery. Down a road, where we saw five abandoned French caissons mired in a field, we had another experience with a most disconcerting sign. Hauptmann Kliewer's automobile stopped and seeing him get out, we followed, joining line in mud that came above our shoe tops.

"It is unsafe," he explained, "to take these motors any further. Knowing we were officers, the French would surely spray the road with shrapnel."

"Then the French observer can see us?"

The Hauptmann laughed.

"They've probably seen us from the moment we entered Houthem, and if our artillery hadn't been keeping them busy, they probably would have thrown some shells at our automobiles. But here we haven't even that chance. We walk to the battery. Separate yourselves at intervals of fifty paces so that if a shell drops on the road we won't all get it."

Too business-like a tone had come into his voice to let you think he was fooling. At once his manner became that of the officer in action, terse and taking instant obedience as a matter of course. We spread out. I found myself walking with Poole. We were approaching a high-banked railroad track, the road disappearing under a trestle. I suppose the field must have been strewn with the objects of war. I did not see them. I was staring straight ahead at the sky, looking for shells, and getting ready to throw myself on my face—as I had been told to—if one came. And then, from behind the railroad embankment, came a terrific explosion and I was watching a whisk of grayish smoke trailing away. I stood for a moment unable to talk. The embankment was only a hundred yards away.

"Poole," I remember saying. "That was close."

"The French must be trying to destroy the railroad," he returned.

He was saying something else when another explosion shook the air, almost in the same place. Badly rattled, for I could see Hauptmann Kliewer and the Second Bavarian Army Corps Staff Officer calmly walking on, where every stride was bringing us nearer the track, I tried to say unconcernedly: "That's wonderful marksmanship. Two in the same place," thinking, "suppose another battery not so accurate, should open up, and missing the tracks, drop one where we stood." "Wonderful shooting," I repeated, adding to myself, "and we're walking right into it."

Whereupon Poole and I decided that if two German officers wanted to commit suicide, good enough, but as for us, we were not going another step further unless there was some other way than by this road that ran under the tracks not thirty feet from the bursting shells. Yet I found myself walking on, although my blood had long ago turned cold; and I wonder now if that is the way some men go into action, ashamed to hold back. But we weren't going into action and there was no hot, nervous frenzy of battle and patriotism to urge us on. Walking towards those explosions was a case of "going in cold."

Disobeying orders, we hurried forward, overtaking the officers, and to our amazement we learned that the explosions were not of bursting shells; but the firing of our own battery hidden behind the tracks! Sheepishly, we trudged under the trestle. We had had all the sensations of being under heavy shell fire, dangerously close, and there had been no shells at all!

Coming out from under the trestle, I saw, sleeping under the high embankment of the railway, a greenish canal. Dug in the side of the opposite bank, that slanted upward forty feet from the water, I saw a hole shaped like a door, and as I looked, an officer darted forth and, scrambling up over the slippery clay, disappeared in a scraggle of bushes. I saw the mud-spattered carriages of two German field pieces, their dull barrels lying back between the wheels and serenely pointing into the blue and gray mottled sky.

Leaving the road, we sank shin deep into a yellow ooze, and standing on some planks about the yards behind the guns, we waited. The boyish-looking artillerymen, rigid gray-green figures, so statuesque that something in the mud must have turned them to stone, they seemed waiting too. And then, from the direction of the hole in the bank, I heard:

"Links! Ein viertal tiefer!"

And the statues by the guns became alive; they darted this way and that. They reminded me of sprinters leaving the mark. One leaped to the sights. *"Links! Ein viertal tiefer!"* And as the man on the bank bellowed again, the soldiers at the sights began tugging madly on something I could not see; and I knew that the range receiving telephones must be in that cave in the bank, for it dawned upon me now what that shouting meant: "Left! A quarter deeper." Sight the gun to the left, advancing the range a quarter—some scale on the gun obviously—and they would get the French! I glanced towards the shouter; he was disappearing into the hole in the bank.

I saw another of the boyish artillerymen bend down over one of the brown straw baskets that stood in neat little piles and lift from it a shell, evidently heavy, for while stripping off a waterproofed cover, he rested the projectile on his knee. As he darted towards the opened muzzle, the waterproof cover fell in the mud, but instantly the soldier who had just lain the brown shell basket upon a pile of empties, picked up the cover and, neatly folding it, saved that too. And I saw a pile of discharged shell cases; copper was too valuable these days to leave in the mud. And as I saw them load and prepare to fire, each man doing his task with the speed and deftness of a whirling gear, I thought of it as one part of the war machine in which individuality was utterly lost in the gun; but that was before I went into the hole in the canal bank.

And then I saw that all the soldiers were holding their hands on their ears; and I was quick to put mine there too. But even then, as the gun discharged, I could feel my ear drums trembling as though they would break—the long red flash, the roar, the frightened recoil of the barrel, the dark puff of quick dispelling smoke, the air flying with black specks, and then a sound like a gigantic coil of wire being whirled through the air and a 7.7 centimeter shell was whistling towards the French line.

As swiftly as they had loaded and fired, the youthful artillerymen withdrew the shell and when one of them stood patting the copper jacket of a new projective and glancing towards the edge of the bank, as if waiting for the man who cried "*Links, ein viertal tiefer!*" to appear, I knew that they were firing shrapnel. They must wait for the range before setting the tiny indicator which travels with the projectile through the air. And as I waited, marveling at the detailed accuracy for shooting at an enemy who must be nearly two miles away, the other gun in the battery went off with a roar, and, while my ears throbbed madly, I watched the village hidden among the dense trees about a quarter of a mile away, for an enemy's shrapnel was spreading its white clouds there. And just above those trees there appeared another white speck, two more and the sky was ringed with curling smoke; then two heavy booms and tatters of black smoke whirled from the trees. The French had opened fire on the village. As I waded through the mud to go down into the bombproof, it struck me uneasily that our officers glanced at each other.

I was slipping down the bank as the "Links ein viertal tiefer" man rushed from the bombproof, bellowing something to the gun crews. Then we climbed down through the hole of a door into darkness. The first thing I saw by flashing on an electric lamp was a dirt wall, a little artificial Christmas tree that stood in a niche in the walls; beside it a half loaf of black bread, a bottle of wine and a picture of the Emperor. And then the man who lived there nodded to me.

He was sitting at a rough board table. He looked as absurdly young as the men under his command. I saw from his shoulder straps that he was an Unter-Lieutenant, and, even as I looked, his features seemed to grow grave with something he must be hearing through the telephone, which was strapped to his head. The stub of a candle guttered on the table and only his face seemed lighted; everything else faded away into shadowy silhouetting darkness. I saw him begin to race his pencil across a little pad and calling the orderly who, standing back in the darkness, I had not seen, he sent him scurrying away. The telephone buzzed. He called into it, lighting as he did a cigarette; from the blackened stubs strewn on the table, it was evident that he smoked constantly. He began scribbling again. I saw that he was looking at me nervously. I was thinking how this little room with the bread, wine, and Christmas tree, and the Emperor's picture, was the very organism of the battery and that this good-looking, nervous young lieutenant was directing it all, when I saw the orderly hurrying in. Another officer hurried after him. I noticed that the Lieutenant at the table looked relieved.

"You gentlemen will have to go now," said the officer, whom I saw was an artillery captain. "The French have opened the village with heavy *grenaten* and two just burst four hundred yards from here."

"What was that lieutenant so excited about?" I asked, as we left the bombproof.

"Why, his observer just telephoned that the French and their aeroplanes were ascending."

Even as I climbed up the canal bank, I saw the young artillerymen reluctantly covering their guns with branches, until, through a distant field glass, they would seem to be bushes. Their battery was "strategically silenced." I saw the under officers scampering down into the bombproof and their guns transformed into big gray leafless bushes, the boyish soldiers ran into hiding behind the blackened brick wall of a shelled house. Boo-oom! Boo-oom! Over in the village the smoke was pouring from a burning house and above the treetops the shrapnel spread their fleecy clouds.

In the next field I saw a patch of blackened smoke; dirt flew.

"Run!" shouted the Bavarian Captain, who had been in America. "Run like hell."

And as we tore pell mell past the ruined house, the artillerymen grinned and waved their hands.

"*Gute Reise!*" one of them yelled.

Pleasant journey!

CHAPTER VI
A NIGHT BEFORE YPRES

The following are expanded pages of the diary that I kept from five o'clock in the evening of January 10th, 1915, to seven o'clock the next morning.

5 P. M.: The motor has stopped, but I wonder why. In Houthem the Bavarian captain told us that we were going to Brigade Headquarters. I can see though only a dirty brick farmhouse; its door is open and the light of a lamp falling on the yard seems to float in a yellow watery pool. But the other gray-green army car has stopped too, and Hauptmann Kliewer is getting out.

So we pile out on the muddy road just as Hauptmann Kliewer beckons us to come on. Behind us the ruined walls of Houthem are hiding in the thickening dusk, but the grayish steeple where the Germans have—and the French used to have—their observers, persistently shows itself.

Hauptmann Kliewer and the Bavarian captain have left the road and are wading through the mud of the farmhouse yard. I thought we were going to Brigade Headquarters. We splash on after them. Hours before at the battery we sank in mud to the tops of our puttees; now the novelty has worn off. Through an open barn door I see a motor and think of it as being hidden there, an impression which grows, upon noticing that all the windows in the rear of the house are covered with boards, so that no light is visible. But the front door is visible. Yes, but that faces Houthem where the Germans are, and these rear windows face Ypres and the English and the French. About that silent house broods mystery. Hauptmann Kliewer is knocking and the door opens just enough for us to pass in one at a time, and is hurriedly closed. I wonder if a French observer could have seen that narrow bar of light. Probably not, for in the room only candles are burning—three stubby candles on a long kitchen table, around which soldiers are sitting. And something buzzes, and picking up one of the many telephones, a soldier says into it, "*Brigade Hauptquartier.*" A moment, and it buzzes again. And once more the monotonous "*Brigade Hauptquartier.*" And it dawns upon me that this dirty farmhouse must be the Brigade Headquarters that they told us we would visit. The kitchen now has a new interest.

Bidding us wait, Hauptmann Kliewer and the Bavarian captain have gone with an orderly into another room. The man at the table with the ragged beard and the boyish face has clamped a telephone to his head and is writing rapidly, pausing now and then to assure the man at the other end of the wire that he is getting every word. I wonder where that other man is? Down in a trench, perhaps, or possibly in the regimental headquarters. What is he saying? Have the French attacked? The other man at the table, puffing stolidly at the briar pipe, is clasping a telephone as though ready should the buzzer call. I wonder how he can be fresh and clean shaven, when all the other faces seen in the flickering candle light look weary and unkempt.

"Come!" Hauptmann Kliewer is calling us, so we leave the men around the kitchen table, who, unlike most of the German soldiers we have met, seem too exhausted to talk, and file through a latched door into a room that might have been in a farmhouse somewhere near Monroe, New York. The little black, pillow-seated chairs, the old-fashioned piano with its rack of torn music, the red-cushioned stool with the stuffing coming out, a hideous colored print of Antwerp on the wall, the oil lamp with the buff china shade, it all seems so utterly un-European. And then the door to an adjoining room opens and a slender, nervous-looking man in the fifties, whose impressive shoulder straps indicate an officer of high rank, begins to bow to us all. "General Major Clauss," Hauptmann Kliewer is introducing us, and at once the General Major dominates the room. It is for him to say whether we must go back to Lille, or spend the night at one of his regimental headquarters.

He begins a long conversation with the Hauptmann. General Major Clauss is shaking his head. I guess it's back to Lille.

"Ask him," I beg the Hauptmann, as he begins to give us the substance of what had been said, "if they cannot let us go to the firing line, if they'll let us stay here until morning."

With a smile, Hauptmann Kliewer is telling the General Major our wishes, but he too smiles, and spreads out his hands—the right one is wounded—as though it were out of the question.

The little parlor is filling with officers. They are all bowing and smiling in a friendly way. I appeal to one of them, a young chap, handsome in spite of the dueling scar across his chin. "We can do nothing," he says regretfully, in English. The General Major, apparently, is reluctant even to ask one of his regimental commanders to assume the responsibility for us. As if to bid us good-by, the staff is standing at attention. We urge the Hauptmann to telephone. "I shall try," he says, with rare good nature. General Major Clauss has closed the door behind him in his bedroom, and the Hauptmann buttonholes a Major. The Staff officers look at each other in surprise. They believed they were well rid of us. Briefly the Hauptmann is making the point for us. The young officer with the scarred chin puts in a word. The Major seems undecided. A lieutenant says something that I imagine would translate into, "Telephone,—anything to be rid of them," but he regards us with the amazing polite smile.

The Major darts into the kitchen where the telephones are and then, smiling broadly, Hauptmann Kliewer comes in followed by the Major.

"Permission has been granted," he says, "for you to go to the headquarters of the Seventeenth Regiment. You will spend the night there, and be here at seven in the morning, where I shall meet you with the motor."

"Aren't you coming with us, Captain?" somebody asks.

"I'm going to spend the evening in the headquarters of my own regiment in Commines," the Hauptmann explains. "One of the officers here will take you to the Seventeenth's headquarters."

Thanking everybody, we leave the parlor, and the officers smile sententiously. We pass through the dimly lit kitchen where the tired soldiers sit around the table, and cautiously opening that betraying light filled door, we file, one at a time, into the stable yard. It is still dusk, and as we follow our officer towards the narrow road, that meets the one we had taken from Houthem, Kliewer bids us good-by. "Be careful," he calls. His motor drives away, and to my surprise our car follows. "Call back that driver," I say to our officer, "he's made a mistake."

"No, he is right," smiles the officer. "No automobile ever goes up this road. The French would see it. It's an easy walk, only a mile."

We follow him through the mud, finally setting foot on the road, less muddy I notice, than the road from Houthem. We are on our way to the headquarters of the Seventeenth Regiment, The dream of every correspondent in this war is about to be realized. We are on our way to spend the night on the firing line.

5:30. We have been walking ten minutes. We have passed a mounted patrol and an unarmed private, walking fast. The long twilight has grayed, but even far up the road I can still distinguish the posts of the wire fence. We have just passed a lonely, brown frame cottage, the last house between the open fields and a fringe of wood, when the Lieutenant stops short and faces us.

"From now on," says the Lieutenant, with that easy way of authority, "we shall walk at intervals of thirty paces."

I know what that means. Only a few hours before, when approaching a battery, Hauptmann Kliewer told us the same thing. I remember his words: "Altogether we make too plain a mark. We must separate."... How uneasy you feel, walking along this way. Not only are you gauging your own interval of thirty paces, but you are careful to keep an eye on the others, ready to warn them if they draw too close; and they are keeping an eye on you. You expect something to happen. Uneasy, you watch the sky, but no shrapnel is bursting nearby. Ahead somewhere the artillery is booming, but here everything is quiet. This walking along, pacing your distance, restlessly glancing to right and left, and listening, is getting on my nerves. No wonder I can't hear anything. The flaps of that aviator's cap are tight around my ears. Expectantly I unloosen them. And then I hear it, above us, a sound that makes me stop short; a sound as though a giant had sucked in his breath.

Above us a shell is screaming on its way to the French trenches. From beyond the woods the cannonading sounds heavier. Through the trees, where the road bends to the right, a row of roofless houses seems ghostly gray in the dusk. "That's what's left of Hollenbeck," I am saying to Poole; "I heard the Major say we'd pass through it." And then it seems as though the air is being sucked in all around us; it shrills to a multitude of strange whistlings. The fence wire rings; a twig rattles along the dried limbs of a tree and floats down; something spats against a stone and goes ricocheting away. I'm positive we're going to be hit; the air is wild with bullets. The trees are closer. There we'll be safe. Why don't the others hurry, so that we can move faster, too?

And then, right on the road, almost where my heel has just lifted, a bullet strikes. The dirt flies high. Instinctively I lurch forward and fall on one knee. Forgetting his blanket, Poole bends over me. "Did you get it?" he asks. I wonder if I didn't, and look at my foot. "It was close," he says, relieved; "I heard the thing hit right behind you."

"I don't think we're seen," I unconcernedly try to say. "They wouldn't have let us come up here if we were. These must be wild bullets flying above the trenches. They're just beyond the wood, you know."

"Too wild," is Poole's comment, with which I agree. We are climbing a slight hill now, the road turning to the right into Hollenbeck, a silent place of unroofed, shell-battered houses. Here you feel safe for the walls protect you, but over our head the loud whining of the German shells keeps up the sound of war. Passing the last house we come upon two squads of soldiers waiting in its shelter, and as we go on out into the open road, they grin. The dusk is turning to black, and ahead it is hard to tell where the tops of that clump of trees leave off, and the sky begins. I am certain that those trees are our destination, and although the bullets are whistling again, one feels safe.

A few minutes' walking and we have turned into what seems to be a wooded lawn. A hundred feet away the vague shape of a low roofed house marks itself by a thin bar of light, evidently from a closed door. The lawn is muddy, and as, walking in single file, we cross on planks, the liquid ground sloshes beneath our feet. As we approach what seems to be the stable of a farm, those in front walk slower, and even slower descend into the earth. Poole and I follow them down a flight of rough stone steps, and seeing two uprights of stout logs standing as a doorway and, level with my head as I descend, a roof of tree trunks and dirt, I whisper, "Bombproof."

The opening of what seems to be an old kitchen door. A warning to keep your head down, and we go stooping into a room dug in the ground, at the other end of which a genial, gray-haired man, whom you instantly decide is Colonel Meyer of the Seventeenth Infantry, is rising from beside a homemade table spread with military maps, a hospitable smile on his ruddy face.

"Welcome," he is saying in German. "So you got up the road all right?"

A sudden suspicion possesses me, and after introductions are over, I ask: "Colonel, there were too many bullets on that road. Where did they come from? Wild?"

"Wild?" he chuckled. "Why, sir, that road is our line of communication. It is watched and is covered by French sharpshooters. We lose half a dozen men on it every day."

And the officers at Brigade Headquarters smiled.

5:57 P. M. The broad wooden benches against the walls seem to us as comfortable as a cushioned lounge, and repeating, with many a *"glaube mir"* — which the Colonel and his Adjutant are quick to catch on to as the "believe me" of American slang—that wild horses couldn't drag us out on that road again, we take in the details of the room. It is about ten feet from where I sit to the strip of burlap covering the earthen wall behind the opposite bench. I should say that from the shelf, where the Colonel has his personal belongings, down to the other end of the room, which the glow from our big oil table lamp only lights faintly, is about twenty-five feet, enough for men to sleep on the benches along either wall. In the middle squats a red bellied stove, its pipe going up through the roof. The door looks as if it came from a farmhouse kitchen; it is paneled with four little squares of glass, one of them cracked, probably from the concussion of a bursting shell.

Yes, the timbers overhead look strong, intensely safe unless a *grenat* should burst squarely on top of them. And only by one chance in a thousand could a shrapnel ball fly down through the door. Yes, it seems safe in here; slowly we began to forget about the road. The Colonel excuses himself to study a map that seems to have been done by a stencil, and I cannot help but notice that it has been executed to the most minute detail, even individual trees and bushes being marked. I wonder what the scale is. I have to compel myself to glance elsewhere, for the fascination of the map is strong.

Above the shelf that runs across the end of the room, just so high that the Colonel who is sitting beside me, can reach up and take from it what he wants, stands a large square mirror. It seems also to be doing service as a visiting card tray, for stuck in the frame are five or six cards bearing the names of officers and their regiments. Somebody is taking good care of the Colonel—I imagine he's married—for the shelf is filled with luxuries, boxes of cigars and cigarettes, bottles of liquor, and there's a quart of sparkling Moselle! Strewn in a long row are all varieties of those wonderful food pastes that Germany began to put up so extensively in tubes, since the war—Strassburg gooselivers, anchovies, rum chocolate. Colonel, you're living well down here!

It's queer how you can, in a few minutes, learn the tastes and habits of a man in a place like this. The Colonel is religious. There is a crucifix fastened to the burlap over my head. The Colonel must sleep on this bench. At the ends of his shelf, I see two other crucifixes, and there, standing on the top of a box of cigars, is a colored print, a Station of the Cross. I begin to know the Colonel better than if I had observed him for months in his Bavarian home. As I gaze at him now, bending over the map, that in his preoccupation he has pushed farther across the table, the lamp's yellow glow shows me his face in relief against the shadowed walls. It is a strong face, and kind; the chin is grim and square, but the eyes are big and gentle, grayish though, the color of a fighter. The gray mustache almost hides it, but reveals enough of the full mouth of one who is not ascetic. As for the crucifixes and the picture; they belong to the eyes. A seasoned man, the Colonel.

With a nervous start, that seems incongruous with his broad shoulders, the Colonel looks up. Then, appearing suddenly to remember something, he pushes the map towards me. I see it is a map of his position.

"There," he says, running his finger the length of a broken line in the upper right hand corner, "are the French trenches." "There," and he points to lines par-

A NIGHT BEFORE YPRES 57

alleling them, "is our position. Here," and his finger travels down the map, to rest on a group of oblongs and squares, "is where we are now. This *unterstand*," and he makes a mark beside the smallest square, "was dug next to the shed where the farmer kept his wagons. This place is known as...." Were I to name this place, it would, upon publication, be cabled to France, and telephoned out to the French artillery positions. "Now," and the Colonel smiles and runs his finger along a thick blue line that makes an angle and then disappears at the lower end of the map, "that is the road by which you came from Houthem, and at this point you were fired upon. Notice the curve that the French trenches make. From the extremity of that trench," and the Colonel indicates an imaginary line sweeping a section of the road, "it is not a thousand meters, easy for a sharpshooter."

"And that," I laugh, and I'm trying to make this gaiety real, "is the point that we don't care about crossing when we return."

"Can we not go back by some other road," Poole suggests, "a longer way, making a detour?"

The Colonel shakes his head with a reluctant smile.

I hear then the same buzzing that I heard in the kitchen at Brigade headquarters. And from the top of a varnished box, on the floor where I had not seen it, the Adjutant picks up a telephone. "*Hier ist Siebzehn Bayrischer Regiment*," he calls, and hands the instrument across the table to the Colonel. "*Hier ist Oberst Meyer*," says the Colonel, "*Ja ... Jawohl ... Adieu*." With a chuckle, he turns to us. "That was Hauptmann Kliewer," he explains, "telephoning from Houthem. Somebody must have told him there about the road. He was rather concerned for you, but I assured him that you were about to take dinner."

Feebly we try to protest. But the Colonel insists that we'll have to eat with him, and we all feel guilty and self-conscious. It's just like these Germans to share their black bread and army wurst with us. But this is the firing line; this bomb-proof is only eight hundred meters from the French trenches, and every scrap of food must count. An electric torch flashes on the wall outside the door; some one is coming down. A black mustached, young Bavarian comes in, and picking up the varnished box, which I now see sprouts with vine-like wires that climb up the wall and out under the roof, he carries the telephone away. The door opens again and another private comes in. Clicking his heels in a salute, he bows low from the waist, and then announces dinner. In bewilderment we look at each other and follow the Colonel up the earthen stairs.

"I always dine," Colonel Meyer seems to be apologizing, "in the farmhouse."

Overhead a stray bullet whistles, and I hear it rattling through the dried tops of the trees.

7:05 P. M. It seems safe, until leaving the shelter of the bar, we see that we have to cross an open space before reaching the farmhouse. I can see, standing outside the door there, the vague form of a soldier. He passes the shaded window, a faint orange square in the shadowy wall, and his bayonet flashes. As we cross this open space the Adjutant is asking us to turn off our electric lamps, for their reflection might attract French observers. So we trust to luck in the darkness and, slipping in mud, dart behind the shelter of the farmhouse. I hear a bullet thudding against the stone wall of the barn.

The door creaks open and we go in. As I gape around, the fragrance of good cooking comes from a coal stove, crammed with tall cylindrical army pots. The room is evidently the kitchen—a typical farmhouse kitchen with a wide fireplace of red bricks and a long mixing table along the wall by the shade-drawn window. Tacked to a slate-colored pantry door is a calendar with the month of October not yet torn off, and on top of the fireplace an old wooden clock that has run down at half past four—was it on the day the Germans came? "Sit down, gentlemen," the Colonel is saying, indicating a round kitchen table, around which six chairs are crowded. On a snow white cloth our places have been set. There are not enough forks to go round so some have soup spoons. I see only three knives, so some of us will have to use our pocket knives. A comfortable yellow light falls from the yellow lamp in the center of the table. We begin to feel as snug as a fireside cat. "Our knives and forks are rather limited," apologizes the Adjutant, who introduces himself as Hauptmann Koller, a tall handsome Bavarian with a scraggy black growth on his chin. "However, there are dishes enough to go around." I begin to have a suspicion that our sympathy has been absurd. Black bread and army wurst never gave out the odors that are coming from those pots on the stoves, and then our surprise is complete when the Colonel offers us a cocktail. Cocktails, and the French trenches eight hundred meters away!

"A German cocktail," smiles the Colonel, as he pours out the white *schnapps*, "not like the kind you have in America. One of my friends had a bottle of them in München—Bronx cocktails," and the Colonel makes a grimace. There are only two cordial glasses, but by passing them around, we succeed in drinking the Colonel's health. As we take our seats at the table I notice that while four of the chairs seem to belong to the kitchen, the other two are richly tapestried. There must be a château near here. The Colonel is sitting in one of them and Dunn in the other. Leave it to Dunn to be lounging in the other tapestried chair. Hauptmann Koller, who is opposite, is hacking off chunks of bread from a round rye loaf. On my other side Reed is looking at the bottle of *schnapps* and wearing his unextinguishable smile.

A soldier brings a pot from the stove and the Colonel serves us. It is an oxtail stew, canned of course, but smells appetizing. "The Colonel hasn't any left for himself," exclaims Poole; but the Colonel is holding up his hand. "There is plenty," he says, and the soldier brings another steaming pot. Magically, tall, dark liter bottles make their appearance and on the labels I see *"Hacker-Brau."*

"Münchener Beer," cries Reed. "Isn't this amazing?" The Colonel looks at Hauptmann Koller and grins. I think that from their viewpoint they are enjoying it as much as we. Canned boiled beef follows the stew; more of the tall, dark bottles appear. I see a soldier open a green door in the wall at my left and, reaching into what is evidently another room, straighten up with his arms full of beer bottles. "That is our Bierkeller in there," explains Koller. Dunn decides that it is the very place for him to sleep.

"Colonel," says Poole, pointing at the wall behind me, "what did you do, have those windows boarded up so that the light wouldn't be seen?"

Hauptmann Koller is laughing and rubbing his frowsy chin in delight.

"Those are not windows," the Colonel says, with a laugh. "They are shell holes." We press Koller to give us the story: "The Colonel was dictating a report in here one morning. That orderly was writing it," and Koller nods towards the smiling, good-looking private with the Iron Cross, who is writing at the mixing table. "Without warning, for our battery was not in action and there was nothing to draw the French fire, two shrapnels tore through the wall and burst in the room. You can see the holes their balls made in the other walls and the floor—and the Colonel wasn't hit!"

With a wave of his hand the Colonel indicates the last of three cots against the wall. "I was sitting on the edge of that bed," he says, "and the shells passed over the other two beds."

Almost incredulously we gaze at him as if to make sure that he is wounded but doesn't know it.

I am staring now at the walls and ceiling, trying to count the little shrapnel holes. Above the Colonel's head there is an Empire mirror that never hung in any farmhouse, and perched upon it a brass-black, hair-plumed helmet of a French Cuirassier.

"Out in the yard," remarks the Colonel, "there is an unexploded shell, one of the French 'twenty-eights.' It fell there one day and didn't burst. We had one of our ordnance experts up to examine it, but he says it won't explode now. If it did, it would blow up the house."

So we sit here thinking of the silent guest in the yard outside. I forget that there is something more to eat. With the cheese and coffee, the evening concert begins. A German field piece in the woods close by has opened fire. Suddenly the night is roaring with the bursting of shells, and down in the trenches the rifles begin their incessant harsh croaking. The Colonel is looking at the tiny watch dial on his wrist. "The same as last night," he remarks to Hauptmann Koller, adding to us, "The French always open heavy fire at eight."

That's the third German officer I've heard make that statement in as many days. The French always shelled Mouchy at three; they put *grenaten* in Houthem every evening at six; they concentrated their fire here at eight. Frenchmen, the last people in the world you would suspect of systemization!

"They'll keep it up," continues the Colonel, "until two, and then they'll stop and begin again at five for two hours. We know exactly what to expect from them. They're hammering on us, for we hold the furthest front on this part of the line. I dare not advance any further until my supports come up."

We ask him to tell us something about the fighting here.

"The French attacked on December second," says Colonel Meyer, "more than a month ago. They came in columns of fours, and you can see them now, lying out there between the trenches in columns of fours. They were mowed down, and for a month the fighting has been so heavy that they can't get out to bury their dead. You can see them afterwards when the rockets go up. They make it quite bright."

"How many rockets, Colonel, do you send up in a night?"

"About a hundred generally."

"And how many men on an average are in the trenches?"

The Colonel considers long. "That varies greatly," he says finally. "At some points only 400 men of a regiment are in the trenches, at a time; at others, 800. I have used as high as 1200 for repelling a hard attack."

"Strange things happen, fighting the French," he muses. "The night after they were cut up so, they were ordered to attack again. As soon as it came dark, one of our soldiers heard a Frenchman calling across to him in German. The Frenchman had crawled across from his own trench on his belly. 'Don't shoot,' he told my man. 'Two hundred soldiers and an officer want to surrender.' The soldier kept him covered, and sent for an under officer. They telephoned me from the trenches and I told them to let the Frenchmen come over if they threw down their arms. And two hundred Frenchmen with their officers, did come over. I asked their officer why they had surrendered, and he told me that the order had come to storm our trenches again that night, and that all day his men had been looking out and seeing their comrades lying in the mud in columns of fours, and that they nearly went mad." And the Colonel slowly shakes his head. "I saw them lying there, too. I can understand how it affected them."

As Hauptmann Koller pushes back his chair and goes to the fireplace, I notice that his shoulder straps are covered with meaningless cloth; no sharpshooter will pick him for choice game. And from beside the old wooden clock Koller takes down a box of cigars, piling on it a tin of cigarettes, while with the other hand he picks up a bottle of Anisette. "They're Austrian cigars," he says, "but they're all right." While we are lighting up, he pours out the Anisette. This time we drink Koller's health and then the officers insist upon drinking ours; we return with a toast to Bavaria. Colonel comes back with a standing health to the United States.

"Tell them," he begs, "that we are not barbarians. I have a sister who lives in Wyckoff, New York, and I'm afraid that by reading your newspapers, she thinks that I've become a terrible ogre." Again the Colonel is the easy smiling host.

The door opens; a private comes in and sits by the telephone. He moves it down the mixing table quite close to us. "Is it time for the concert?" asks the Colonel.

Hauptmann Koller nods. "At eight thirty. It's that now."

"*Gut!*" and the Colonel indicates us with a wave of his hand, "Gentlemen, be my guests at our regular evening concert."

We look at each other blankly. The Colonel seems to have a huge joke up his sleeve. He is bustling about the telephone like a man dressing a Christmas tree. He takes up the instrument and holds it to his ear. "Come," he says, beckoning me. I pick up the receiver and almost drop it in my amazement. Somewhere an excellent pianist is playing the *Valkerie*. In a spell, I listen to the music, each note retaining its sweetness over the wire. The music stops; I hear a flutter of handclapping.

"Where is it?" I gasp, coming over to the table.

"That comes from the headquarters in Houthem," explains Koller, while the Colonel nods, smiling, as with a surprise well planned. "That was General Major Clauss at the piano. He was playing under great difficulties."

"The man with the wounded hand!" I exclaim. Poole takes up the 'phone.

"He is playing Tristam," whispers Poole, and outside I hear the growing fury of the shells and the crash of the German field piece close by. The Colonel is telling me how on Christmas Eve they played "*Heilige Nacht*" for them, down in Houthem, and that while he was listening to the music a heavy shell burst down in the trenches, killing eight of his men. But I am not following half of what he says. Everything seems to be in a daze. It is all too incredible. We have finished what seemed to be one of the best savory dinners I have ever eaten. The supply of golden-brown Münchener beer seems to be limitless. We are finishing with coffee, cigarettes, cigars, and a cordial; and now a concert. And outside the sky is hideous with war, and eight hundred meters away are the French. And this is war.

Koller is at the 'phone now. "When General Clauss is through," I tell him, "ask him to play something from Chopin." In a moment Koller nods for me to come over. And I am listening to the opening bars—perhaps my nerves are overstrained—but I hear a noise that sounds like a bullet hitting a wire fence, and the music is still. Snatching up the 'phone the orderly tries in vain for a connection and finally transfers it to another wire. Perhaps, after all, I heard only a normal snapping of the wire. Imagination plays strange tricks in this world of uncanny and violent impressions.

The door opens and an orderly comes in with the mail. There are two letters for the Colonel, and while he is reading them Koller opens a bottle of cognac. The Colonel is stuffing one of the letters inside his coat. His eyes are wet and, not to embarrass him, I watch Hauptmann Koller measuring out the cognac. Probably a letter from the Colonel's wife. The door opens again; the room fills with officers, who click their heels and bow to us. "The relief," whispers Koller.

A thin, gray-mustached man, whose precise speech makes you think of a university professor, comes forward; the Colonel remains on his feet. The room seems to stiffen with military etiquette. The Major is making his report to the Colonel. I catch the words: "They put heavy shells on us, beginning with eleven o'clock last night and lasting until one." What time is it now? Ten thirty-three. Soon the shelling starts. It is a very detailed report and, unfolding his map, the Colonel spreads it on the table and indicates a position. The Major studies it and offers some thoughtful comment. How like those Civil War plays played in New York years ago, in fact identical in situation. The Colonel gives some orders, asks if there are any questions, and to the clicking of heels and polite adieus, the relief officers file out. They are going to the trenches.

The good looking private with the Iron Cross salutes. "Sir, the concert is ready."

What! do they keep it up all night? But the Colonel is getting up, leading us out of the room. We follow him out into the night—and the sky seems faintly luminous with weird light—going along the farmhouse wall until we come to a short flight of steps into the ground. Descending, we are seated in an extremely low-roofed bombproof, in which five soldiers, half in uniform, are sitting around a wooden table. They look like the comic band of the music halls. One has a harmonica, another a flute, another sits before an inverted glass bowl, which he is ready to tap with a bayonet tip and beside him is the guitar man—a wonderfully made guitar, its wires, telephone strings, its box, a case for canned goods, planed thin; and there is a serious-faced drummer. But facing them, blasé and autocratic, is a man with sensitive features and pince nez. He has discarded his uniform for an old black coat, and with a dirty hat pulled down over his eyes, he suggests the Jewish comedian of burlesque. Evidently he is the leader for, raising a bayonet scabbard, counting, "*Ein, zwei, drei,*" he brings it down and the concert begins.

You recognize *Puppchen*. Leisurely beating time, sipping a glass of coffee that our orderly with the Iron Cross has filled for him from a pot that simmers on the squat coal stove, the leader is having the time of his life. They play some old German Folk songs, and once the harmonica man is late in starting and receives a boisterous reprimand from the leader. They are singing now, "*Röslein auf der Heide ... Morgen Rot,*" and you think how sinister the words are, "leads me to an early death." Red morning! Will it ever be for them? Even here under the earth I can hear the hungry growling of the shells.

Modestly the leader is telling us that the Bavarian musicians are the best in Germany, "therefore our band is the best in the trenches," and the Colonel is beaming on them all. The orderly with the Iron Cross, who, unable to speak a word of English, has been smiling at me all night, urges us to take some more coffee; and it's "Good-by, boys! Good Luck," and we're out into the battle-shaken night.

"Want to have a look at it?" Hauptmann Koller asks me. I nod, yes. Hugging the wall, Koller and I turn the corner of the barn and slowly go down the open space between the buildings, that we had rushed past earlier in the evening, plastering ourselves against the walls. As if that would do us any good! We can hear the French bullets whistling by, and the air is shaking with heavy guns.

"After eleven," remarks Koller, "I fancy the French are at it with big *grenaten*," and as he speaks I see a flash in the trees not two hundred meters away and a field piece discharges with a crash. "Our seven answering them," Koller is pointing towards where a greenish light seems to flash in the sky. "Over there about a mile," he says, "is the Ypres Canal. The Thirty-sixth Division is on the other bank, and as soon as they push back the French, we'll go ahead again," he speaks with a quiet confidence that makes you feel that the advance of his regiment is a matter of course.

"Come down here," he suggests, "and you can see the battle. Don't scorn the shelter of those trees. Keep them between you and the trenches. Go from one tree to the other."

I hear him splash through the mud; he is waving from behind a tree. I plow after him, going so fast that I almost slip and fall. The whistle of a bullet will make you move faster than you ever thought possible. Out of breath we come to the edge of the little grove and look out on the battlefield.

It is all color and noise—unearthly colors, unearthly noises. I stand at the edge of an Inferno. The heavens streak with a sulphurous green, and the earth is scarred with flame. I see the rockets swishing up from the trenches, breaking with the weird light that would reveal any enemy creeping up, and falling in a shower of sparks, like shooting stars. It gives a strange confirmation of an old saying that when a star falls some one dies.

I see the steady, streaming, reddish line of rifle fire and the yellow flash of shells. I hear their fierce, harsh croaking and their deafening boom. I see, in the burst of a rocket, the wet fields glistening with mud; and the night crashes and rolls with awful clamor.

Koller is handing me his binoculars. Through them I can see the Ypres Canal, a monstrous glistening water snake, sleepily drinking the blood of men. It is a green night, a green land, a universe gone mad, for the sky was never meant to shine with those hideous lights. And the rockets spread their fiery trail and spill their hideous glare; and the line of fire brightens and grows dim and brightens again; perhaps as men are falling and others are springing to their places, and I turn my glasses on the glistening fields, and think I can see the columns of fours, the mounds of the dirt, the color of the mud, and I can hear the bullets panging in the mud at our feet. How they must be riddling the bodies of the dead!

"I've had enough," I tell Hauptmann Koller.

We say good night and cross the farmyard. The din of the battle seems to have died down, although the bullets still whistle and rattle among the dried trees. We lie down on the benches in the bombproof, with our clothes on, with the dirty blankets over us. Our night of nights is done.

12 P. M. to 6 A. M. Bits of dirt from the ceiling fall on my face. Hauptmann Koller is snoring.... The guns are rumbling again. Koller snores blissfully on. The cannonading is terrific. Those poor devils down in the trenches.... The cannonading sounds fainter and fainter.... The handsome orderly with the Iron Cross is flashing a lamp on Koller's blanket. "All right," calls Koller, but in a moment he's snoring. Only stray rifles are crackling now. The glowing phosphorescent face of the watch on my wrist shows six o'clock. Morning! Hauptmann Koller is already out of bed.

"Good morning," he says, with a yawn. "The orderly was in a minute ago. Breakfast will be served at six-thirty."

In the trenches it's the hour when they pick up the dead.

CHAPTER VII
IN THE TRENCHES

By the first of October, 1914, every European war map had become a bore. After Von Kluck had conducted what a United States military attaché in Berlin told me was the most masterly retreat in the history of the world, the black fishhook line stopped moving across northern France and fastening its barb in Belgium, it ceased to move. Day after day, as we read the newspapers we saw that the line was the same; perhaps near Dixmude or Mulhausen it changed from time to time, but by November first it was evident that it was there to stay—for a time at least—and war maps became a bore. The reality of that line of ink is not, I assure you.

The next time you read your newspaper, glance again at the map of the West front. Follow the line that begins on the Channel above Calais, turning southeast above Ypres and ending in the passes of the Vosges in Alcasse; and then think of it in this way. On the dunes you can enter a ditch that has been dug across Europe from the English Channel to Mulhausen. You can walk about three hundred miles under ground, eat three meals a day, and sleep on officers' cots without once having to expose yourself in the open. You will realize as you see second, third, and fourth trenches parallel and connecting by labyrinthine passages that the amount of excavating required would dig a subway. The labor involved in the New York Aqueduct, the Chicago Subway, the irrigation works of our West seem trivial when you consider this work was done under fire.

Before I came to Germany I was told: "There is not much doing in the West. Both armies are marking time." Since then the battle line has become about three hundred miles long. A surgeon in the *Feld Lazarette*, in Vis-en-Artois, told me that they had on the average ten wounded a day and that their hospital was fed by a segment of the front about two miles long. When you recall the terrific fighting near the Channel ports, this average is not high for the whole line. So when you glance at the little map in your newspaper think of it as meaning three thousand wounded men a day, ninety thousand a month, and a tenth as many dead. Remember also the Ypres Canal, where soldiers have gone mad and thrown themselves into red water, and at the same time the field of Soissons, strewn twice with the dead; of men in the trenches of the Argonne, undermined, dynamited, their bodies blown as high as leafless forest trees.

Again, when any one says to you, "There is not much doing in the West," imagine a three hundred mile line with three quarters of a million soldiers standing in muddy brown water, and three quarters of a million more, too, whom they

IN THE TRENCHES

have just relieved, lying on beds of straw, too exhausted to remove their uniforms until it is time to wash; think of that line in which for every five minutes of every day a German is being killed—and God knows how many English, French and Belgians.

For two days I had been in the vicinity of Lille with Ober-Lieutenant Herrmann of the Great General Staff. Near Labasse I had seen the trenches at night, but I wanted to see them by day; for at night the soldiers are all keyed high; it is then that the hard fighting is done. What did they do with themselves during the day? It was at Lille, the fifth night after I had left Berlin, that I met five other American correspondents, a Hollander and a Norwegian, who were in Hauptmann Kliewer's party. After dinner in the Hotel de Europe, Ober-Lieutenant Herrmann, who had gone with Hauptmann Kliewer to the Staff of the Second Bavarian Army Corps, told me that from now on the two parties would travel together until we reached Brussels. "In the morning," he said, "we go to the trenches in front of Arras. You must be here in the lobby ready to take the motor not later than six."

In the inky darkness of a clear, cold morning three army automobiles left the Hotel de Europe and roared away through the streets of Lille. A Second Army Corps officer whom Bob Dunn, the New York *Post's* correspondent, was apologetically explaining as being a cousin of his, rode in the first car. This officer, who had never traveled the road to Arras before, was acting as our guide; soon we understood Dunn's apologetic way, for after one challenge upon another came ringing out of the night, and we had stopped to have our papers read in the lantern light of sentries and patrols, Dunn's cousin lost the way. "I knew he would," remarked Dunn. "No one related to me could go straight."

The officer tried again. He took us along the crumbling path of war, along a road where under a dark centered half moon we saw in the silvery graying light the lanes of abandoned trenches and rows of gaping shell torn houses, while one by one the stars turned to tiny icicle tips, and day slowly came on. I think after crossing the Ypres Canal at Douai, that we followed every blind alley between there and Vitry, for turning one corner after another, with each new row of poplars coloring clearer against a brightening sky, we seemed to come no nearer to the boom of the guns.

As we plowed through a heavy cross road to Mouchy le Preux and came out on the highway to Arras, we saw a German battery. The last stars had withdrawn, and in the grayish morning light the clanking field pieces lumbered by, a ghostly company with vague gray ghostly men on ghostly horses. I imagined they were moving parallel to the firing line, changing position. How close were we now? Probably six kilometers. Two miles riding up the road to Arras with the battlefield of October 1st, the muddy, desolated fields on either side. It was up this road that the French artillery made its retreat, across those fields that their infantry poured with the Duke of Altenburg's Saxonians in hot pursuit. Ober-Lieutenant Herrmann had told me that the French had given way all along the line here before the German second drive, retreating to Arras, which they now held. I remember that he had spoken of Arras as an objective and that the Germans were constantly drawing nearer. How close were they now? How far from the French would we be in the trench? One began to feel a tremulous excitement.

Hauptmann Kliewer and Ober-Lieutenant Herrmann told us that this was as far as they dared go with the motors. To approach closer than two kilometers to Arras with automobiles, and we easily would be discerned by the French artillery observers. Evidently having been telephoned that we were coming, two gray cloaked officers were waiting for us outside a little brown shack that I guessed was regimental headquarters. The Captain, an intelligent looking Prussian—and, by the way, I've yet to see one of the upturned mustached bullies of whom our cartoonists are so fond—spoke perfect English.

"Leave your overcoats here," he advised. "It's rather warm going up to the trenches." Then he glanced at our feet and gave an approving nod. "No pumps or gaiters, I see. That's good; you'll be up to your knees in water," and as I walked up the road towards Arras, he told me that two Italian journalists—any newspaper man is a journalist in Europe—had visited the trenches at Arras. And the Captain laughed. "One wore a pair of gray spats and the other had one of those artist ties, those black fluffy things. One of our soldiers drew a sketch of them." When we had gone about a hundred yards, we turned to the right, descending by an abrupt runaway into a trench that dug in a plowed field, led away at right angles from the road. More than a thousand meters from the French trench, and with rifle fire yet to begin, and shielded by the very fact that you walked in a narrow pit seven feet under ground, comparatively less in danger than you had been in the motor from Mouchy le Preux on, you nevertheless tingled with a strange exhilaration. Keeping one eye on the top of the trench, prepared to duck, lest it suddenly became uniform in height and expose your head to the open field, gazing the rest of the time at the bottom of the pit, lest you slip in a hole and go sprawling in the yellow liquid ooze, we followed the officers, slavishly imitating their movements of progress. Then we came to another trench that made a right angle with our own, advancing towards the firing line, parallel to the road we had left as unsafe, exactly as in the approach trenches at Labasse. But as we trudged on, splashing now and then through water to our knees, we no longer imitated the officers. They walked as before, unconcernedly and erect. We were going along ducking our backs, for shrapnel was beginning to fly in a neighboring field, and I heard it panging in the mud on all sides.

It was light now, although a fleecy white moon still hung in the sky, and as it grew brighter, one after another, the batteries began the forenoon cannonade, and as I heard the bursting shrapnel ever growing more numerous, I guessed it was the same as at that other point on the line where I had been two days before, where the French cannonade before and after luncheon, always beginning at the same time. And then directly above me I heard the disconcerting burst of shrapnel and I saw the pretty billowing white clouds that the explosion always makes, and knowing that to be directly under shrapnel is to be out of danger for the little balls spray like the stream of a watering cart, I comfortably watched the smoke until it drifted away, thinning like blown silk.

From the field the trench sloped up into a deserted house. Obviously a part of the trench, I saw the wall of the house had been pierced to make a passage the same width of the ditch, and that in the far wall there loomed a similar passage doubtless leading down into the trench again. As I walked through the ground floor rooms of the house, it reminded me of something I had seen from the windows of the military train that had brought me from Metz to Lille. There the survey of the German pioneers had hit through the middle of certain villages, and I had seen houses flush against the track, with their side walls torn off so that the trains might pass without smashing into them; and I had seen everything in the disordered rooms of those houses. Here it was the same, only this time war had invaded homes with a trench instead of a train. First one, then through a doorway into a second room in utter disorder. I saw concentric holes that marked the entrance and exit of a shell and the confusion of turmoil and pillage. A bureau with the drawers emptied out, clothing strewn on the floor, a baby's high chair overturned, a crucifix lying broken in a heap of fallen plaster, those rooms seemed to be a contrast, a chaos, the picture of the illimitable dissolution of war in one home. Into the trench again, up another slope through another silent house, through a stableyard, vile with blackish typhus water, and so on along a path of desolation, if not where the trench led through farmhouses where it pierced unharvested beet fields, with the panging of shrapnel and now the sucking whistle of rifle balls until we came to another and wider trench. This at right angles to our own, crossed the road to Arras.

"This is the line," the Captain explained. "The French are only two hundred meters away. Don't expose yourself, and when you hear shrapnel close, it is best to stoop down a little. Come," and turning into the pit, he led the way towards the highway. We were walking parallel to the French, and they were only two hundred meters away. And I thought then of it being the great ditch, burrowed under Europe for three hundred miles, and I was soon to feel that I was among the inhabitants of a new and terrible world.

Your pulse quickened. Back there where you left the road and the brown muddy walls about you there had come a thrill; as you floundered on up through the approaches hearing the burst of shrapnel and the spatter of the balls on the soaked field, you were uneasy; but now as you gazed up and down the trench, which you have thought of not in so commonplace a way as to call it "trench," rather "firing line," as slowly its impressions came upon you, they left you amazed. This goal that you had been striving for during a whole month was a place where men looked bored!

And how can any one be uneasy or frightened when every one else seems as though the very safety of their existence is torturing them to death? But that was before I went into the advance trenches, for out posts make a difference in the soldiers, as I was presently to see.

"This position," explained the Captain, as we walked in single file, "was a French trench. We did some work on it. Made bombproofs out of some of their old rifle pits and dug new ones along what was the back of their trenches. Now the French see our guns sticking out where their stove pipes used to be."

I noticed one little square doorway after another cut in the back wall of the trench, curtained with burlap bags, and as we passed, the curtains were pushed aside and I saw the soldiers sitting inside playing cards by candlelight or smoking and talking, and all looking so comfortably bored; just as you would imagine them sitting in a Friedrichstrasse café and watching the crowds go by. "There's no attacking now," explained the Captain, "so only half the men are on duty in the rifle pits. The others lounge in their dugouts."

And as we went further along I saw signs of idle time when soldiers revert to childhood and remember that they used to dig things in the dirt and sand. Here in the trench wall four nitches had been dug, three in a line and the other below. And in the upper nitches, tiled in various attitudes suggestive of destruction, were three toy battleships, flying tiny Union Jacks and below them a toy submarine with U 9 painted on his gray hull. And I was positive that I knew the store in Leipzigerstrasse from which they had been sent by *Feld Post*.

To the right I saw the short wide passages leading up to the rifle pits where two soldiers stood on a platform cut in the dirt. One was cleaning his gun while the other squinted along a rifle barrel that protruded through a narrow port reenforced with bags of sand, and watched. His manner, the stiffened pose of the gray-green shoulders, the boot braced in the ground, set him off in increasing alertness and vigilance. In one of the dugouts I heard the whine of a harmonica; it was the waltz from "The Dollar Princess." And as I came along the line the impression grew on me, the men in the rifle pits, crouching statues of war; and the men in the dugouts behind, wondering what to do with their time.

The trench sloped upwards and we were crossing the road to Arras, but I could not see the village, for there loomed a barrier of sandbags six feet high; and thrust through this gray wall, I saw a machine gun, with a soldier dabbing it with oil, while another peered through a slit towards Arras. It was obvious that the gun was trained on the road. A Lieutenant came to meet us.

"The Lieutenant," said the Captain, after he had introduced us, "is in command of this section of the trench."

As we followed up along the line, I began to think of the French as being only two hundred meters away and that it was uncanny not to see them. Every now and then the whistle of a bullet told you that they too were watching this trench just as the Germans were watching theirs, and in an empty field, a quarter of a mile away, *grenaten* were bursting with terrific din. Yet perversely you half doubted that the French were there at all. Subconsciously the thing didn't seem possible, a line of armed men just across the field; and you had been walking opposite them for more than a quarter mile without any more of a realization of their presence than that caused by the suck of a rifle ball. Where were they? What did they look like?

At the next rifle pit, with a nod to the Captain, I turned in. The soldier who sat with his gun on his knee, smiled in a friendly way. I said something in German and his comrade at the oblong porthole, relaxed his vigilance long enough to look around and grin. Carefully I listened for bullets. On this point there was apparently no firing. With absurd stealth—I imagine they must have both grinned—I stuck

IN THE TRENCHES

my head up over the top of the trenches. I saw about a quarter of a mile away a fringe of trees with white and yellow houses showing through, and further forward, just off the macadam road, a house of grayish stone. The sky was blue and in the bright sunlight the furrowed rain-soaked field was a golden brown. I could see a black wisp of smoke curling from a red brick chimney, but where were the French?... Something slapped against the mud in front of me, and a shower of dirt flew over the trench. Down I ducked. Yes, the French were there.

The soldier at the porthole was talking excited German. "He says," smiled the man with the gun across the knee, speaking English now for the first time, "that you kept your head up too long. It's all right to look quickly and get down, but the other way they see you."

His growing beard did not conceal his smiling mouth. I wondered at his easy dialect, spoken without the London accent noticeable in so many Prussian officers. I asked him where he had learned to speak American. He told me he had worked in the Bronx—which those who are not New Yorkers may or may not know—and that he was a joiner in a piano factory. Every Sunday afternoon he played baseball in Claremont Park; his team had won a Church League championship. Bullets began to whistle overhead. Doubtless thinking that a reckless officer had exposed himself, the French were covering the pit. "Do you hear them?" grinned the Bronx piano joiner, as the whistle of the bullets kept up. "Fine, isn't it?"

"You like to hear bullets?" I asked. He nodded. Well, I suppose it's a cultivated taste, like German hors d'œuvres. I began to think of him as of the Saxonians whom I saw drilling in the courtyard in Vis en Artois. Of course he liked this better than piecing together colorless bits of wood in a factory. Not a day passed, probably, but that he got his little thrill, and when the war was over he could go back to the Bronx—if he lived—and be a hero among his friends for the rest of his days. And as I wished him good luck and turned to overtake the others I wondered if this war is going to change the workingman in this way; if he is going to become so accustomed to a spicy existence that he never tasted before, that he will not follow to the humdrum of shops and mills as inevitably as before; rather demanding something more?

Beside the door to a dugout I saw on the wall a page torn from a French periodical *L'Illustration*. It was a lay-out of actresses and bicycle riders and it struck you as incongruous until you remembered that the trench had been captured from the French. I saw a profusion of mottoes lettered by the soldiers on their writing paper—*Gott mit uns*. You could not pass a rifle pit—and they are about ten yards apart—without seeing those words of the Emperor that have become the slogan of the German army; and you thought as you saw them, not printed under some official orders and sent to the soldiers so that they would ever have them before them, but written by the men themselves out of the feeling in their hearts, you thought that it is going to be a tremendous job to hold at bay an army, that thinks the Divine is on its side.

I noticed that the soldiers try to outdo each other in the individuality of their dugouts. There was one that had a little sign over the door "*Gasthaus zur Kron*" and the soldier inside told me that it was the name of the hotel he owned in his home town. I saw another with three inches of stove pipe protruding from the roof that billed itself as the *Schmaltz Kuchen Bäckerie*, under which was modestly written in pencil "Here is the best kitchen in the world." Delightful these signs, for presently I came upon an exceedingly frank one, the tenant of a dugout having stuck over the door, a shingle upon which was written "*Gasthaus der Wilde Wanze*," which means "The Inn of the Wild Bed Bug."

I went down into one of the dugouts. I saw a square hole in the earth where one had to move about stooped. A candle flickered on an empty box and in the corner I saw two piles of mud-caked blankets. A pair of wet socks hung from a string that had been fastened in some miraculous way from wall to wall and a soldier was straining his eyes in the candlelight, reading the tiny Bible which is part of the equipment of every German private. Perhaps I do the man an injustice but I imagined he was reading because he was bored; and that by the time this war is over, more Germans will know their Bible from cover to cover because of hours in the trenches when they had nothing else to do. I saw no crucifix in that room in the ground—and I have seen crucifixes in bombproofs—but I saw another cross, the Maltese outlines of the Iron Cross dug in the dirt wall, and I thought of it as that soldier's dream.

At the next passage to a rifle pit, the officers stopped and I saw that here were no soldiers on watch and that a narrow passageway opened up into the field.

"That is the way we advance our trenches," explained the Captain. "At different points we dig out like this and then after we have gone out awhile, we dig sideways in both directions, parallel to this trench. Soon the different little trenches that are being dug that way, meet. Then they are deepened and the soldiers leave pits here and take the new position."

It was the method, as old as fortifications that the Japanese gave perfected, to the military world at Port Arthur and that the Bulgarians copied around Adrianople, and it is the way by which the —th Infantry finally closed in Arras, the way the whole German line, meter by meter, is moving France, creeping this time, not running wild over the country side, as during those wild August days, but gaining slowly here, losing slowly there, instead of being driven back across their own frontier, as the English newspapers promised they would be long before this writing. I went up into one of the little outpost trenches. The approach was shallow and you had to walk doubled over. I passed a door of solid iron that slid into a groove dug in the mud, and through another gate, this one of wood and tangled with barbed wire.

"In case anything should happen during the night," offered the Captain with a smile; and then we came to the new trench where soldiers were digging, while a squad of eight stood guard with leveled rifles and a machine gun lest the French attack by surprise. It was not yet a trench in the military sense; only a ditch in which you dared not stand erect for even your chest would be exposed above the bags of sand that lined the top. Crouched beside a soldier I peered through an opening between the bags. I felt that the gray stone house that I had seen before,

IN THE TRENCHES

was approaching nearer. Where were the French? I stared across the plowed field. Finally I made out a furrow that was different from the others. It seemed higher and more gray than the color of dirt and I saw that it extended as far as the eye could see, and as I watched it I suddenly saw a speck of blue. It was the hat I had seen by the thousands in the prison camps. I had seen the French.

The soldier beside me seemed engrossed in the gray stone house. He muttered something to the next man—there were not separate rifle pits here—just a line of men. I too watched the gray house. I saw on the roof the rack of a wireless, and in the middle of the wall where the garret must be, a circular open window looked almost as if it had been made as a shell. I became conscious that there was somebody in that room and the next moment I saw a figure slowly approach the big gaping window, and a head cautiously appeared. I had a glimpse of a pallid blank face and then a rifle roared in my ear, and three more went off in a salvo. "French officers in that room," remarked the soldier wisely. "We get them."

As I turned to go back to the main trench, I saw that already in this little ditch the irrepressible German soldier had been at work. There in the mud wall was a heart, outlined with the ends of exploded cartridges, and as I looked at it, a boyish man smiled sheepishly and turned away. On the battleline, less—here in the outermost ditch—than two hundred meters from the French, they draw pictures and trace hearts, these sentimental people; and yet they have been accused of wantonly burning houses, these Germans, to whom the home is the biggest thing in all existence. Were every American who believes those Belgian stories, to live with the German soldiers as I have, and to know them off duty, and to watch them in the trenches, he would be utterly at sea. The stories of Belgium do not agree with the men of the German army.

Back in the main trench, I turned off with the Lieutenant, going down what seemed to be a retreating trench until he stopped before a wooden sign that read *Kamp Fuhrer*. The sign marked his bombproof, and descending a flight of dirt steps, I entered his quarters, different naturally from the private soldiers. He lived in a warren of straw and mud-caked bags and the walls of his ten by ten room in the ground were covered with genuine Afghanistan rugs. The carved desk, strewn with personal belongings, also had the château look, although the rickety washstand seemed to have come from a farmhouse. There was even a tiny window looking out away from the French, a mirror, a hatrack and a stone, and when upon coming out I saw that the door to this strange abode could be locked and that a little weather vane fluttered from the roof, I gave him up. He was too wonderful. He had been watching me with the quiet smile with which all these German officers regard you when they show you the marvels of their army front, and he said: "Would you like to telephone anybody in Berlin? I shall have my orderly get the connection."

I began to catch on and when he said that I could stand at the field telephone which lay in a niche in the trench wall, near his bombproof and get a series of connections that would terminate in Germany and that I actually could carry on a conversation from the firing line with somebody in the Hotel Adlon at Berlin—well, you come to expect anything possible of achievement by these people. I thanked the Lieutenant, but told him I knew of no one to telephone and he said with a laugh that he felt sorry for me, that one always knew a Charlottenburg telephone number in Berlin.

To get back to our motors, we used other approach trenches, and we had not gone a hundred and fifty meters from the trenches, when Bob Dunn and I—we had lingered so long to talk to a German soldier who spoke American that our party had gone ahead—discovered that the water in the pits was rising above our knees. The only thing then that occurred to us when the trench ran close to a road was to climb up out of it. Dunn was hungry and took some bread and cheese from his pocket; munching it we walked along. The sky was white with tiny clouds hanging over the trees ahead. For January it was too warm; we unbuttoned our coats.

"Amazing people," Dunn was saying. I happened to look behind me. The gray stone house! "Do you know," I said feeling cold, "that we're exposed to the French trenches?"

"What of it, they're not firing now," remarked Dunn, who would no more have said that two hours before than I would. And we walked along the road, eating our bread and cheese with the French to look at our backs if they cared to, a quarter of a mile away. There was no danger; the only danger was potential. We had let ourselves feel comfortable in the lulling security of the trenches, which paradoxically kills men....

You have read that trenches have changed war, that the life of a soldier is regarded as so precious by those who devise the war machines, that everything is done to protect him. "Digging in" and "trench-work," reassuring phrases for those who do not know, or for those who do not think. By statistics I tried to show how safe the trenches are. Yes, everything is done to safeguard the soldier; he is valuable to the State, which is not a cynicism, for feeling the tremendous national spirit of Germany, you come to think that there is only one thing worth while in these years, and that is the State; and you feel that such a thing as national pride is more worth while than dollar pride; which is something which would come shamefacedly to most Americans were they to walk through the German trenches from the Channel to the Vosges. But if trenches were devised to save the soldier, modern artillery and explosives were devised to kill him; and the only thing that makes you wonder about the trenches and their relative value to life, is how a man can go into them and be alive at the end of the war. At Labasse one night I talked to a captain who told me something of these things.

"Yesterday," he said, "the English fired a hundred and fifty shells over our trench. One hundred and forty-eight burst harmlessly. The other two dropped into the trench and killed fifteen men. It took one hundred and fifty shells to do it, but fifteen men," and the Captain shook his head. I asked him what the effects of shell fire were on the men and he told me: "The moral influence of shells in breaking courage is terrific. That's why a heavy cannonading always precedes the storming of a trench. Especially is this so at night when you have to keep sending up rockets that light the ground between the trenches so the enemy cannot creep

IN THE TRENCHES 73

up. You see, during the day, the soldiers sight their rifles on different points and at night they simply sweep those points with fire. We only use machine guns to repel air attack, but further down the line where the French are, officers have told me that the French will waste ammunition firing a machine gun for hours, apparently satisfied if they kill only one man."

And in conversations that I had with officers at the different brigade and corps headquarters where I dined while in the West, and from things I heard in Berlin, I formed an opinion about the trenches. They are tremendously important to Germany. I would go so far as to say that everything depends upon that three hundred mile ditch in the West. If the Germans hold it, it means this: the war is going to end with Germany in possession of Belgium and a big section of industrial France; and somebody has to pay Germany's bill for this war; and German troops may not leave captured soil until the bill is paid; whereupon billions of dollars depend on a six-foot hole in the ground that twists and burrows across Europe....

I had seen the trenches by day; later I saw them by night. A tedious, slipping walk through half a mile of muddy, unroofed tunnels and I was in the front German line near Labasse.

When I had accustomed myself to the steady cracking of rifles in the firing pits which I could not see, but which I knew must be close by; when I had nervously counted the bursting of twenty shells, all in an appalling few minutes, yet had heard no plop of fragments burying themselves into the mud above, I began to be able to look about me. By turning my indispensable electric torch this way and that, I could see in the rear wall of the trench a series of caves dug in the earth, their entrances so low that a man would have to enter them on hands and knees, and in some I saw the yellowish gutter of candles and others were pitch dark. At Unter Officer Ochsler's suggestion I went down into one of the caves.

"Later," he said, "you won't want to be moving around much. It'll get hotter then and you'll want to remain in one place where you're sure the shelter is good."

From one of the candle-lighted dugouts, I heard part singing, a lively air, doubtless from some German operetta, and above us shells whined and burst roaring in the fields. It was while we were walking thus, peering to right and left into the life of the catacombs of mud, that a stentorian cry behind us seemed to spin the Lieutenant round on his heels and I followed him thumping heavily back down the slippery pit. "It's an attack," he shouted over his shoulder. "Get into one of the dugouts and stay there. And, if they get us, wave your passport if they find you, and yell you're an American."

Indicating one of the little passages towards the firing pits, he gave me a shove and spattered away to take command. Down on all fours I went. I wondered if the two soldiers in the pit saw me. Apparently not. Their shoulders were hunched to their guns. I hesitated. Of course the dugout would be the safest place, but shells had been flying over the trench for an hour now and nothing had happened; and their shriek and heavy boom no longer seemed so terrifying. But then the Lieutenant had strongly hinted about my being in the way. He had told me to get into that dugout and remain there. Was I not really under his orders? Strange things to be reasoning out with yourself, points of military etiquette, with the skies raining death and the whole line of the trenches blazing with a red, repelling flame. But war is strange, and now I wonder if in the firing line, cowardice and bravery do really exist; if it is not rather one man's nervous system responding to reckless hysteria quicker than another's?

You forgot the Lieutenant's request; you forgot that perhaps you owed it to some one to remain where it was safe—and dull. You forgot that these were not American soldiers leveling their guns not a stride from you, and that they were Englishmen who were pouring up over the trenches across that muddy field and storming towards you; you never thought of nationality, that was a creation of man's. You thought of nothing; you only felt things. You felt something chaotic going on, an inchoate impulse possessed you. It was to fire a gun. If only there was something to shoot, something to throw you into the surge of this fight so you could be thrilled the more. The men in front of you were fighting away; but it was not your fight.

And then came the quick banging beat of the machine guns and you ran to where they were, your pulse beating with them. As you ran, stumbling down the slippery trench, there seemed to jump out of the ground a soldier with black belts of cartridges slung over his shoulder. Then another darted up from another pit and you knew they were bringing ammunition for the gun. In an ecstasy you followed them. At the second little passageway they turned and you turned too and found yourself crouching behind an armored wall of mud, above which the machine gun lay between heavy bags, and you saw a man's elbow jerking round in a circle and you knew he was firing the gun. If only your arm could move like that!

And above even that incessant hellish clamor you heard the crackling report of rifles, one report seeming to run upon the other, as though trays of dishes were constantly being dropped downstairs, and then the heavy booming of shells would deafen all, to the fierce spurting of shrapnel and the slapping impact of fragments of *grenaten* in the mud. Then a swift rush of air, as of a mighty exhalation, and rockets from our trenches began to swish, one after the other, in short flaming arcs that terminated in a burst of greenish light, turning the night into a mad radiance so that we might better see to kill. I crowded forward, wanting to peer through a slit between the bags, but a soldier pushed me back. I was in the way. I cannot convey how that makes you feel, a realization that you are indeed in the way with these men fighting for their lives and you just there watching them.

I ran from the machine gun, ducking in at the first pit I came to, and here I saw men who without a word, their movements as regular as machines, were loading, firing ... loading, firing. They were shorter than I, and by raising a trifle on my toes, I could squint along their gun barrels and see the patch of the open field that their loop hole framed. I saw a confusion of color—the green, unearthly haze of the rockets; a wavering red hue of fire that had a way of rushing at you, vanishing and then appearing further back, rushing at you again; and I saw a patch of mud, glistening like mottled tarnished silver in the rain, and once when a whitish rocket burst, the air seemed to be sparkling with myriad drops of silver and diamonds. And the rain poured down; and the guns shook the sky; and the rifles rattled on.

I began to notice then, by craning my head from left to right, that the red wavering lines of fire, which had a way of rushing at you and vanishing to appear again further back, was slower now in appearing after it lost itself somewhere in the mud, and then it became even slower in showing itself and finally when it came, you saw that it had disintegrated into segments, that it was no longer a steady oncoming line, rather a slowly squirming thing like the curling parts of some monstrous fiery worm that had been chopped to bits and was squirming its life away out there on the mud. And it dawned upon you in horror that the fiery red lines had been lines of men, shooting as they had come; and that, when one line had been mowed down, another had rushed up from behind, so on almost endlessly it had seemed until they came broken and squirmed like the others had done, into the mud, and came no more. And the spell that you had been held in was broken; and you remembered that there was a God, and you thanked Him that your hands had found nothing with which to kill....

And coming across that stretch of mud—only one hundred and fifty meters were their trenches—broke forth the rattle of the English machine guns and the fever of it over, you could reason out what that meant. The English attack had failed and now they were sweeping the field with machine gun fire so that the Germans could not form and storm in turn. Their shells, too, no longer exploded behind our trenches, but in front, and you knew that the English had telephoned back to their artillery to shorten the range about fifty meters, making that field a muddy Golgotha in which nothing could live and upon which their own wounded must be being slain by the score.

We had almost ceased firing. In the pits I heard the straggling shots that mean "at will," but our machine guns were silent. The rockets still swished upward, making their parabola of sparks and keeping the night hideous with their bursting green. The Lieutenant was running down the trench towards me. "You're not hurt?" he asked. I told him no, and he seemed immeasurably relieved. What a futile outsider you felt!

"I think our losses were, by comparison, slight," he said, leading the way towards the passage that turned back into his bombproof. "I shall have an exact report on them in a few minutes." From out of the pits, as we passed, I heard a groan. Thinking the man might be alone, I paused and turned on my lamp. Its white light found a circle of brown mud and then moving down, it shone upon the grotesquely hunched up form of a man in soiled gray green, and wavering across the pit it rested then upon a pair of boots, their soles turned towards me.

"Probably shrapnel," remarked the Lieutenant, as he looked over my shoulder. "Both dead."

You caught a professional lack of emotion in his voice and you experienced a moment's unpleasantness before you realized that a kind providence makes the spectacle of death seem as commonplace to the soldier as it does to the surgeon; otherwise he should go mad. There was a business-like air about the Lieutenant now, rather different, you thought, from that rush through the mud when first the alarm sounded. By the way, how long ago was that; not more than twenty minutes? But when you looked at your watch, the hands shaped more. Two hours!

I followed the Lieutenant into his bombproof.

"We're safe here," he said in a dutiful way, "unless a shell should strike the roof. But I think they'll soon cease their artillery fire altogether."

He twirled the spark wheel of one of those patent lighters that the German soldiers carry and the glowing coal at the end of the chemically treated cord began to seek the wick of a candle. I flashed on my lamp to help him, and in a moment the little dirt walled room was faintly luminous with yellow light. It was possible to stand without bumping your head against the logged roof, and while he picked up the field telephone, whose slender tendrils crept up through the roof like a vine, I glanced around me. Over there in the corner one saw a red rubber wash basin, evidently folding, for it was creased in many places; it rested upon an empty ammunition box, and above it a tiny mirror gave out the reflection of the candle. I heard him call for regimental headquarters and then in a very calm voice he proceeded to give the details of the engagement insofar as he had been able to collect them in such a brief time. He begged me to excuse him while he wrote out a report.

"This must be delivered at once by a soldier to my Colonel," he explained. "I shall leave blanks for the number of our killed and wounded and telephone it to headquarters to be filled in as soon as the under officer brings me the figures."

I told him that I would go out and take a look around while he was writing his report. "I'll only be a minute," he begged.

"I'll be careful," I replied, and he smiled in a way that showed he understood. I then went down the line of the trench for perhaps fifty meters, stopping here and there to go into the firing pits, where by now most of the rifles were silent, one man in each pit watching through the oblong hole between the sand bags, lest the enemy creep up, for their cannonading had ceased and shells no longer fell upon that narrow zone between the trenches. They appeared to take turns watching, the two men in each pit, the one on relief sitting on the ground, his back against the dirt wall, as though fatigued.

It was in one of these pits that I stuck up my head—for the enemy's bullets no longer whizzed by—and looked out upon the little battle field. The rain had ceased; the stars were coming out. It was quiet out there now, but in the distance, north and south, you heard muffled uproars as though what had begun and ended here was happening there now. It was quiet out there, too quiet, not even the wounded groaned; there were no wounded; the artillery had turned them into dead. In the feeble starlight nothing was visible, only vague outlines as of a rise of ground, just at a distance, you imagined, for the English trenches to crest; only that and close by the short, shadowy posts across which the German barbed entanglements were strung. Slowly the silence grew upon you.

And then I heard the hiss of a rocket. I watched its arc of yellow sparks. I watched its burst, and in its light I saw that which I pray my eyes may never behold again. I saw in that eerie radiance the glistening, puddled field and across it, on the upward sloping ground what you might have thought were innumerable graves, but which you knew to be the bodies of men, fallen as they had come at the charge; in twos—threes—I counted ten in a perfect row; and behind them were more of these lumps which seemed to be of the earth, for they were the color of that blackish field; and there the mounds seemed higher, as though a pile of them lay there; and you heard the hissing rockets, and their greenish fires seemed to be now of that green which sometimes burns on an altar's rail. And then the rockets stopped, and the field of the dead was shut from your eyes.... If only a sound would come from out there....

I found the Lieutenant in his bombproof.

"I have been waiting for you," he called in a cheery way, and he reached down under the empty cartridge box. "Cognac," he exclaimed, producing a flask. "It will taste good now."

"I suppose," I nodded.

I admired his unshaking hand as he poured out the liquid. "There's only one glass," he smiled. "Go ahead, I insist."

I gulped down the stuff and hoped he had not noticed my manner. I watched him pour out his own drink, holding it like the connoisseur you felt him to be, before the candle flame. He must have been admiring the amber color when footfalls came from without. The under-officer saluted and handed him a bit of paper. Putting down the cognac and returning the salute, the Lieutenant picked up the telephone. I heard him call regimental headquarters, and then reading from the paper, he reported in German: "Fifteen dead—thirty-eight wounded." And laying aside the 'phone he picked up his cognac, slowly sipping it down....

I had seen the men in the trenches and it was at Commines that I saw them out. With a tall young Prussian officer, who told me in entire sincerity that before this war was done Germany was going to invade England and that the plans had all been perfected, but what they were he naturally could not say—I walked along the cobbled street of the old French town until I came to a gray stone factory. Through the paling of a picket fence I saw soldiers moving about in the yard, and going in we walked along a narrow cobbled driveway between dingy workshops until the officer opened a door, and we went into what had been a storeroom. I saw rows of pens, each as wide as a cot and filled with straw, and in the straw lay men. You thought of them as being too exhausted upon coming back from the trenches to take off their uniforms and wash before lying down. I saw their cartridge belts, knapsacks and guns strewn in the straw beside them, and I became conscious of a faint sickening odor that minute by minute became stronger in that stuffy room, the stench of men who had not been able to as much as unloosen their clothing for days at a time.

As I walked between the pens I saw further on that some of the men were awake. I saw their faces; the others seemed all to sleep with their faces buried in the straw; and they were wild, unshaven faces, yellowish with mud, and bleary with sleepless eyes that somehow could not sleep now. There was one munching on a big chunk of black bread, and another who had been leaning on his elbow, writing a letter, jumped up as I passed.

"You're an American, aren't you?" he called after me.

I saw from the blue and white button on his cap that he belonged to one of the Bavarian regiments.

"I lived in the United States," he told me, "until the war came. Then I joined my regiment. I was the cashier of a bank in Juarez, and I lived across the river. I used to make my money in Mexico and live in America."

He went on telling me of his experiences and obligingly answering certain questions that must have sounded foolish to him.

"We work here in the army," he said, "seven day shifts. We're in the trenches forty-eight hours and then out for twenty-four hours' rest; in again for twenty-four and then out for three days."

I asked him what the men did during the last three days and he told me.

"To-day, for instance, we get paid. Then we wash up and go out and buy cigars and cheese and things, though I'm afraid some of the boys will be laid up this time with the typhoid vaccine. We're fresh troops, you know, and haven't had it yet. I suppose when spring comes on, they'll have us working as farmers when we're not on duty."

I asked him what he meant, and he told me that all the captured farmland of Belgium and France that could be planted during the fall had been sown by German soldiers, and that when the crops were ready that the soldiers would harvest them. And again the marvelous details of this German machine amazed me.

I said good-by to the Bavarian who had made his money in Mexico, spent it in America, and did his fighting with Germany in France, and went down the damp cobbled alley where you thought the wagons used to drive into these mills with their supplies; the officer told me a thousand soldiers rested, bathed and were fed every day in the factory. We saw the room where they bathed, one tub running the entire length of the machine room—overhead the motionless belt wheels looked self-conscious—this tub for the legs, another for the feet, while in the middle of the stone floor the army barbers, daubed white with lather, were shaving the soldiers and clipping their hair to the scalp.

"These are three companies of the —th Bavarian Infantry who have the room for this hour. They must be bathed and shaved within that time."

Outside I saw three soldiers picking mud off their uniforms; and when we returned to the street, waiting for our car, three of them passed with shiny shaven faces and puffing on long cigars. We saw three girls and the soldiers smiled. It was their day off....

When I think of the trenches again I think of the bombproof, near Labasse. The English have attacked, to be beaten back. The young German officer has just telephoned his report to his Colonel, and is pouring himself a second glass of cognac. They are the same at night as they are in the day, these trenches; they have the same bored men lounging in the dugouts, waiting for an attack; the same tensely watchful men in the rifle pits, scanning the enemy's line. I heard a harmonica. The dead still lay where they fell, the wounded were getting first aid, and you could hear the whining harmonica above the scattering spatter of the shrapnel. Yes, in the trenches it was the same; they had settled down once more into the lulling secure feeling of the protection of a dirt wall, six feet high, which paradoxically ends by killing them. Only the night was different.

Hideous night, pierced with flame, serried with a rocket's gleaming train, weird with bursting bombs that light the glistening fields a grayish green; awful night, shaking to the booming of heavy guns, blotched with the red of splitting shells, quivering insanely to a machine gun's steady beat; night of death, with the wounded turning white, waiting for the hours just before the dawn when the firing stops and their comrades may be spared to carry them back; with the field of the soaked dead, a nightmare of lumpy things, seen hellishly in the rocket's glow.

But in the trenches—all along the big ditch from the dunes of Flanders to the foothills of the Vosges—it is the same night and day; and bullets are whistling and harmonicas are playing. I heard them both at Arras and Labasse.

CHAPTER VIII
CAPTURED BELGIUM AND ITS GOVERNOR GENERAL

"The Governor General will receive you at four," said Ober-Lieutenant Herrmann, explaining things; "I shall accompany you."

As we had just come up from the front around Lille, the only clothes we had were those on our backs; and to Ober-Lieutenant Herrmann's officer's boots and my puttees, the mud of the trenches still clung in yellow cakes. Hardly the most proper clothes in which to meet King Albert's successor; but in field gray we had to go. Through the busy streets, up the long hill, to the Government buildings, we skirted the edge of that rectangle of stone buildings where Belgian officials used to conduct Belgian affairs. At the corner we turned, passing up the Rue de la Loi, where King Albert's palace frowns down upon two black and white striped Prussian sentry boxes, and then entered the Belgian War Ministry building. A German private ushered us up a flight of marble stairs to an antechamber, where we waited, while an adjutant disappeared through a pretentious white double door, to tell His Excellency that we had come. I noticed two marble busts in that antechamber, white busts on pedestals in opposite corners—the King and Queen of Belgium, and I wondered if they ever visited this city again, would it be an official visit, the guests of another nation, or a home-coming.

The Governor General received me in a dainty, Louis Quinze room, done in rose and French gray, and filled incongruously with delicate chairs and heavy brocaded curtains, a background which you felt precisely suited His Excellency. In the English newspapers, which by the way, the Germans do not childishly bar from the Berlin cafés, I had read of His Excellency as the "Iron Fist," or the "Heavy Heel," and I rather expected to see a heavy, domineering man. Instead, a slender, stealthy man in the uniform of a general, rose from behind a tapestry-topped table, revealing as he did, a slight stoop in his back, and held out a long-fingered hand. As I looked at Governor General von Bissing I saw that he wore the second class of the Iron Cross and no other decorations; at the same time I imagined he had been awarded about ten orders which he could have strung across his narrow chest. His black, glistening, almost artificial-looking hair, was brushed back tight over his head, and when I noticed his eyes, I saw that they were of bluish gray, heavy and unrelenting, pouched and lined, glowing in a way that either made you want to turn away, or else stare, fascinated by their powers. He struck me as being rather longer headed than most Germans, and his straggly grayish mustache only half hid the thin, straight, ruthless lines of his mouth; but when you tried to study his face, you could discern only two things, features thin, but intensely strong, pierced with two points of fire, sunken, glowering eyes. And I knew then what they meant by the Iron Fist.

General von Bissing spoke no English. Somehow I imagined him to be one of those old patriots who would never learn the language simply because it was English. Through Ober-Lieutenant Herrmann I asked the Governor General what Germany was doing towards the reconstruction of Belgium. I asked Herrmann to explain to him—for I dreaded attempting my ungrammatical German—that America, when I had left it, was under the impression that Belgium was a land utterly laid waste by the German armies; in America the common belief was that the German military Government meant tyranny; what was Germany doing for Belgium?

"I think," replied Governor General von Bissing, "that we are doing everything that can be done under the circumstances. Those farmlands which Lieutenant Herrmann tells me you saw, coming up from Lille to Brussels, were planted by German soldiers and in the spring they will be harvested by our soldiers. Belgium has not been devastated, and its condition has been grievously misstated, as you have seen. You must remember that the armies have passed back and forth across it—German, Belgian, English, and French, but I think you have seen that only in the paths of these armies has the countryside suffered. Where engagements were not fought or shots fired, Belgium is as it was. There has been no systematic devastation for the purpose of intimidating the people. You will learn this if you go all over Belgium. As for the cities, we are doing the best we can to encourage business. Of course, with things the way they are now, it is difficult. I can only ask you to go down one of the principal business streets here, the Rue de la Neuve for instance, and price the articles that you find in the shops, and compare them with the Berlin prices. The merchants of Brussels are not having to sacrifice their stock by cutting prices, and equally important, there are people buying. I can unhesitatingly say that things are progressing favorably in Belgium."

And although I felt General von Bissing could be a hard master, he impressed me like a good many hard masters, as being thoroughly sincere. Thinking of Schleswig, I asked him if he thought that Belgium could ever be Germanized. Suppose after the peace treaty was signed that Germany decided to keep Belgium, would the Empire ever be able to assimilate the new people? Before replying, General von Bissing appeared to be thinking hard; he dropped his eyes and hesitated long, finally saying: "I do not think that it is the time for me to discuss this point."

The conversation turned upon Belgian and English relations before this war. The Governor General mentioned the documentary evidence found in the archives in Brussels, and proving an understanding between these countries against Germany. He talked briefly about the point that the subjects of King Albert had been betrayed into the hands of English financiers, and then laconically said: "The people of Belgium are politically undisciplined children. You may know of the high percentage of criminality in Belgium. You may have heard that the slums of Antwerp are considered the worst in the world. Apparently education was never designed in Belgium for the mass of the people. They knew nothing, they could conjecture nothing, about what was going on between their rulers and the rulers of other countries. Even now they believe that relief is at any moment at hand. They think the English will deliver them," and the Governor General sneered. "They are the victims of subtle propaganda that generally takes the form of articles in French and neutral newspapers," and General von Bissing looked me straight in the eyes, as though to emphasize that by neutral, he meant the newspapers of the United States.

"I can understand the French doing this," he said, "because they always use the Belgians, and do not care what happens to them. It is beyond my comprehension, though, how the Government of any neutral country permits the publication of newspaper articles that can have but one effect, and that is to encourage revolt in a captured people. A country likes to call itself humanitarian, and yet it persists in allowing the publication of articles that only excite an ignorant, undisciplined people and lead them to acts of violence that must be wiped out by force," and the Governor General's mouth closed with a click.

"Do you know that the people of Brussels, whenever a strong wind carries the booming of heavy guns miles in from the front, think that French and English are going to recapture the city. Any day that we can hear the guns faintly, we know that there is an undercurrent of nervous expectancy running through the whole city. It goes down alleys, and avenues, and fills the cafés. You can see Belgians standing together whispering. Twice they actually set the date when King Albert would return.

"This excitement and unrest, and the feeling of the English coming in, is fostered and encouraged by the articles in French and neutral newspapers that are smuggled in. I do not anticipate any uprising among the Belgians, although the thoughtless among them have encouraged it. An uprising is a topic of worry in our councils. It could do us no harm. We could crush it out like that," and Von Bissing snapped his thin fingers, "but if only for the sake of these misled and betrayed people, all seditious influences should cease."

I asked the Governor General about the attitude of officials of the Belgian Government, who were being used by the Germans in directing affairs.

"My predecessor, General von der Gotz," he replied, "informed me that the municipal officials in Brussels and most Belgian cities, showed a good cooperative spirit from the start. The higher officials were divided, some refusing flatly to deal with the German administration. I do not blame these men, especially the railway officials, for I can see their viewpoint. In these days, railway roads and troop trains were inseparable, and if those Belgian railway officials had helped us, they would have committed treason against their country. There was no need, though, for the Post Office officials to hold out, and only lately they have come around. Realizing, however, that without their department, the country would be in chaos, the officials of the Department of Justice immediately cooperated with us. To-day the Belgian civil courts try all ordinary misdemeanors and felonies. Belgium penal law still exists and is administered by Belgians. However, all other cases are tried by a military tribunal, the *Feld Gericht*."

I asked Excellence von Bissing if there was much need for this military tribunal.

"We have a few serious cases," he said; "occasionally there is a little sedition, but for the most part it is only needle pricks. They are quiet now. They know why," and slowly shaking his head, Von Bissing, who is known as the sternest disciplinarian in the entire German army, smiled.

And then I urged the most important question—Belgian neutrality.

"It would have been a very grave mistake," said Von Bissing, slowly, "not to have invaded Belgium. It would have been an unforgivable military blunder. I justified the invading of Belgium on absolutely military grounds. What other grounds are there worth while talking about when a nation is in a war for its existence? If we had not sent our troops into Belgium the English would have landed their entire expeditionary army at Antwerp, and cut our line of communication. How do I know that? Simply because England would have been guilty of the grossest blunder if she had not done that, and the man who is in charge of England's army has never been known as a blunderer. It was the only way. Subsequent events, the finding of diplomatic documents, have proven the English agreements with Belgium. In the captured fortresses at Namur, Lüttich (Liége), and Antwerp, we found stores of French guns and ammunition. Germany would have been much worse off than she is to-day if she had not gone through Belgium. A great state like Germany could not permit holding back at such a time in its history."

This led us into talking about the situation in America. We talked about the burning of Louvain, which I later saw and found to be comparatively little damaged, roughly, but one-twelfth was destroyed, and I saw the paintings that German officers risked their lives in fire to save. We talked about Louvain and then about General Sherman's march from Atlanta to the sea, when a whole state was burned and laid waste.

"The truth will come out," said Von Bissing slowly. "Your country is renowned for fair play. You will be fair to Germany, I know. Your American Relief Commission is doing excellent work. It is in the highest degree necessary. At first the German army had to use the food they could get by foraging in Belgium, for the country does not begin to produce the food it needs for its own consumption, and there were no great reserves that our troops could use. But the German army is not using any of Belgian food now."

I asked the Governor General if the Germans had not been very glad that America was sending over food. I told him that when I left New York, the number of unemployed there was huge—largest, so Mayor Mitchell had said, in the city's history—and that some Americans were so unsentimental as to think that this food for Belgium might better be distributed in their own country. This seemed to disturb General von Bissing.

"It is most important," he repeated, "that America regularly sends provisions to Belgium. Your country should feel very proud of the good it has done here."

Somehow I had the idea that His Excellency was indulging in quiet amusement at my expense. He impressed me as being far too clever to make such a statement in entire sincerity. "I welcome the American Relief Committee," he said. "We are working in perfect harmony. Despite reports to the contrary, we never have had any misunderstanding. Through the American Press, please thank your people for their kindness to Belgium."

General von Bissing held out his hand; the interview was over. In the next room I saw on a little table a pot of tea and a plate of little cakes. I wondered if the Governor General really ate cakes. I bowed my way out of the rose and French gray room and walked with Ober-Lieutenant Herrmann down the marble stairs. I was thinking of a story that I had heard of His Excellency. A few years ago he was having great difficulty in keeping orderlies; they all found him too strict. Finally he obtained a new orderly, a grim looking individual.

"What were you before you entered the army?" Von Bissing asked him.

"A lion tamer," replied the orderly.

"Good," exclaimed Von Bissing, "you stay."

Try to think of a slender, slightly stooped military man, perhaps a trifle foppish, with his sleek, brilliantined hair, sitting in a delicate gold and tapestried chair, and directing the affairs of a captured nation. His face is sallow, and his sunken eyes always seemed to smolder, and his mouth is so thin and straight, as almost to be cruel, but you feel that he is absolutely fair, and it is hard to think of him as breaking his word. I cannot imagine Governor General von Bissing doing that. I think he is ruthlessly honest, ruthlessly just, hard, a rigid disciplinarian, and scrupulously fair, and if reprisals are necessary no sentimentality will stay his hand. "They are only needle pricks," he says of seditious Belgians,—"they know why." The ideal man for a military government, his is an Iron Fist; but if the fist were of softer stuff, all Belgium would be in chaos.

CHAPTER IX
PRISONERS OF WAR

Promptly at two o'clock the gray army automobile emblazoned with Prussian eagles in black, left Wilhelmstrasse. Half an hour's run—and the drivers of those army motor cars know not a speed law—and we were at garrison headquarters on Doeberitz Road. One saw a fence of white palings, a lawn surprisingly green for winter, symmetrically laid out among gray gravel walks that lead up to a square business-like house of brown stucco, over the door of which was printed "*Kaiser Wilhelm Soldatenheim, 1914*." Off to the right loomed a long weather-beaten line of huge tents, one of which was open, showing the tail of a Taube monoplane. Across the road behind us, unpainted barrack sheds and soldiers showed through a grove of pine trees, and then while Dr. Roediger of the Foreign Office, my escort, went to find Major General von Loebell, commanding the entire Doeberitz camp and garrison, I heard something that reminded me of the riveting machines on the skyscrapers in New York. Imagine your state of mind with twenty riveting machines, all making their infernal clatter at the same time, only each capable of double the usual noise. That is the sound that suddenly broke in upon us at Doeberitz Road, and off in the fields we saw battery after battery of machine gun men, learning their deadly trade. While we waited Dr. Roediger's return, more guns broke loose, and by the time the General came, he could scarcely make himself heard. He began by explaining from his military point of view the Doeberitz camp.

"We have seventeen thousand prisoners here," he said, "and there are more coming every day. The war office thinks it fine to take so many Russian prisoners. Out here we don't like it," he smiled. "They are coming too fast for us. Every day we are building more houses for them, but each house costs $2500. Already we have spent nearly $800,000 in this one camp on sleeping quarters alone, and we've got twenty other prison camps in Germany, and nearly three quarters of a million prisoners. Here at Doeberitz we are building a bathing place for the prisoners that is costing $17,500, and when you figure up what it costs to feed those fellows, the expense of this camp runs up into the millions."

Perhaps to put us in the proper mental state before visiting the prison camp proper, Major General von Loebell went on to say something about the prisoners.

"The French and Russians," he explained, "are easy to handle. They don't mind working. In fact, they are always asking for something to do. And remember that whenever a prisoner does any municipal work, labor on the roads, for instance, he is paid for it, thirty or fifty pfennigs a day, and he can use the money to buy tobacco." And for an instant the General grew wrathy. "In France and England, though, they don't pay German prisoners a cent, no matter what work they do. Our English prisoners, though"—and the General dolorously shook his head—"Oh, they are more difficult. Always they have a grievance. The first thing they asked for was a place to wash. We were glad to give it to them," and the General grinned. "The Russians never bother you for a luxury like that. Then we gave the English coffee in the morning, and they protested again; they wanted tea. Gott, I was glad enough to give them tea; it is cheaper. But when we want them to work, they sulk. Really, the Frenchmen work for us as if they enjoy it. So do the Russians. On the whole, though, we don't have much trouble here at Doeberitz." Pausing, he added: "I shall now put you in charge of Lieutenant Colonel Alberti, who will show you around the camp." And with the usual German military bow, the General bade us adieu. With the Lieutenant Colonel, a most accommodating man, we proceeded by motor down the Doeberitz Road. Near the prison sheds my cigarette burned down, and I opened the limousine window to throw out the stump. Four Russians, guarded by a soldier, were passing, and suddenly I heard an excited clamor. There, on their hands and knees, punching and cursing each other, while the soldier prodded them with his bayonet, the Russians fought for that inch of tobacco, oblivious to everything, bayonet and all, until it was won.

Leaving them, we came to a gate in the barbed wire fences, and passed on foot through a double line of sentries into the main street of the prison camp. One saw on either side rows of long, newly erected, unpainted sheds, separated by side streets of muddy ground and fenced off from the main camp street by more barbed wire. One's first impression was that prisoners of war are among the piteous objects on the face of the earth. You see swarms of shuffling men who before the fortunes of war went against them must have looked smart and soldierly. Now in their uniforms they seemed self-conscious and absurd, sheepish almost because they had to wear regimentals in the presence of the enemy. What must have been a trim-looking British marine caught my eye. His olive drab was tattered and stained; he must have lost his cap or sold it to buy tobacco. What he wore was a battered derby, picked up Heaven knows where! It was characteristic, I afterwards learned, of the entire camp.

As we walked up the main street, groups of prisoners ran down the side streets and gathering by the barbed wire fences, stared curiously. We saw a whole battalion of English jackies, more marines, and then swarms of Russians, heavy and stupid looking. Only one enclosure, the Colonel explained, was filled with Frenchmen.

The first place that Lieutenant Colonel Alberti put at our disposal was the camp kitchen. We entered one of the long sheds and came into a steaming room, where instantly the chief cook and his assistants stood at attention. The chief cook, following the fashion of his kind, was dressed in white from head to foot, but his assistants wore the field uniforms of Russia, smeared with grease. The eye took in a cement floor that supported three enormous caldrons, each one big enough for three men to hide in and brimming with a white-looking mixture.

"They are getting supper ready," explained the Lieutenant Colonel, and he went on to say how the prisoners were fed. "That is a stew made of cabbage and meat; you can see the pieces of meat in it. At four o'clock in the afternoon, and at six-thirty in the morning, the prisoners are given a soup similar to this. Then in the middle of the day they get sausage and bread. Of course we change the diet; very often they have coffee in the morning, also."

It did not sound very promising; nor did the stuff in the caldrons look inviting. I asked the Lieutenant Colonel if I might taste some of the stew. To my surprise he was perfectly willing; and to my further surprise I found it to be excellent. Far from being tasteless, it was evidently prepared by a good chef, and there were sufficient pieces of meat to provide ample nourishment for a man partaking of that dish twice a day; certainly he would not be underfed, and in a prison camp one does not expect delicacies.

As we left the cookroom, the Lieutenant Colonel told us that the eight thousand five hundred men in this particular section of the camp were fed in fifty minutes, a statistic suggestive of German efficiency. From the kitchen we visited one of the sheds where the prisoners sleep. Leading the way, the officer threw open a wooden door. Instantly some one shouted a command in Russian; there was a scuffling of feet and the prisoners jumped up from their mattresses, struck attention and saluted. At the thought of being compelled to sleep in that room, cold chills ran up one's spine. In justice to the Germans it must be said that they build the place clean; they furnished it with new clean bedding; they do everything humanly possible to keep it clean.

Given that same number of Russians, two hundred and fifty, put them in that same sized room, their mattresses in four rows, each mattress flush against the other, transport that shed into Russia and leave those men there without German supervision to make them keep reasonably clean, and you would get one result—cholera. As it is, every prisoner at the Doeberitz camp and every other prison camp in Germany—and I later visited many of them—can thank fortune that he was taken prisoner by a nation that knows how to keep things clean.

Passing through the long room with the Russians standing on either side, bewildered at the sight of foreigners, noting the many windows for ventilation, one was glad to get out into the open air. There the Lieutenant Colonel confirmed something you had been thinking.

"It's best not to get too near those fellows," he said. "We do our best to make them keep clean, but they've all got lice." Then the officer had his little joke. "For a few days before we had these quarters ready we had to keep all nationalities together, so the Englishmen caught it from the Russians. They've been scrubbing ever since, but then they should share everything. Are they not allies?"

Walking up and down the side streets of the Russian section one saw faces pressed against the window panes, others peering from behind the doors, while others boldly came out to view the Lieutenant Colonel's guest. Here one noticed the difference in the Russian soldier. Two distinct types, one with the predominance of Tatar blood, heavy faced and tiny eyed, as devoid of expression as a pudgy Japanese; but there was the other Russian, the man from the North, more alert looking, who grinned at you as you went by, and seemed to see something funny in it.

We next came upon a temporary tent where two hundred men were quartered in a place a hundred feet long and thirty feet wide. It was dark inside the tent, but by the aid of a candle that probably burned with difficulty in that air, one could see rows of excelsior mattresses packed in as close together as possible on the bare ground. The place was a nightmare, and the thought of two hundred and fifty men sleeping there was incredible. What impressed one, though, was not so much the conditions in that tent, for we could see near by a new shed, intended for them, needing only a day's work to complete it, but the policy of entire sincerity on the part of the War Ministry in permitting an American correspondent to see this section of the camp.

We then came upon the Englishmen. Their quarters were just the same as the Russians, and as we later saw, equally as good as those occupied by the comparatively few Frenchmen at Doeberitz. The Germans had given them their quarters clean, and they had kept them clean. It was a relief to go among them. It was with an odd sensation, too, that an American heard these men, these prisoners of war, speak his own language. Like the Russians, those who had been sitting, sprang on to their feet, but there was no salute. There was none of the unctuous servility noticeable among the Slavs. There was no attempt to curry favor with the officers of the camp, and one admired the English tremendously for that. They had played the game of war, lost, and they were taking their medicine. Their attitude, you saw, as you looked down their line of faces, was admirable.

To my amazement the Lieutenant Colonel turned to me and said, "You can talk to these men if you like," adding, "I know now what they'll say to you."

And standing off he listened to the conversation with a smile.

"Well, boys, how do you like it here?"

"Rotten," was the answer given together.

I looked at the officer; he seemed not surprised.

"Where were you captured?" I asked a particularly boyish marine.

"At Antwerp, sir."

"Then you fellows are the new recruits that were sent over there?"

They all said, "Yes."

"How long were you drilled?"

"About two weeks, sir."

And one was struck with the pitiful side of the blunder that made the First Lord of England's Admiralty the laughing stock of military experts the world over. In America we had read and only half believed that Winston Churchill had taken five thousand young men, practically greenhorns, and thrown them into Antwerp, a mere handful compared to the German hosts. That needless sacrifice of men, that useless waste of five thousand, their number making them practically useless, came home now in another way. Every boy there—and they nearly all look like boys—could blame the high-hatted strategist of the Admiralty for their predicament. And many of them openly did.

"The grub here," said a voice from their ranks, "is swill; it's nothing but skilley, and poor stew at that. Slops, I calls it, sir."

Having tasted the "slops," I could not agree with him and put it down to his inherent animosity towards all things German. I should have said that Dr. Roediger of the Foreign Office seems more the good-looking, young Englishman of the university type than German; also his accent and intonation is entirely English. I noticed that when he spoke to me, the prisoners looked at him queerly. Then I saw two of them go off into a corner of the room and begin whispering; the chances are that they decided he was an English journalist who in some miraculous way had been granted permission to enter Germany and visit the Doeberitz camp. Hope is eternal with any one who is a prisoner. As we left the room, the officer going first, this was confirmed; beckoning Dr. Roediger, the two prisoners who had been whispering said to him, "When you go to England, won't you tell them over there that we get their letters all right, but that we're afraid the Germans are not going to let us have our parcels?"

Dr. Roediger asked them what they meant.

"Why, the folks write us that they are going to send us packages as Christmas presents—tobacco and things a chap can't get here. Now it would be a rotten Christmas if a chap didn't get those, wouldn't it? Can't you help us?"

Dr. Roediger assured them if any packages came they would be delivered, but the prisoners seemed to doubt this, and when we left them their faces fell. As we were going out, one of them whispered to me, "See if you can get us our Christmas packages, won't you?"

Christmas in a place like that....

Drawn up outside another of the unpainted sheds, we saw two men whose appearance instantly contrasted with the half slouch of those about them.

"You're a regular, aren't you?" I asked a tall, powerfully built man who wore the chevrons of a sergeant.

"Yes," he replied. "The boys here are just new recruits."

I caught the sympathy in his voice when he spoke of "the boys." His very manner, his stiff, unyielding, soldierly bearing, made me understand better than ever before what Kipling meant when he called the British soldier a king. More than ever one marveled at the system that takes men out of the London gutters and transforms them into regulars, into a sergeant who could stand amid the humiliation of that prison camp and not once forget that he was a soldier of England. That single man was one of the greatest tributes to the regular army of England that I have ever seen.

I found myself talking to a browned, deep-chested sailor, whose red insignia told me he was a gunner's mate.

"What are you doing here?" I asked, surprised, not knowing how a man from a war ship could have been made a prisoner.

"I was with one of the English naval guns at Antwerp," he said. Then he made his complaint. It was different from the way the younger men had talked, based on a different thing, a different way of thinking; in fact, his one way—the question of discipline.

"The Germans expect me to keep good discipline here. I try to, but if they would feed us a little better, it would be easier. Every so often the lads kick on the grub."

"It isn't really bad," I said to him. "I tasted some of it."

His manner was earnest. I knew he was sincere.

"Well," he said, "I can bear up under it, but with some of the lads here it is pretty hard. They are used to better."

"But," I argued, "they can't expect what they get at home, can they?"

He agreed with this himself, but persisted, "If they'd give us better grub, I could give them better discipline."

It seemed to be the thing that concerned him most.

As we went along talking to these English people, one heard all kind of stories. There was the marine, who, when he was captured, had seven pounds, and in ten weeks he had spent it all but one mark, buying himself little luxuries at the camp; now he was wondering what he was going to do with his money nearly all gone. There was another marine who, when I asked him why he had enlisted, did not say, "Because my country needed me," but rather, "Because I thought it would be a bit of a lark, you know." There was another fellow who had a grouch because the Germans would not let him write long letters home.

"Yes, that's the fellow," Lieutenant Colonel Alberti commented. "The first day he was here, he wrote an eighteen-page letter. The officer in charge of the camp has to read every letter sent out by the prisoners. For the first few days these fellows had nothing else to do but to sit down and write. You can imagine the result. We were inundated with letters, so we had to put a limit on them. You see they all have to be translated. Now they are allowed to write every so often."

The camp at Doeberitz Road only opened my eyes a little. Two days later I was watching the gray shape of a Zeppelin soaring two thousand meters above our motor, as we hurried down the Kaiser Wilhelm Road towards Zossen. This time a good friend had gone to General von Lowenfeld, the Commander of Berlin, and from him had been secured the exceptional privilege to take photographs in the prison camp at Zossen.

If my first sight of Doeberitz was sinister, Zossen was farce. As our motor drew up before a gate similar to Doeberitz, we were put into a light mood by the spectacle of a baggy, red-trousered Frenchman balancing himself on a little box and nailing a gap in the wall of his own prison. He was busy nailing a strand of barbed wire to a post and near him stood another Frenchman, who looked up at him, poked him in the ribs with his stick when the sentry wasn't looking, and made faces like a mischievous boy. The humor of the situation was not out of the picture, so we afterwards learned, for the Zossen camp has a surprisingly good time of it. A handsome white-haired baron, who spoke excellent English, and who was introduced to us as the Lieutenant Baron von Maltzahn, was as genial as the spirits of the prisoners. With Captain von Stutterheim, who has charge of the Weinberger section of the huge camp, they made an escort that was willing to do everything possible to show us every detail of Zossen. One quickly saw that the Captain and the Baron, who was the aide of the General in Command of the Zossen garrison, were proud of the camp.

One saw at once that to all exterior appearances Weinberger camp was just like Doeberitz. There were the same dirt center street, same side streets, the same rows of unpainted sheds. But there was a difference that we later saw. At Doeberitz, as far as the eye can see, the flat land stretches away unrelieved only here and there by trees, but this Weinberger section of the Zossen camp is set down in a pine forest, as the Captain boasted, "One of the healthiest places near Berlin." Here, although the same number of men live in a shed—two hundred and fifty—they seem cleaner, which is because here they are mostly Frenchmen, although, to our delight, we later found a streetful of their black allies, the Turcos. At Zossen, too, I found a few Russians and Belgian civilians, although in Belgium, as I came to know, civilians and soldiers are synonymous—both firing upon the Germans. As we walked up the street, we were surprised at the few German soldiers.

"We don't need so many," the Baron explained to me. "Eighty guard, eight thousand prisoners. That's only one per cent., you see. And then over there," and he pointed to a tall wooden scaffolding, "we are going to have a searchlight on that, and another on the other side of the camp, so if everything happens to go wrong with the electric plant we can sweep the searchlights on the camp streets. Also in case of a disturbance we are going to have some rapid firers and a big gun. Over there, now," and he led me towards the fences, triple fences of barbed wire, "one of those wires on the inner fence—you see the soldiers and prisoners are protected from it by the outer wires—one of those wires is charged heavily with electricity, so that anybody trying to escape will be electrocuted. The prisoners have been warned."

As we continued on up the street, we were impressed by the number of Frenchmen. Everywhere one saw the baggy red trousers and the Baron told us that they were all prisoners from Maubeuge and Rheims. I noticed that squads of Frenchmen were marching up and down in command of a corporal and extending their ranks to go through the military setting-up drill. They seemed to move with a jaunty air, which contrasted with their nondescript appearance, and which spoke wonders for their spirit.

"They weren't like that at Doeberitz," I said to Captain Stutterheim. "There everybody slouched around. Here they have some life. How do you explain it?"

Luncheon is served at twelve.

Prisoner making flowers for the chapel altar.

Calisthenics instead of rifle practice.
WITH FRENCH PRISONERS AT ZOSSEN.

The Captain didn't know. "They are taken the best of care of. They have plenty of money. We give them all the privileges we can and they seem to have made up their minds to enjoy themselves."

Whereupon one decided that this marked difference in the spirit of the two camps was due to the fact that here they were nearly all Frenchmen, ready to enjoy life no matter where they were.

"Yesterday," remarked the Captain, "there were 6000 marks sent in the mail for these prisoners, and last week we had a day when 9000 marks were received. We are careful to do everything we can to make them comfortable; for instance, the French Catholics have streets to themselves; so have the Protestants. We also separate the Russians and the Poles. We have to be very careful to keep the Turcos in a street of their own. They don't like the French, now, since they've heard that a Holy War has been decreed in Constantinople."

Eating is one of the best things the Germans do, so it did not surprise me when the Captain led the way to the prisoners' kitchen. It looked the same as at Doeberitz, only here the huge cauldrons were filled with a whitish semi-liquid substance that made you wonder, until the cook explained that it was rice. I was deciding that the prisoners were fed more substantially over at Doeberitz, when the Captain remarked, "We have many Catholics here, you know, and to-day is Friday, so we give them rice instead of a meat stew." He went on to explain that the men received a pound and a half of bread every third day, as well as receiving the sausage and soup diet of Doeberitz. The men were doing things, not slouching around. They were either making little articles or playing games. I saw them weaving slippers of straw and cutting out things with pocket knives; in one corner of the room a bit of gay color met the eye. A soldier was making paper flowers. In poor French I asked him what the flowers were for.

"They are for the chapel altar," he replied with dancing eyes.

I turned to the Captain. "What! Have you got a chapel here for these fellows?"

"You will soon see it," he said. "They built the altar themselves, and among the captured soldiers are three French priests."

At the end of the kitchen street I noticed an adjoining structure, which the Captain explained was the canteen. In there I found a wonderfully equipped little place, where all sorts of articles were for sale. Soldiers were sitting around just as farmers hang around a country store and talk. There was a gossipy air of snugness about the little place that made one think it belonged in the midst of a well fed garrison and not in a prison camp. There was a counter behind which stood a German salesman, assisted by a French interpreter, and this little canteen bore no relation whatever to the system of company stores in vogue in the mining camps of America. In other words, it was run to give the men the best possible for their money.

On a blackboard I saw chalked different prices, 10 Cigarettes for 10 Pfg., which is almost five for a cent. I saw sponges strung on a string, which convinced me that the men in the camp were doubly anxious to keep clean. I was reminded of Coney Island by a little griddle of sizzling hot dogs, which could be bought for two cents each. I saw a basket full of segments of thick German wurst, 5 cents for a piece 2 inches in diameter and 4 inches long. They even sold butter in that little store ½ lb. for 12 cents, cheaper than you can get it in America. Sides of bacon, hams and long dangling wurst hung from the ceiling, and near them a wooden aeroplane tried to fly, while below on the floor, a pair of wooden shoes waited the owner who had the necessary 45 cents. On a table in a corner I saw where the games came from, checkers and cards, absurdly cheap. They even sold beer. I remarked on this.

"It's not an intoxicating beer," the Captain explained. "It's what we call in Germany—Health Beer. It is used in cases of illness when a doctor wants to give a patient strength."

It was after we had inspected a little room which one of the French soldiers had converted into a barber shop, where one might be shaved for 10 centimes, and where if one had 50 centimes he might be tempted by a sign that read, "Latest Parisian Haircut here"; it was after we had talked with the sparkling-eyed barber, happy these days—was not money plentiful among the prisoners?—that we came upon the sculptor.

Opening a wooden door upon which was written in French that only officers might enter, the Captain bowed us into the last place that you would expect to find in a prison camp. Had the damp odor of clay not told you, you would have seen from the unfinished gray pedestal that stood by the window, that this little twelve by twelve room was a studio. There, standing beside his work, a make-shift sculptor's apron over his soiled red and blue uniform, stood a young French soldier. The Baron explained to me that in 1908 this man had won the second prize at Rome. He told me that his name was Robert L'Aryesse, and in my notebook he wrote his autograph so that I might not misspell his name. I asked him if he knew Paul Manship, the young American sculptor, who only a few years ago took the prize at Rome. At Manship's name the Frenchman's face lit up and he began eagerly to talk of the quarter where they had all lived in Italy. How was Manship? What was he doing? Oh, he had been very wonderful, that young American! The admiration of Monsieur L'Aryesse was great.

The Frenchman was so happy to hear news from an old comrade that he forgot that my command of his language was elementary and launched forth in a glowing appreciation of Manship which left me far behind.

A photographer meanwhile caught sight of the statue of a Turk standing on the shoulders of a Russian soldier with arm extended (the Baron explained it was to be used as a guidepost to the Zossen prison), and with a keen sense for a good human interest picture began to focus his camera.

M. L'Aryesse was in alarm; it would never do to take a picture. What if his friends should see it! He began wringing his hand and then nervously running his fingers through his hair. To think of such a specimen of his work being photographed and published in America. But the photographer assured him that the statue was wonderful, and in an incredibly short time a flashlight powder boomed in the room and the job was done.

From the studio we walked up to the end of the street and entered a shed where a swarm of roughly-clad prisoners divided into groups were standing around a post pulling at something. They were braiding straw. One of them exhibited a round mat made of braided straw about five inches in diameter, which, it appeared, were mats to put in the hoofs of the horses to keep out the snow.

And again you marveled at the German system, this obvious weeding out of men who knew how to braid straw and putting them to work making a winter supply for the army horses. These men were the worst type of Belgians from the Antwerp slums and from the farms. One black-haired, evil-looking fellow had two yellow bands sewn to the sleeve of his coat, the badge of their spokesman and officer.

This black-haired gentleman was known as Lulu. Lulu was very proud of his rank. I doubted at first whether the man had a forehead; his black hair hung low; he was of the type—and there were many more in that room like him—of the hereditary criminal. Our gunmen would look like saints in comparison with this apache of the slums. Through an interpreter I was permitted to talk to the Belgians, and I chose the mildest looking man of them all. He said that he was perfectly satisfied to be where he was. The other men in the room nodded assent. This puzzled me a little, for they looked sullen enough to be unafraid to speak their minds even in the presence of a gray coated Prussian officer. But the Belgian explained, "Here we have a place to sleep, we get food, and we are not in danger of being killed."

Another black-browed fellow volunteered his story. "When the war began I was a reserve. I was told to hide my uniform and shoot at the Germans whenever I got a chance. Then I was called into regular service, and I put on my uniform and fought in the ranks. After that, with hundreds of my comrades, I was told to put on my civilian clothes again and go back home or any place where I could hide and take shots at any stray German soldiers I could see."

This seemed to me to be a confirmation of the German charges, that soldier civilians had been making war upon them.

At the other extremity of the street I found the other feature of the camp. Here were the Turcos. Dressed in outlandish costumes I saw some still wearing the burnooses of their tribes, others natty little, light blue, gold-embroidered jackets, some with the red fez, others with turbans, a motley collection that did not look at all the terrible Turco we had heard about. It happened to be what Captain Stutterheim called "Lice day," and thoroughly enjoying it the Turcos were standing in the street beating their blankets.

The leader of the Belgians was Lulu; but the Turks had a handsome gentleman who looked as if he would cut your throat for two cents, who answered to the name of Jumbo. Like Lulu, Jumbo was very proud of the two yellow stripes sewn on his arm. It was Lulu who posed his comrades for the photographer, arranging them with a nice sense of values. And when I looked the length of that line, glanced from one brutish face to another, I need no other confirmation of the statement that out of two hundred Turcos at the Zossen camp one in every four had been captured with ghastly trophies in his possession. The same charge of savagery has been made against the Turk, but from everything I can learn about the Turkish soldier—and here in Berlin I have talked to three American correspondents who have traveled with Turkish armies—there is a vast difference between the German trained Turkish soldier, and the French Turco.

Presently we selected a grinning, black villain and the most dapper Frenchman in the camp. All his comrades roared with laughter when they understood, and the whole procession came up the camp street as if they were going to a workman's Sunday picnic. Nicely posed, they made a splendid picture, which provoked the Baron's *"Allies!"* and roars of deep-throated Germanic laughter.

Possibly with a stage-manager's instinct to relieve the setting, the Captain walked us a short distance to a model little hospital camp in the pine woods. The surgeon in charge amazed us by saying that fifty per cent. of the captured French soldiers were tubercular. After walking with the wounded through the pines, we returned to the camp. We passed Frenchmen busy at landscape gardening. It seemed incredible. On every camp street they had made a long box design of evergreen and lettered to read the name of the company and the regiment.

It was then that I saw the man who had been making the paper flowers leave his shed and cross the street. Remembering what he had told me that the flowers were made for the chapel, I suggested that we go there. Following the soldier, we found ourselves in an anteroom at one end of a scrupulously clean shed. From the anteroom a door opened into a long unpainted room, at the far end of which I saw a crude altar. I noticed a square of red cloth of some cheap material, half covering the wall, and against this, in white and gold relief stood different figures of worship, candles, crucifixes, a host covered with a roughly cut piece of the same red muslin, and surmounting it all, high on the wall, an Almighty crown.

I saw the soldier with the flowers enter by a distant door and give them to the priests. When the priest handed him a plain vase and let him fill it himself, the soldier seemed ready to cry out with happiness. Silently the three figures at the altar went about their devotions. Again the door opened, a line of prisoners appeared, walking on tip-toe, their rough boots creaking; they filed across the room, and making two lines before the altar, dropped on their knees, their lips moving in a monotonous monotone of prayer. Rising, they tip-toed out and another file came in, and among them the vivid garments of a Turco. Making a sign to the Captain, I left the chapel. Presently they brought the Turco to me. He could speak French. I asked him why he had turned Christian and he said something to the effect that he had seen the way to the one real religion. He was explaining volubly about his conversion just before a battle in France, when the Captain pulled off the Turco's fez and grabbed a little braided pigtail concealed beneath.

"Christian, eh?" laughed the Captain. "What are you still wearing that thing for, then?"

The Turco began to grin.

"This religion," he said, "makes it pleasant among the Frenchmen, and then when I get home—well, how can I be a good Mohammedan without this?" and lovingly he patted his braided hair.

Prisoners of war? Are they ill or well treated? I leave my reader to judge the facts. I have tried to give you accurate pictures of the varied camps, typical of the German system. Of the camps in England and France, I do not know; of the camps in Russia no man knows. To silence the stories of ill-treatment that official press bureaus intermittently produce, why not apply a remedy?

Why not standardize the prison camps? As it is a task for humanitarians why should not the suggestions come from Switzerland, the home of the Red Cross, with the tacit understanding and backing up of the United States. A standard set of prison camp recommendations could be drafted recommending certain quantities and kinds of food, certain conditions for sleeping quarters, certain limitations to the enforced labor. The old Geneva document is out of date; its compilers could not foresee a World War; no nation to-day could meet its recommendations; the problem of handling prisoners of war has become too vast.

CHAPTER X
ON THE HEELS OF THE RUSSIAN RETREAT

The Russians were retreating! In Pschoor's our waiter told us; on the Linden great pennants began to appear; an hour and Berlin had bedecked itself in flags.... The Russians were retreating! In front of the newspaper offices the crowds stood twenty deep, their faces turned to a bulletin which said that Hindenburg was driving the enemy from East Prussia. Magically, vendors selling little photographic buttons of the German hero, swarmed on to the streets. *"Bilder von Hindenburg! Bilder von Hindenburg!"*

The great cafés which an hour ago had been empty, were suddenly filled. The air was tense with excitement. At every table the "beer strategists" were discussing this newest of great victories, which they were calling a second Tannenberg. Unable even to get a place of vantage from which to overlook this ecstasy of patriotism, I returned to Adlon just in time to receive a message from a blue-coated page boy; Major von Herwarth, of the General Staff, wanted me at the telephone.

"Good afternoon, Mr. Fox," the Major was saying. "I am very happy to say that everything has been arranged and that you start to-night for the East." Thanking Major von Herwarth, who has done everything in his power to help every open-minded American correspondent locate the facts, I hurried to my room to get my luggage together.

And an hour later we were completing arrangements for the most amazing piece of reporting done in this war. With the cooperation of the Foreign Office, the Staff had decided to permit Herbert Corey and myself to send collaborated reports from the front to America. Subsequently filed at different points on the battle line, they went by military telegraph into Germany, thence by the regular Government lines to Berlin, thence by the great wireless to Sayville, Long Island. Only a limited number of words a day are sent by the transatlantic wireless but the Foreign Office gave us one hundred and fifty of these which is why thirty-seven American cities read as swiftly as science could bring it to them, the truth of the terrific smash of Hindenburg's army.

That night, my only luggage, a change of clothing wrapped in a sleeping bag—for we had been cautioned to reduce what we had brought to the barest necessities—I went at eleven to the Friedrichstrasse Bahnhof where I met the officer who was to take me to the front. I found Baron von Stietencron, a captain in the 5th Regiment of the Prussian Guards, the crack infantry of Germany, to be a light spirited devil-may-care type of officer, gifted with a touch-and-go sense of humor, high

ON THE HEELS OF THE RUSSIAN RETREAT

strung and imaginative. Since the war he had let a reddish beard grow around his chin but one could see he was young and never happy in the field unless he was leading a charge. Indeed, later that night I learned that Baron von Stietencron had been shot through the throat when the Germans stormed at St. Quentin!

Troops swarmed on the platform; new recruits going out to fill the gaps in the line, officers rejoining their regiments. The train for Königsberg glided into the arc lighted shed; we managed to get a first class compartment.

"I tried to get sleeping accommodation," apologized Baron von Stietencron, who spoke good American, "but we were too late."

To the waving and calling of good-bys, the train glided past the pallid faces of soldiers' loved ones, and clanking over the switches, turned its headlight towards the Eastern night. It was near three before any of us thought of sleeping. In that short space of time we came to know Baron von Stietencron amazingly well. And I heard some things of war that made my blood run cold.

"The Russians are in retreat now at this point," explained the Baron, tracing his finger over one of those marvelously minute staff maps. "We arrive at Königsberg in the morning and from there we shall go south to Lyck. It was at Lyck that the first big engagement of the battle took place."

Lyck from which only a few days ago the Russians had been sent flying! There was no bed that night; we slept sitting but the drowsy rumble of the car wheels seemed to be the clatter of the Russian retreat and when the big light glared through the window into my eyes, I had to awake fully before realizing that it was not a searchlight seeking out the retreating soldiers of the Czar, but only the station lamp at Dirschau.

BURYING RUSSIANS ON THE EAST PRUSSIAN FRONTIER.

REINFORCEMENTS FOLLOWING OUR MOTOR INTO RUSSIA.

Morning found us in the beery dining-room of the old station at Königsberg, breakfasting on coffee and wurst, and watching through the window a bivouac of young soldiers who had spent the night outside. We were walking down the platform to take the train for Korschen, when we saw a little boy tug at his mother's arm and stare with mouth agape into the sky. There to the south what seemed to be a stub of black pencil was slowly dissolving into the snow gray clouds. "Zeppelin! Zeppelin!" In a clamor the waiting rooms emptied but already the great bag was a thing of the mists, vanishing, with its cargo of death, towards Warsaw.

Half an hour and we were on the train for Korschen.

Running almost due south from Königsberg, the railroad enters Masurenland where swamps and lakes still hold the Russian dead of those terrible August days, when Tannenberg turned East Prussia red. There the empty yellowish fields, undulating from hillock to gully, across the picture that the car window framed, bristled but five days before with Russian lines. There at Korschen where we changed cars, they had burned the station. There we saw on flat cars, ready to be pulled to some point behind the front, three black painted motors that the Russians had abandoned in their flight; coupled to them a heavy truck, bearing a long German howitzer; beside that a Belgian freight car, marked Louvain. Somehow it seemed quite natural that they all should be there—the Russian motors, the Belgian car, the German gun.

It was just as we were leaving Korschen that a smiling slender young man who wore glasses, bowed outside the compartment door, and said: "You're an

American, aren't you?" And when I told him yes, he said: "I am too." He went on to say that he was from Passaic, and I found myself recalling Gus Schwing of Newark, the Lieutenant Brevet whom we had met in Brussels and wondering if all the Americans in the German army came from New Jersey.

"I am an architect in Passaic," he said. "I happened to be in Germany on August 3rd. Before coming to America I had served my time in the army, but I, being born in Germany, offered my services at the outbreak of war to the government. They are using me to go behind the army, building up what has been destroyed. I have just come from France where we're rebuilding everything behind our battle line."

Captain von Stietencron, who had noticed my amazement, smiled and added, "In France and Belgium our soldiers planted the fields with a winter crop, last fall, and they're planting an autumn crop now."

Which seems to be a case of harvesting machines following the howitzers. At Stürlack where the railroad strikes due east for Lötzen we were made to feel the growing intimacy of the front, by being shunted on a side while troop trains rumbled by for an hour. It being four o'clock then and not having been able to eat since morning, the Baron led a foraging expedition into a track-side farmhouse, which resulted in more wurst and heavy black bread. I can still see the expression in that old farmer's eyes as, opening the cottage door, he saw the Baron outside. It was as if the gray officer's cape, hanging over the Baron's broad shoulders, at once made him in the eyes of that old man, something superhuman and to be idolized. And I did not wholly understand this until I learned that the Russians had spent a rioting night in the farmer's house and that thenceforth to him, the German troops had become avengers and deliverers.

"They are swine, these Russians," he told the Baron. "Further on you will see."

Beginning with Lötzen, the railroad became wholly military. No passenger cars went further than Lötzen, a direct feeding point to the front. Learning, upon leaving our car that a military train would pull out for Lyck in a few minutes, we ran down the tracks, stumbling on the ties, for it had become dark, trying to find a place to get on. But every freight car filled with food and ammunition was sealed and even on the flat cars there was not room to stand between the caissons and guns.

"Next to the engine," some one shouted, but even as we ran towards that car, where we now saw the pale glow of lantern light framed by an open door, the train pulled out.

"It's an hour," remarked Captain von Stietencron, "before there's another."

Picking our way back over the rails we made towards the dimly lighted station, its platform swarming with soldiers, gleaming with bayonets as they moved in a path of light. Entering a dingy waiting room, we stood beside a crowded lunch counter while the Baron went in to see the station Kommandant. Around the little stained topped table officers were eating dinner.

I wondered first at the contrast of their uniforms stained and worn with the field, and the immaculate cleanliness of their persons, at their finger nails which each man must have manicured, for they shone, at their clean shaven faces, and glistening combed hair; one fancied their eyebrows were brushed too. These officers in the well worn uniforms stained by six months of field service had obviously made their toilettes as for the opera.

We saw Captain von Stietencron coming out of the Kommandant's office.

"There will be no troop train leaving for Lyck," he said, "until to-morrow. However, in forty minutes a big supply train is going and if you can stand riding in a freight car," and the Baron paused with the unspoken question.

"Anything at all," I assured him. "When do we reach Lyck?"

"With a supply train," he smiled, "one never knows." Whereupon, being a soldier, and having a chance to eat, the Baron proposed taking advantage of this chance.

A steaming platter of an amazing good goulash, and we were picking our way over the rails to find the freight car in which we were to ride. We found it coupled to the engine and behind us, car after car, filled with ammunition, fodder and food, stretched endlessly up the track. We were in a freight car that had been painted inside and fitted with three long benches. From the white roof, two lanterns swung their flickering light across the brown walls, and at the farther end near a stiflingly hot round stove, I saw a big pile of straw where doubtless the train crew spent the night.

So we sat under the swinging lanterns, while the light car rattled and shook as with a disorder. Time never passed more quickly, listening to the Captain's stories of the war. And later I knew of many things concerning that first great drive into France, of how Namur was taken by storm, but the Iron Cross that hung from Von Stietencron's coat did not appear in the narrative, although I referred to it many times.

And with the shadows trembling on the wall and the two tired soldiers sleeping in the straw, it seemed the way to go to war, not as in the West, in a train on a soft plush seat. I involuntarily shuddered at the thought of the potential death we carried in the cars behind, the tons of ammunition coming now to make Russian dead. As the engine drew its heavy, dangerous load slowly on, through the partly opened door, I saw a drift of white falling snow beginning to blow past us in the night.

By the time we reached Windennen, the fields had turned white and when a soldier told us we would be delayed here twenty minutes, we got out. A sullen murmur, almost as of animals, met the ear, and walking up the tracks in the direction of the murmur, we saw presently, the glisten of bayonets and beyond that in the obscured light of a station lamp a horde of Russian prisoners. Herded within the confines of a barbed wire square that gave the impression of having hastily been built as a *Gefangenenlager*, the Russians watched our approach with suspicious eyes. Splendid types of the human animal, deep chested, tall fellows, with mighty physiques and stupid faces, the Russians of that greater Russia, who exist in the fiction of those who portray the "beautiful Russian soul." One recognized the great coats of sheepskin and goat, the round shaggy fur hats, that had succeeded the natty peaked caps of the first mustering in; one recognized the Russian smell which sickens you in the great prison camps all over Germany. As we looked at them the muttering ceased and uneasily they shifted about seeming to be waiting for something and instinctly you thought, upon realizing the utter ignorance of their faces waiting for a sentence of death.

"Over here are the officers," remarked Captain von Stietencron, and we followed him to a separate enclosure where a yellow bearded Russian glowered at us from the doorway of what had been a signal tower, while another drew his tall form up straight and smiled. The Captain spoke to this man in German. I caught the words: Doctor of Medicine, Esthland, which is one of the Baltic provinces of Russia, where five centuries ago the inhabitants were German.

"As a surgeon," the Captain was saying to tall, smiling, beardless Russian, "you might be returned to your country. There is a possibility."

Emphatically the Russian shook his head.

"No," he replied. "I've had enough of their army. I want to remain in Germany."

And then both evidently having interest in some proper noun that happened to fall into their conversation, they talked with increasing pleasure and speed.

"Queer," mused Von Stietencron, as we walked back to the freight car. "That Russian's father is the priest who gave me my first communion—and I meet him here."

But then anything is possible in this war.

From Lötzen to Lyck, by rail is twenty-five kilometers; in times of peace, the average passenger train takes little more than half an hour. In times of war, the run of a heavy supply train such as ours, is about an hour. We left Lötzen before seven; four hours and Lyck was still away. Rattling along, jumping the switches into sidings while coaches filled with troops rushed clanking past, faintly luminous phantoms in the snowy night, stopping at one little station after another, the weirdest ride of my life, even before we came to Iucha.

The village of Iucha, typical of that section of East Prussia which is known as Masurenland, hides behind the trees half a mile from the railroad. There being forty minutes before our train would leave, we gratefully accepted Julius the station master's invitation to visit his house. It would be cozy there. "Just up the track aways," he said. Imagining a comfortable half hour of lounging on some pillowed German chair, we followed the station master who led the way with a lantern. Outside his house, a squat two floor, stone structure, I noticed in the yard, a sofa, from which the plush cover had been removed. "A frugal man," I thought; "saving it no doubt for something else."

We followed him into the house. Nauseated by a stench we stared bewildered into a room. In the lantern's light, it was a place of pillage and filth. Torn papers made soft the floor, the walls seemed ragged with torn pictures, hanging shredlike from their frames—torn plush covers from old chairs, torn curtains—everything torn, broken or slashed.

"The Russians," he remarked, "they lived in my home," and I thought his eyes filled. "I lived here fifteen years. My boy was born here."

Following the station master into the room where the Russians had eaten, I saw the little brass meat cans of the Russian commissary, strewn around the floor amid an overpowering clutter of cooked meat and decaying vegetables. I opened a little closet in the wall and stood looking at something that my electric torch picked out on the floor. It was a pair of cow's hoofs, cut off a little below the knees. Probably left there until they got ripe enough to be cooked in a stew.

We found every room in that little home destroyed and filthy, and as we made our way across the snow to the village, we felt certain that we were to look upon even more depressing scenes. Little Iucha, a pretty place on a crest of the rolling country, we found to be utterly and wantonly devastated. We learned there was no fighting in Iucha, yet home after home we found destroyed. We visited the shop of G. Geydon, and found all the goods missing from his shelves, all the counters smashed, all his business papers torn and strewn on the floor. We went into another store, where amid a ruin of splintered wood, stood the owner's safe, blown open as by cracksmen.

In another house, a private dwelling, we entered a room that the Russian officers must have used as a council chamber, for chairs were drawn around one end of a long table. Beside the table, on the floor, I noticed a Russian map of this section of Germany. Here in this room, beyond doubt, the staff officers were in conference when the alarm rang through the town—"The Germans are coming!" Everywhere were signs of the panic in which they had fled.

"On that hill over there," said the station master, pointing across the snow, "the Russians had a trench. The morning after they retreated, we went up there and found it filled with loot and the dead bodies of three good women of the village whom they had taken up there, outraged, and slain."

"How long," I asked him, "were the Russians here?"

"From November sixth," he replied, "to February twelfth."

Six days ago! The trail was getting hot. As we passed the station, I looked in at a window and saw sitting on the floor there, their backs sliding down on the wall, a room filled with sleeping German soldiers, obviously two machine gun squads, for the guns were in the middle of the room; and beside this another room where in the light of a candle stub, under officers were playing cards with ten pfennig pieces as the stakes. Feeling as though I had been walking through a dream, I followed the others back to the car.

It was after midnight when somebody said we were in Lyck and clambering down from the car, we began packing our way across the tracks towards the station. Even at a distance we could perceive the marks of destruction, with one jagged wall leaning against the night. Leading the way past the burned building, Captain von Stietencron asked us to wait while he went into a rude shack where a light burned. Out of the night stalked a shadowy form and the electric eye of a powerful torch gleamed in my face, hesitated and darkened, while with a "*Gute Nacht!*" the shadowy form stalked on. It was the Lyck greeting—friend or foe?

In a few minutes, the Captain called us to come into the little shack.

"Be good enough to wait here," he said, "while I go out and find the officer who was to meet us in Lyck, and tell us where we will be quartered for the night."

He was gone and we were looking around the little board walled room. In a darkened corner I discerned the sleeping forms of three soldiers and along a wooden shelf, sat two others with heavy lidded eyes, field telephones clamped to their heads. A large white shaded lamp, evidently from the same house as the sofa on which we sat and the three upholstered chairs, stood upon a rough board table in the center of the room. Getting up and walking around, I saw that the wooden shelf had been the table for the Russian field telegraph, for two of their despatches obviously left there in the excitement of retreating, had been pasted by the Germans on the wall.

The time passed with Captain von Stietencron plodding somewhere through the snow. A young officer came in, a big handsome fellow, who looked at me in polite surprise, and seating himself at the table, began to write a letter. I saw that his pencil was of gold and flashing with little diamonds.

"An American, I take it," he said after a pause. "I know your country well. I like it." I talked with him about the cities he had visited while he hesitated over his letter. "It is so difficult," he remarked, "when you are writing your wife from the front. You want to tell her all the news, and then," with a grim smile, "you don't."

We watched him deliberating long over the composition of the note which, finally sealing, he gave to a soldier and sped him away.

"I am leaving now for Russia," he said, drawing on his great coat of beaver; "I must be at headquarters by morning. Good night, I am most happy to have chanced to meet you."

We heard the muffling snort of his motor die away in the snowy night. It was after three before the Baron returned.

"I am so sorry," he apologized, "but there has been a mistake. They know nothing here about us. We must go in the morning to the —th Army headquarters at Goldap. And now," and the Baron looked about him in dismay, "we must sleep."

So we stretched our sleeping bags on the floor of the shack and in a moment were sleeping like the soldiers, whom not even a cannon could awaken....

I awoke to find the brown coats of Russian soldiers passing outside the window. Rubbing the drowsiness out of my eyes, I saw follow, larger men in goat and sheepskins, and then a squad of black hatted, slit-eyed Siberians, a squad of strapping fair haired Finns. A guard of mature looking *Landsturm* complacently puffing at big German pipes were watching them shoveling away the snow.

It was the second night I had not been able to take my clothes off, and as for the civilized luxuries, given a tooth brush, a morning shave is not a matter of grave concern.

"Roll up your bag," advised Captain von Stietencron, "and leave it here. We'll go to the Officers' Casino for coffee. There a motor will meet us. We can pick up the baggage here and then we start for Goldap."

As we walked down the long shaded street that seemed to be the main street of Lyck, a gray transport train of "prairie schooners," slowly but steadily rattled by. The way was strewn with discarded cartridge clips and smashed rifles. On the walls of the houses we began to see the spatter of shrapnel.

"This is where General von Buelow's army broke through," explained the Captain. "One division of our soldiers rolled up four Russian divisions here and put them in retreat for the frontier."

An automobile of the Flying Corps shrieked past. We came into a zone of looted shops. We entered a store where bottled liquors had been sold, a chaos now of smashed glass. On the day of the battle when all discipline flew to the winds the Russians had evidently sought their solace or courage in vodka. We became aware that not a house nor store in Lyck had escaped their pillage. As we crossed a little public park we found they had vented their revenge at defeat by smashing every bench in the square. Since we learned that no Germans had remained in the town of Lyck, and no sniping could have been possible, this orgy of broken shop windows, blown up safes, and robbery, before our eyes, was the indisputable evidence of Russian barbarism.

We had our coffee in a little inn that had been the Russian Officers' Casino where a squad of Germans were already at work cleaning out the filth. Black coffee, black bread, in a room where the wall was riddled with bullets, from the pistols of drunken Russian officers who had sat there making a target of a portrait of the German Emperor, now lying on the floor. A tired officer of the Hussars came in as we left and I heard him say to Von Stietencron, "So their officers were here, were they?" And Von Stietencron replied: "I'm afraid they were as bad as their men...."

We climbed into the automobile, one of the gray-green army cars that I had seen in the West, and in a few minutes we were rushing by the never ending transport train. We left Lyck with its pillaged houses and shelled walls behind and swept across the open country. But we could not put the war behind us. We overtook a long shuffling column of Russian prisoners and further on, the Germans who were slightly wounded walking with almost a springy step in contrast to the dispirited Russians. We passed another of the gray supply trains, where the sleepy horses of the Uhlan escort pranced on its flanks. We came to a bridge which the engineers were rebuilding, and had to make a detour, crossing further up the stream beside a burned mill, its twisted, charred, water wheel a mute witness of the devastation that the Russians have brought to this land.

On the left the ground fell away into a gully and on the bottom of this I noticed a farmer's sled, the horse in a dead tangle beside it. I noticed a second sled, a third, a fourth; apparently these sleds having been met on the road by the beaten

ON THE HEELS OF THE RUSSIAN RETREAT 107

Russians were hurled with their drivers into the gully below.

As we drove into the great square at Goldap, a "goulash cannon," one of the German field kitchens, was smoking. It was the only smoke we saw in this once busy town of eight thousand people. We seemed to be standing in a burned sepulcher for all around us the houses were black with fire and on the streets no human thing stirred, save soldiers.

"I must go to the Kommandant," said the Captain, and noticing that I was staring at the desolation, he added, "There was no fighting in Goldap, not a shot. All this that you see has been done by the Russians."

I wondered if there would be a roof to shelter us. Where could the German general and his staff have their headquarters? It seemed impossible that they could find a single habitable house in this awful desolation. We left the motor and walked around. On one of the side streets we questioned one of the victims of Russian brutality. She found us another. And we heard from their own lips black tales of Russian savagery and violation of defenseless mothers and daughters—too ghastly for these pages.

I saw Captain von Stietencron coming across the square. He looked perturbed.

"I cannot understand it," he said. "There is no Oberkommandant here and in the office of the Etappen Kommando they told me that I must find a Rittmeister Tzschirner."

We went with Von Stietencron to find the Rittmeister, which means Captain of Cavalry. We found him standing beside a long rakish motor car, outside a looted bank. Von Stietencron held a long conference with the officer at the end of which I thought the Baron looked a trifle disappointed.

"I must say good-by to you," he said, coming over. "New orders from the staff. I must return to Berlin, and Rittmeister Tzschirner of General Hindenburg's staff will be your officer from now on."

I remembered that first night in the train to Königsberg, how Von Stietencron was constantly reiterating his boyish delight in the trip. And now with a glum face he was saying good-by. "Look me up when you return to Berlin," he said. "We'll have dinner together," and waving a farewell from the gray car he disappeared down the road.

My new guide and councilor, Rittmeister Tzschirner, was a short, springy, fair haired, young officer, of the ideal cavalry build. I saw that his were the cold steady eyes of the fighter, yet not without a twinkle, and the good natured mouth that the little mustache could not hide, suggested that here again we were in luck—another of these wonderful German officers with a sense of humor.

"Captain von Stietencron," I remarked, "said that headquarters were no longer here."

"No," said Tzschirner, "they have moved up with the pursuit of the Russians. We start now, if you like, for Suwalki, Russia."

If we liked! Suwalki was on the very dust of the Russian retreat.

"It is fifty kilometers to Suwalki," said the Rittmeister; "we should make our arrival there by seven o'clock."

He must have forgotten that it was on the line of communications.

As we set out on this road it was growing dark. Turning in a southerly direction toward Kowahlen we began a ride through a vague, darkening country, peopled—except when our searchlight picked them up—with indistinct beings. Through the trees that fringe Goldap on the east, there gleamed a huge campfire that spread its yellow light on a ruined wall; as long as we could, we watched the black forms that must have been soldiers, passing across the flames. The motor rumbled on; signs of the retreat began to appear. In the ditch beside the road, I saw a dead horse, a second dead horse, a third dead horse. An abandoned Russian cannon leaned against the night, its long howitzer barrel pointing an angle of ruin into the sky. One thought of that as a symbol of the Russian rout.

Along the road there commenced a strew of clothing, a trail of discarded hats and coats, the dirty brown of the Russian soldiery. I saw rifles, cartridge bones, single shoes and then a broken caisson, a hooped roofed transport, overturned in the ditch; and then even whiter in the failing light, the scarred trees torn with shrapnel and shell.

"Did your artillery harass their retreat?" I asked Rittmeister Tzschirner.

"Oh, yes," he replied. "It was very fine."

And the strewn débris of war continued in a silent clutter of horror; and an inky darkness closed round shutting it all out; and we sat listening to the motor's rumble. Where were the dead? In the fields? We strained our eyes but the damp night was impassable; yet we felt they were there.

"Rittmeister," I asked suddenly, "were many men killed here?"

"Oh, yes. The losses of the Russians were very great. Our artillery shot very well. I cannot give you the exact number. We do not know. The Russians did not wish us to know the regiments engaged so they carried away their dead. I mean they carried away as many as they could; but our soldiers came very fast and the Russians had not always the time. Yes, they left many dead but we cleared the road of them."

"And the fields too?"

"Oh, no," he said quickly as if unwilling that I should make a mistake. "In the fields here are many Russian dead. We shall bury them."

We were passing between the fields of the unburied dead....

It was when we had made the turn of Kowahlen, which is where the road strikes due east toward the frontier, that we saw silhouetted against the sky a man, a woman and a girl. Caught by our headlight, they stood beside the road, as if they had paused there to rest. The man in the heavy coat of an East Prussian farmer leaned on a cane, watching with suspicious eyes. The woman, stout and motherly, sat on a stone, her hands folded in her lap, her eyes blinking from an awakened sleep. And the girl seemed to draw a cheap shawl as if to hide her face but not so quickly but that I saw she was astonishingly pretty. This sudden protective movement had its origin perhaps in some horrible experience. Had the Cossacks —

The road tunneled through a vista of trees. We passed another peasant family — a father and a mother bearing packs, three children, one carrying a bird cage in which there was no bird. They too were on the heels of the retreat, only they were going back to the homes which they had fled in those terrifying November days when the Russians had overrun the land ... going back to what?

The sledge had stopped. A scrawny girl held the cow by a rope. As our searchlight glared into their faces, the children, piled among the household goods, frowned and blinked. The man was holding the horse. The woman was staring off into the night.

Our gaze followed hers. Our headlight was shining on a roofless house with charred windows as the empty sockets of a skull and revealed the outlines of a jagged wall that had been the barn, and a huddle of fence palings and soft earth, once the garden. The woman who sat with her children on the loaded sledge, must have sobbed — although we could not hear it above the motor's din — for the man holding the horse turned, and the girl holding the cow turned, and the frowning, blinking children turned in her direction. And after we had passed we looked back and they were standing there in the same postures, transfixed, gazing at the blackened chaos once their home.

There are many villages between Kowahlen and the frontier — the villages of Lukellen, Drosdowen and Mierunsken. But to-day they are only names by which may be characterized certain works of Russian arson. Not a house did we find intact on this road to the frontier, not a home but that was ashes or if of stone whose walls were black. Not even the church at Mierunsken had escaped the torch. In a few moments more we were in Russia. We did not need the striped frontier posts to confirm this; nor the holes and lumps, that marked the end of German road building. Something more significant revealed to us that at last we had come to the land of the Bear. For we passed through two villages but a kilometer apart and in these not a house had been burned, not even a fence smashed; they were Amt and Filipowa, in the Czar's domain.

"Rittmeister," I asked, "did German soldiers follow the Russians down this road?"

"All the way to Suwalki," replied Tzschirner.

"German soldiers," I persisted, "who passed through Goldap and all those villages to the frontier."

"Naturlich. That was the line of advance."

I was silent.

"Rittmeister, you have wonderful discipline in your army."

Tzschirner seemed surprised. "Why?"

"I cannot understand," I said, "how your soldiers, seeing what the Russians had done to East Prussian villages, could refrain from taking vengeance on the first Russian village they entered."

I think the Rittmeister was a little offended.

"We are soldiers," he said with dignity; "not criminals." He paused and perhaps guessing that Belgium was in my mind, "We only make war on non-combatants when they make war on us."

Near Jemieliste we overtook the army. Visible at the extremity of our long, yellowish light, there grew out of the darkness, the grayish tops of transports, rolling as on a sea; and as we came up with them we distinguished in their muffled clamor, the clanking of chains, the cries of the drivers and the cracking of whips on the horses' backs. Throttling down until we barely crept along, our soldier chauffeur dexterously guided the car between the maze of wagon wheels and balking horses, so on, until after I had counted twenty wagons struggling hub deep through the frozen snow, we came to the head of the column, where the serene officer, utterly oblivious to the confusion behind him, leisurely rode the lead. And I thought of that other great general who dared the Russian snows without railroads and all that modern science has given war, penetrating the land to Moscow and across such frightful roads through the heart of the Russian winter; in that night one was awed with the name Napoleon.

The yelling of the transport men died away. The gloom thickened; rain fell. Milanowizizna passed, a ghostly village. Torn, by heavy wagons, furrowed and frozen into icy ridges, the road became almost impassable. It was like going over a huge washboard, with the corrugations running in crisscrosses. Jumping insanely from ridge to hole, our motor stood up wonderfully, until we came to an abrupt hill where nubbles of frozen snow impeded the way. Three times did Gelbricke, the chauffeur, try to make it; and three times the wheels spun helplessly. Finally with reluctance the Rittmeister said it would be better if we all got out. And then in the pitch darkness and cold rain, we put our shoulders to the car, but with futile effort.

"Let's find some wood for treads," I suggested.

The Rittmeister would have none of it. He seemed to be mortified that we should be put to this inconvenience while guests of the German army. "Seyring!" he called the mechanician by name.

"*Jawohl.*"

Of course, out on a Russian plain, in pitch darkness, it was quite easy to find wood; but one thought that Seyring's "Jawohl" would have been equally as cheery had the Rittmeister ordered him to find a bottle of wine.

I too went to find wood. Only my foot stumbled against something in the ditch and I almost fell upon it. And when I flashed on my electric torch I saw that it was a Russian soldier. His face was buried in the snow, his stiff, extended arms pawing the frozen ground. On the shoulders of his long brown coat I read the number of his regiment, 256, and on his feet, from which the boots had been stripped, were wound with strips of knitted wool. His black, bare head, intensified by the contrasting snow, seemed the blackness of a raven.... The others found the wood.

ON THE HEELS OF THE RUSSIAN RETREAT 111

The car climbed the hill. Near Mlinisko we passed a clanking transport, near Turowka, a mired limousine of the Flying Corps. The rain froze to hail and as we crossed the great open plain to Suwalki, snow came, a slow, steady fall, unnaturally white in the headlight's glow. Progress became even slower. Ahead the road seemed choked with wagons, but always there opened up a lane through which drove this soldier shaving the hub of transports with the nicety of a race driver.

And then we came up with the artillery, two batteries to pound away at the crumbling Russian front. We saw the drivers, each with a carbine slung over his shoulders, astride the straining horses, while the heavy caissons and guns rumbled behind. Our headlight shone upon a gray and red cloaked soldier, sitting on the gun carriage, his spurred boots dangling, his body jumping and jouncing, while quite complacently he munched on a bar of chocolate. The battery blocked the road; Seyring blew his horn; Rittmeister was shouting, "*Los! Los!* Away! Away!" But the soldier with the chocolate simply ignored us and went on munching that sweet of which the German army is so fond.

"*Abspannen!*" the command gutturaled from driver to driver. It was the order to unhitch the horses. It being impossible now to drive ahead, we watched the tired carabineers slide down from the saddles and loosen the horses from the spans, while the gun crews poured out oats from big gray bags and gave the horses their meal. And, two by two, the drivers led them clanking off into the night, with the gun crews following on foot, with the caissons and cannon let standing in the snow. They were going to sleep. Where? On either side the rolling snow covered plains seemed to spread illimitably, before graying into the black Russian night.

The horses gone, a gap opened in the road.

"*Los!* Gelbricke! *Los!*"

To the Rittmeister's urgings, the car sped forward, and we rushed past the battery, so silent now, in the snowy night, but on the morrow to roar forth death. Through the gray white curtain of snow, the lights of Suwalki came twinkling to meet us, and as we drove down a shaded street, even there I could see the débris of war — discarded uniforms, guns and shells. And when finally we stopped before an old stone building and followed the Rittmeister through a damp archway into a dirty looking café, where we had ham and tea; after I had seen two German officers pay for their meal and then bow courteously to the sullen proprietor of this Europiski Hotel, after I had stretched my sleeping bag on three chairs and said good night, I heard a swift succession of heavy reports.

"The Russian artillery," said Rittmeister Tzschirner.

"How do you know?" I asked.

"Because the Russians fire like this — one-two-three-four, then — one-two-three-four. Listen."

I caught then the quick but measured beat of their guns, but having just ridden down the road of their retreat, I could not think of their artillery as firing so methodically; rather, to me, those quick salvos seemed to be the firing of desperation, the frantic gunnery of men who knew the enemy was closing in — an enemy who upon their heels had followed the red Russian trail through East Prussia, across the snow swept plains to the pine forests of Augustowo, where even now the guns bellowed that a hell on earth was there.

CHAPTER XI
THE BATTLE OF AUGUSTOWO WALD

This is the first complete account of a great battle that has been told in this war

The battles in the East are so vast and the movements of the troops are so swift and secret that up to the middle of February the war against Russia was, to all correspondents, only a thing to be seen in unimportant fragments. Through sheer good fortune I saw the Battle of Augustowo Wald, which historians may or may not write of as being a decisive conflict, but in which a Russian army of 240,000 men was annihilated; only one intact division escaping to Grodno, there to be swallowed up by a new Russian army, which became the new Tenth. And because of these huge reinforcements the Germans did not break the line of the Niemen, flinging it back on Warsaw. Russia has denied this annihilation. With another American, Herbert Corey, I saw it.

The story I shall tell is a story of this battle, of its strategy, as told to me by Rittmeister Tzschirner of Field Marshal von Hindenburg's staff, of its actual fighting, which I saw, and of its celebration. For on the night of victory I was the guest of Excellence von Eichorn, commander-in-chief of one of Von Hindenburg's victorious armies, and with his staff I sat around a strange banquet—a little room in a Russian inn, with candle-light flickering on the wall, and for music, the rolling of the guns, while the victors celebrated the battle in a way that I could not understand.

The Road to Augustowo

We awoke to hear the guns, great drums beating a sinister roll.

"To-day," said Rittmeister Tzschirner, "I take you to the front. Do you wish?"

I was for a quick breakfast.

"Oh, no, Mr. Fox. There is much time. The battle will endure all day."

Nevertheless I hurried the Rittmeister to breakfast downstairs in the Europiski Hotel. Quantities of black coffee, served in long glasses, platters of white buns coated with some tasteless powder, suspiciously Russian, and Ober-Lieutenant Lieckfeld of the Eighth Battery of the First Guards, joined us—a handsome, healthy skinned, smiling man, who spoke a fair English. He told us what an officer had seen on the road back from Augustowo this morning.

"Just this side of Augustowo," explained Lieckfeld, "the Captain saw a Russian gun that had been hit by one of our shells. The horses and men were all killed and the carriages smashed. The Captain said they looked very bloody and all sort of mixed."

This was the kind of war I had seen for years in pictures—the war of de Neuville and Verestchagin. I wonder if the officers noticed my impatience to be on the road to Augustowo. And then the Rittmeister did a significant thing. Drawing his Browning, he drew the clip from the magazine to see that it was full.

"And now," he said, "we go to Augustowo," adding with a tantalizing smile, "Do you wish?"

"Don't kill any Russians," Lieckfeld called after us and chuckled.

Following the Petersburg Prospeckt, a wide unpaved highway, obviously the Main Street of gray, squat housed Suwalki, our motor bumped out on the road to Augustowo—a road of frozen brown snow in the middle of a dreary snow covered plain and tunneling ahead into a green forest of pine. We passed a huddle of miserable huts and a great Russian church with bulb shaped cupolas, slender minarets and a dome gleaming with gold. We passed the deserted garrison barracks, places of filth, in which the Germans would not live. We ran along a line of pretty pale blue fence palings; and then we saw the boys. They seemed to be playing a game. A little fellow, whose round fur hat and brown pea jacket was typical of his chums, was poking at something with a stick. Greatly excited, he called the boys, who seemed to be looking for something across the road in the snow. Stridently he called to them.

"That boy is saying," explained Tzschirner who understands Russian, "that he has found another one."

And we saw that the youngster was poking the snow away from a big bearded man in a sheepskin coat. The game the boys of Suwalki were playing was hunting the dead....

The woods opened up; a funeral stillness closed in. A Uhlan on patrol passed at a canter. Tzschirner gave a command and the motor stopped. "*Laden*," he said, and while the red haired mechanician was loading the two carbines strapped to the car, Tzschirner said, "The battle is continuing. Russians cut off from their regiments are in the woods. They are fugitives. They are hungry and if they see us, they'll shoot. I must say you this."

We began to take an interest in the woods. We saw that the slender trunks of the pines gave poor concealment to a man but in the snow we discerned many tracks. Somewhere in their depths a rifle cracked. Tzschirner stopped the car. We listened; everything was still. We drove on. We came upon an abandoned howitzer and in the snow a magnum of unexploded shells, a great stain that had turned black, and a yellow mound of fresh clay.

"A gun position," said Tzschirner briefly. "Our soldiers made advance too rapidly for the Russians to retreat."

There are thirty kilometers on the road from Suwalki to Augustowo and the thirty kilometers were strewn with the tangle and débris of war. I found myself

THE BATTLE OF AUGUSTOWO WALD 115

counting caps—round Russian caps of goatskin and fur, and the black peaked caps of muster day. I counted these caps until I counted thirty-three in an unbelievably short time and I found myself thinking of them as thirty-three dead. For a soldier will discard his coat before his cap.

Near Szszepki which is where the forest opens into a brief snow gray plain, ringed with a dreariness of sky, we met the woman, a young peasant woman, her loose hair wreathing her sullen eyes with thick black curls. As she saw us, she made the sign of the cross.

"Stop the car," I called to Tzschirner.

He got out with me, the woman gave a scream and fled down the road. We ran after her.

"Please, Madame," the Rittmeister asked her, "why did you make the sign of the cross when you saw us?"

She began mumbling a prayer; her shaking finger traced the sign in the air.

"Why," said Tzschirner gently, "do you fear us?"

When she spoke it was without looking up. "Our soldiers," she said, losing her fear, "told me you were devils, so I thought if I made the cross you could not pass it. They told me you would burn my house and kill me."

"Has your house been burned?"

"No-o."

"And you will not be killed, Madame," said Tzschirner, touching his hat. "I promise you."

We left her looking after us in a bewildered way and when we climbed into the motor she fled up the road.

"They have bad minds, the Russians," remarked Tzschirner. "They know what they have made in East Prussia."

And then near Szczobra we overtook the "clean up squad." We saw them advancing, as in extended order, the teeth of a great comb, cleaning woods, fields and ponds, of the dead. We saw segments of the line abruptly stop, and come together and begin digging in the snow.

"How," I asked Tzschirner, "did they miss the dead we saw along the road?"

"They have not been there," he explained. "They first work where considerable actions have occurred; then they take up the more isolated points of the line."

All this time the grumble of the guns had grown more distinct. We were nearing Augustowo. A horde of prisoners stolidly shuffled and I saw that their hands and faces were black with the battle. The German light wounded commenced to straggle along, holding a white bound hand, or unconcernedly handling a cheap cigar while the other arm hung cradled in a sling. I thought they all looked tired but their step was alert. And always the roll of the guns grew louder, monstrous drums insanely beating their Miserere from somewhere beyond the tops of the pines.

Finding at Szczobra a field bakery, we ate. Seated around an empty box with two officers of the commissary, we ate from deep tin dishes filled with a stew of white beans and beef; there were chunks of a brown bread made from Russian meal. And the floor almost in the long shed that the engineers had built in a night, was covered with loaves of the brown bread baked fresh in the twelve oven transports outside; while at the other end of the shed, white aproned bakers were mixing their dough.

"They are all volunteers," the commissary officer was saying. "By trade they are bakers and when war broke out they at once put themselves at the disposal of the government. I am sorry," he went on, "that I cannot give you better bread, but here in Russia," and he shrugged.

"I like the Russian meal," I told him. "What did you do, commandeer quantities of it?"

"We bought it," he replied a little indignant, "and paid cash for it. As soon as we occupied Suwalki, all the Jews took their meal out of their hiding places and brought it to us. Here," and opening a wallet he handed me a receipt that showed how Herr Friedmann, of Suwalki, had received 10,000 marks cash for meal delivered to the German army.

We continued in the motor. I saw a trooper's grave—his lance upright in the snow, the black and white Prussian pennon snapping in the wind. We passed a frozen pond where Russian prisoners were breaking the ice to fill their canteens. We stooped at a great wooden cross, on which an officer's Rosary hung; and then I saw the birds.

They were gray bellied birds with black wings and heads. They were waddling birds that grotesquely marched across the snow, pecking as they went. They were fluttering winged birds that you thought of as being too heavy to fly strong. And as I noticed one near the road, I saw that his gray breast bulged plumply; he seemed to have eaten well.

Further on in the field,—in the same field where waddled the birds,—I saw a shapeless heap of men; and then another heap, and another, until I had counted six. I saw a bristle of barbed entanglements trampled in the snow and just behind them a trench, a deep long grave that days before the living had dug for themselves—a pit filled with clay and snow and men. I had never seen such men before. They were men postured like jumping jacks only their legs and arms were still. They were men who seemed standing on their heads, their feet over the trench top, turned soles up to the sky. Somehow, they gave you the impression of being all legs and arms,—stiff grotesque legs, stiff grotesque arms. They all seemed lumpy, all but one, and he was standing up, his grayish face turned in the direction the clean up squad would come; and he was standing because the piled dead braced him so that he could not fall....

The Road Through the Forest

THE BATTLE OF AUGUSTOWO WALD

"Eighty thousand prisoners by to-night—I think," added Rittmeister Tzschirner. He had just left the office of the Kommandant in Augustowo, a little gray building, the walls chipped with shrapnel. From the East rolled the steady boom of the guns; the battle was two miles away.

"I have just looked at his map," continued Tzschirner, and he glanced at his watch. "One o'clock.... I think by to-night we make eighty thousand prisoners—perhaps not so many, *naturlich*. But from the position of the lines, I think yes.... And now I think I can take you to the battle. You wish?"

Above the bluish walls of Augustowo the tops of the green pines laid against a leaden sky. Over there was the battle, the dense forest an impenetrable curtain, through which reverberated the pang of shrapnel and the roar of *grenaten*.

"I must tell you," hesitated Tzschirner, as our motor, lurching through the mud of Augustowo, turned toward the woods. "It is very dangerous. The forest is filled with Russians and they will shoot. It may not be agreeable."

"Let's have a try at it," I suggested.

The Rittmeister smiled.

"Seyring!" he called to the red haired mechanician. "*Fertig zu feuer!* Be ready to fire. Gelbricke!" and he tapped the chauffeur. "If I say turn back, turn instantly and drive fast!" With a smile he turned to me. "Mr. Fox," he said, "you know how to use German rifle, do you not?"

Then making a turn to the left, we entered a better road that tunneled away through the trees.

"This is the road to Grodno," said Tzschirner, "the Russian fortress. Our soldiers make their advance here."

We rattled across a wooden bridge that the German pioneers had thrown on top of a dynamited ruin across the Augustowo Canal. The road dipped to a lower level, that pointed toward Grodno, a straight brown band finally seeming to terminate where rows of distant pines, meeting like converging railway tracks, closed across the last thin slit of sky. At a slower pace, as though sensing danger, the car passed into the woods.

There came a German soldier. He was on foot. He had no rifle and his right hand squeezed the left as though it were asleep and he would waken it. But as we drew near, he dropped the left hand as though it were of no importance—and I saw the blood spread all over it—and the right hand flashed to his cap.

"Where," asked the Rittmeister, returning the salute, "are the Russians?"

"In the woods," said the soldier, and walked on; he was holding his hand again.

Watching the woods, we drove slowly on, past the few huts, which are Bealobrzegi, until we heard a noise like a bunch of Japanese firecrackers confusedly exploding in the woods.

"The Russians!" I exclaimed.

"And our soldiers," added Tzschirner. "Our men are going through the forest hunting them down."

And I began to understand the fresh tracks in the snow that crisscrossed in among the slender trunks of the pines, until they darkened with the forest gloom. And I began to think of this battle of Augustowo Wald as another Battle of the Wilderness, although here the ground was free of underbrush; and I realized that on both sides of us a grim game was being played, that we could hear but could not see; a long pursuit in which Germans and Russians stalked each other from tree to tree, to find the quarry and kill.

A battery clanked by at a canter, and the gunners, swinging their legs, seemed stolid and tired. I began to see traces of death in the snow—discarded clothing, broken rifles, clips of cartridges, a profusion of shaggy Russian hats—all the frightful débris of war. We met a Huzzar and he too seemed tired and lethargic.

"*Aus wo fahren sie?*" called Tzschirner.

"Von *Promiska*," shouted the Huzzar.

"*Ist der Weg frei?*"

"*Jawohl! Nach Jamine.*"

"The road is clear of Russians as far as the village of Jamine," explained Tzschirner.

And then I saw the dead Russians. There was one who had fallen in a heap and you thought that his face, buried in the cold snow, had found solace there. I saw another who lay in a ditch, his waxy bearded face staring at the cheerless sky, his arms wide stretched as if impaled on a cross; and I noticed that his boots had been stripped from him, and that one foot was wound with a white stained cloth, as though bruised with the rush of retreating miles over the frozen roads ... and now he could rest.

And out of the gray drizzle down the road there emerged an old woman and a child. The old woman was a grotesque figure as she hobbled along in a vain attempt to run. The little girl at her heels looked incredibly old. She was carrying a schoolbag, bulging with hastily packed belongings. In the old woman's arms there was something covered with a red cloth. She had a way of staring at this bundle and breaking into sobs. And as I watched them fleeing down the road, a swarm of bullets sung overhead with a sucking sound and spattered among the trees. "They will see the dead men," I thought.

A grimy trooper was galloping down the road. "Halt!" ordered the Rittmeister.

"Where are the Russians?"

"In the woods, everywhere, in front and behind you," called the trooper, and galloped away. I heard Tzschirner ask the chauffeur how quickly he could turn round the car if we were attacked. The chauffeur stopped and tried. The result was painfully slow. "I must warn you," said Tzschirner, "it is very dangerous. Entire companies of Russians that have been cut off from their regiments are in the

THE BATTLE OF AUGUSTOWO WALD

woods. They might easily surround us before help could come."

"Let's try it a little further," I suggested, for as yet we had seen no living Russian.

"*Langsam* Gelbricke," called Tzschirner to the chauffeur, and then the Rittmeister drew his pistol and sat with his hand on the trigger, a precaution which until now I had never seen a German officer take in the tensest situations of the Eastern or Western front. From Jamine, the roar of the guns broke through the cold rain in a monotone of clamor, but more distinct became the rattle of rifles among the pines. A bullet kicked up the dirty snow.

At that moment I glanced toward the edge of the trees at the left, where I saw a Russian lying on his back in the snow. He wore a brown army coat with red shoulder straps, sewed with the yellow numerals of his regiments. His gun was leaning against a tree and I thought that it had been torn from his hands or placed there. For with upraised arms, rigid in the struggle with death, his clawing hands seemed to have been turned to stone. At the same time, with odd irrelevance, there flashed into my mind the remembrance of the lead soldiers that I had played with as a boy—a soldier whose gun I had broken off and whose arms I had bent, to signify his death. And I thought of the lead soldier until we passed a yellow haired Finn, whose hands were folded on his great chest, as though a comrade had fixed him for burial before fleeing among the firs. Now the crack of the rifles came closer and with more frequency, and we began to see blood upon the snow, and then a big red hole around which fragments of clothing and fragments of stiff things were strewn. "A shell burst there," remarked Tzschirner.

A few paces on we came upon a dead horse from whose flanks a square chunk had been cut, presumably by a fugitive who, with this first food of days, had crept into the woods. All around we could never see the men who were shooting or the dim outlines of their human targets. And then, from out of the trees, a German soldier came stumbling, and fell limply into the snow. Jumping out while the car was in motion, our red haired mechanician ran toward him. "Dead," called Seyring, throwing up his hands. Tzschirner seemed to come to a decision.

"I think," he said, "that this is as far as we had better go. You have seen it. It is the same."

"But, Captain," I urged, "isn't there some place from which we could see an artillery position?"

"You would go into the woods," bantered Tzschirner. "I will take you, but it is very dangerous."

"No, Captain," I said. "We would like to see the battlefield from the position of one of your batteries in action."

"That is possible," said Tzschirner. "But we must return to Augustowo and journey by another road."

The rifles were cracking not two hundred meters away—so the Rittmeister said—as the car turned and raced down the road to Augustowo. We passed a rumbling ammunition train; and the soldier sitting beside the driver of the first car was munching on a huge chunk of black bread. We noticed more of the fresh dead as we came to a lonely shack set in a little clearing among the pines. I saw outside the door a fallen man who, like a wild animal, had crawled to some hidden place to die. Always guns were booming in the direction of Jamine, their song rolling over the sky an immeasurable travail. Here among the pines, to the right and to the left, the ruthless game of tracking and shooting went on with a cracking sound, and the snow became more cluttered with coats, and I counted furry, shaggy Russian hats until I could count no more. If a bird still lived in that forest, it did not sing; only the black winged birds with the gray bellies of carrion were there, hovering cautiously above the trees with weird instinct that a grewsome feast was near. As we left the great green forest, and rushed the grade toward the bridge over the canal made by the German engineers, we suddenly stopped and our red haired boy of a mechanician got out and lifted a dark object which barred the way and which had not been there when we crossed the bridge before. I saw him dragging at a German soldier whose feet grotesquely bobbed against the boards, and he was careful, the red haired boy, to lay the soldier at the extreme edge of the bridge, as if to make certain that no wagon would pass over him; he was very careful of that, was the red haired boy. But when he was through I saw that the soldier's head dangled over the bridge as though needing but a push to flop into the muddy canal below....

The Battle

We had left the forest, where the rifles croaked and chugged again between the pale blue houses of Augustowo.

"*Chausee nach Raygrod?*" cried the Rittmeister to the sentry by the Kommandant office.

"Links gehen!" was the reply.

"We must go toward Raygrod if you would visit with the battery," explained Tzschirner. "Perhaps the road will not be good, all the way. I hope, yes."

From east and south rolled the thunder of the guns and across the street from a muddy yard that was strewn with Russian dead, I saw five German soldiers, picking the caked dirt from their boots and singing a song. And as we left behind the last squalid house of Augustowo I saw a squad of smiling soldiers crowding around a captured Russian field kitchen. But the odor that assailed my nostrils was not of steaming food; in the road nearby lay the carcass of a horse.

There opened a great grayish plain, serried with hastily thrown up trenches, filled with melting snow and the lying, the kneeling and the sitting dead; a wilderness of sky closed in, grayish like the earth, and across it an aeroplane came, the black crosses painted beneath its wings, crosses of death—for would not the bombs fall?—and it cackled away, the bird of destruction toward the eastern sky. Through Naddamki and Koszielny, into a brief dense forest, and we drove toward Bauszcke to the growing clamor of the guns.

"It is better," said Tzschirner, "that we leave our auto in Bauszcke and proceed on foot. To Tayno we must journey five kilometers. It grows dangerous and the

THE BATTLE OF AUGUSTOWO WALD

auto might be observed by the Russians."

Leaving the car on the highway to Raygrod—Seyring, the red haired mechanician begging in vain to be allowed to come—we tramped through the snow and mud of a narrow Russian road toward Tayno.

"I must tell you," was Tzschirner's note of warning, "this is very dangerous. The Russians no longer have any orders. They are everywhere, little bodies cut off from their commands and trying to escape. You must remember there exists no line like the West here. Everything is movement."

Still the only Russians we had seen were dead or prisoners, so we went on. Two Uhlans passed at a trot, turning from right to left with alert eyes.

"*Ist der weg frei?*" called Tzschirner.

"*Jawohl. Alles ruhig!*"

Satisfied, the Rittmeister thought we could go on. The grumble of the guns became clearer; a *grenat* burst not half a mile away, emitting its terrifying grinding yelp, and staining the air with an ugly spume of brownish smoke. The road turned, skirting a pond, the Drengstwo See, beyond it a grove of pines above which shrapnel was breaking in beautiful billowing clouds. And then just ahead, reverberating in a bowl in the rolling ground, I heard four crashing reports, first two, then two more; and wisps of grayish smoke rose in the air and as quickly thinned away. Hurrying up the road and into the hollow, we joined the battery. Four 10.5 field pieces, set in pairs with thirty feet between, the battery was shelling a Russian position on the Bobr. Moving with a feverish ordered haste, the black striped gunners drew the empty copper jackets of the shrapnel, returned each to its oiled cloth case, and glancing toward an officer who was kneeling beside a tree, seemed waiting for something. I saw that the officer had a telephone clamped over his ear, and then two slender wires, which led from this to another tree, festooned from one to the other like the tendrils of a vine, He was furiously scribbling in a despatch book that rested on his knee and once he looked up to fling some words to the orderly standing by. Whatever they were, these words seemed to fire the orderly with a purpose, for, leaping toward the battery, he called: "*Bischen rechts. Vierzig metres tiefer!*"

For this information the impatient gunners seemed to be waiting. At once they broke into the same feverish motions at the guns, setting the hand on the shrapnel clock, so the burst would come "*Verzig metres tiefer*"—or forty meters further on—then the breeches snapped shut, and I saw them clap their hands to their ears—just as I had seen the boyish gunners of the 7.7s do in the West—while in salvos the guns roared and a multitude of specks filled the air, and there came back to us the loose rattling sounds of four shells, getting under way on their trip to the enemy's lines. In the unreal stillness that followed, I heard the telephone buzz and drone. "*Schön!*" called the officer to his battery. "*Viele Russlanders tot!*"

"Do they get back the results so quickly?" I asked Tzschirner. "How is it possible?"

"You would wish to see?" he asked. "I shall try."

He said something to the officer, who immediately telephoned something to whoever was at the end of the line. After a brief conference Tzschirner saluted the officer and came to us with a smile.

"We shall go now. We can see the battle—if you should like."

What a wonderful little officer he was!—a Miracle Man, who now was granting the one great desire. "What luck!" I was saying, "a battle!"

With his pistol drawn—for, "were we to meet Russians, they would not know who you were and I should have to protect you,"—Rittmeister Tzschirner followed the telephone wires, along the edge of the woods until skirting a frozen reed grown pond, he moved cautiously into the forest, pausing every few strides to listen, while the feeling came upon me that I was utterly hollow and my throat was dry as a board. Once we saw tracks in the snow, a wet red stain and a sleeve of a Russian army coat, which seemed to have been slashed off; once we heard a shrapnel pang behind us on the tops of the trees; and then there came no sound to break the crunch of our boots in the snow. As we proceeded I began to experience a curious sense of security in contrast to the passage through the forest that croaked with rifles. By the time we came out on a ledge that overhung a yellowish frozen swamp, I forgot myself in the interest of the drama before me. As we gazed across the kilometers of the Netta swamp toward where the Bobr lay among the weeds, a monstrous smoking serpent, the shrapnel puffed like the clouds of June, drifting with serene white beauty, while those who had stood near, lay stricken below....

I heard Tzschirner call to some one. From the great pine at our back there came an answer in German.

"You may go into the observing post," said Tzschirner. "Do you wish?"

And I climbed up a ladder that had been nailed on the pine and squeezed my way up through the floor of a little house, hidden amid the boughs of the tree; and there I found the captain of the battery, crouching, for the pine thatched house was tiny, and staring with his glasses through a hole in the wall.

"Come in," he said pleasantly, without looking around. "You will not find it comfortable, I fear. Will you excuse me, please, a moment? It is important. I must see."

While he made his observation, I noticed that a field telephone was strapped to his head and that a writing tablet covered with figures dangled from his belt. I watched him lower the glasses and speak quickly into the phone. "Pardon me," he said when he had finished talking, "it was very necessary."

And then he went on to explain that his battery was doing great damage to the Russians now; that the shrapnel was breaking over their trenches.

"You would like to see?" he said, unstrapping his binoculars.

And now I was looking upon the battle. I saw on the edges of the great swamp two villages in flames. I located the German columns issuing from the south Augustowo woods and breaking into extended order, spread across the snow toward

Mogilnice, a multitude of creeping specks of brown; and toward the south, out of Grezedy, they seemed suddenly to spring up from the earth, as if a Cadmus had sown them, and roll in a cloud toward a point beyond the yellow weeds, where now all the shrapnel seemed bursting, as if by fantastic intent, making beautiful the sky with the fleecy clouds that brought death. And in the din of it all, I heard now the harsh pecking of machine guns, and that which had been a rolling gray-green mass of men became jagged and wavering; and then as suddenly the earth gave up another armed harvest, and the wavering mass of men was caught up in this and hurled forward. Suddenly for the first time that day the sun streaked through the greasy clouds, and the bayonets flashed it back. Was that roar a cheer? As the gray-green mass rolled on, and there came a mad clamor as if all the machine guns were pecking away at once. Then it was as if the mass, swept over like a mighty inundation, for you could hear their volleys no more—only the shrapnel, which seemed suddenly to have lengthened its range, panged ever more faintly away, wreathing a covert where fugitives might flee in a halo of pure smoke.

I felt my arms growing tired. The officer looked patient. I thanked him and climbed to the ground. Tzschirner, too, looked patient.

"I thought you would remain there for the night," he smiled.

"Was I long?" I asked, surprised.

"Half an hour," he said.

But it is not the battery of 10.5's, not the village in flames, not the death stalking amid the pines, not the storm of the Germans near Grezedy, that will be my memory of the battle of Augustowo Wald. Rather it will be of an old woman—an old woman who lives in a little hut on the big farm, to the right of the road as you enter Augustowo. As we started for the battle I saw this wizened little figure with her red shawl wrapped around her head peering from the shelter of the door, like a hen thrusting its head from a coop. Two hours later, while returning, I looked toward the hut again and saw the little woman who wore the red shawl. She stood as before, her head cautiously peering through the crack of the door, as if she feared that her body might present too big a mark for the battle fire. As I looked again when our motor snorted past, I realized that she stood there frozen in terror. At the noise of our coming she turned her face to the road and I saw that her mouth was open wide—as wide as my hand.

The Feast of Victory

As we drove into Suwalki, the muffled rolling of the guns followed us through the damp twilight. Stopping at the Europiski Hotel, a faded building of painted stones, we passed to the clicking of sentries' heels under a dripping archway, opening into a filthy, watery court. One saw bare-legged women, yoked with double pails, picking their way between the shiny automobiles of the staff, to a typhus menacing well beyond. On the right of the archway a flight of heavy stone steps ran up to a dingy drinking room; a tea room now, since the days of the vodka *ukase*. A greasy proletarian smirked a welcome from behind a counter, laden with platters of food, as sour as his smile. Excusing himself, Rittmeister Tzschirner opened the door to a larger room on the right, which we had seen open during the day, but always closed after six at night. Taking seats at one of the little round topped tables, I watched the German officers filing in, taking plates from a high stack, and helping themselves from the large platters on the counter, always paying the price without comment and in money, while the greasy proprietor rang a merry tune on his cash register, and contemptuous, no doubt, that the conquering Germans paid his outrageous prices without protest. I knew the man with the smirk was thinking that had the Russians been the conquerors they would not have bothered about the score. No, not the Russians. They would have had his daughters dance for them, and they would have eaten their fill in the name of the Czar. To give him full measure, they might have beaten him with the flats of their swords. Bah, these Germans, they were fools!

"Excellence von Eichorn," said Tzschirner, returning, "begs that you be his guest at dinner."

I could scarcely credit my good fortune. Dinner with the Commanding General of the 10th German army on the night of his triumph.

"We shall eat with Excellence and his staff—in celebration of the victory," added the Rittmeister.

This latter was a bit of gentle irony that for the moment I missed. I later learned that the room which always closed at six, was the dining hall of General von Eichorn and his staff. As we passed in with Tzschirner, the officers showed a polite curiosity and then bent over their food. "*Amerikaner!*" I heard some one say. Soon I was shaking hands with the hero of the battle of Augustowo Wald. A tall white haired man, who must have been over sixty, whose face betokened more of the scholar than the soldier. The clear twinkling eyes and the fine thoughtful forehead, were those of a serene doctor of laws who was living out his life among the flowers of some pretty university town; and yet his jaw was a buttress of steel and his mouth had a way of thinning in a straight grim line—a strange combination of the humanitarian and militant elements.

"I congratulate your Excellency" (what a feeble attempt it was!) "upon your wonderful victory." Telling me I was very kind, he then by some trick of his marvelous personality almost succeeded in making us feel that we, not he, were the heroes of the evening. While we were meeting different members of his staff, we learned what the Russian rout was. The entire Tenth Army under General Russky had been smashed. One hundred thousand men had been made prisoners; eighty thousand wounded, forty thousand dead, ten thousand fugitives. About three hundred and fifty cannons had been captured, with munition and with machine guns, so vast in numbers that there had not yet been time to count them. An entire army annihilated! The white haired man, who, sitting at the table at the end of the room, from which radiated other tables like those at a banquet, and he who was now raising a cup of tea, and smiling about him with gentle eyes, he had directed it all—the smashing of almost a quarter million men—making ninety thousand of them captive and killing or wounding or starving the rest.

And this was the feast in celebration of victory. In English and American newspapers I had read of the drunken revels with which the Barbarians made the nights of their triumphs more terrible. I had read that the first great drive into France fell short of Paris, because entire staffs had gone drunk; and then I recalled Rittmeister Tzschirner in extending Von Eichorn's invitation had added with genial irony—"*in celebration of the victory.*"

And this was the feast, stewed hare and fried meat cakes, mashed potatoes and rice, all covered with a brown gravy and served all in the same big platters, a slice of black bread, tea, the sweetened whipped white of an egg, and one glass of a cheap Bordeaux for each man—that was the menu with which the battle of Augustowo Wald was celebrated.

I was busy at the hare when the Rittmeister said to us:

"Excellence von Eichorn would drink wine with you."

Tzschirner told us afterwards that it was a great honor.

"I know I made a mess of it," I lamented to him. "What should I have done?"

"Oh, no," said the Rittmeister. "You are American and we do not expect you to understand our military customs," which made me feel a little easier.

On my left, Captain Kluth, who early in the morning would leave for Augustowo to bring back four captured Russian generals, spoke English, like an American. Kluth, a merry eyed, dark skinned Rheinlander, smiled when he said he was sorry that they had no grape juice—and then he did not smile when he said:

"In America, you want peace. You could bring about peace if you would stop selling ammunition. To-day we captured so much ammunition that Russia would be in a bad way for more, were it not for America."

"Did you capture any American ammunition?" I asked him.

"Quantities," he replied, "and the trouble with it is that your ammunition is good. It kills more men."

And then came the champagne, not in honor of Von Eichorn or the victory, but in honor of the American guest.

"I have," smiled Captain Kluth, "two pints of champagne in my room. We shall drink together."

Knowing that in the Russia of to-day, that next to cleanliness wine is the rarest commodity, I begged Captain Kluth to keep his treasure hidden; but he would have none of it, and when he returned with the bottles he told me their story.

"When we occupied Suwalki," he said, "I asked an old Jew if he knew where there was any champagne. He said, no. I gave him two marks and he said, yes. From somewhere he produced these two pint bottles and wanted twenty marks for them. I gave him ten. It's enough for two pints of bad champagne, isn't it?"

In response to a query of mine, a captain of the telegraph corps gave me his story of the battle.

"This morning," he began, "one of our corps telegraphed here that they were without food. They got an answer that the Russians were in the woods with plenty of food. Two hours later they telegraphed again. 'We are enjoying our dinner,' was the message."

"Yes," added Captain Kluth, "and that corps was made up of volunteers. The Emperor sent word to them that they had battled as well as first line troops."

Then we talked of many things concerning the war, while one by one the officers of the staff, leaving the table, bowed and went to the rooms. During this unique feast there was frequent laughter at witty sallies, but no boisterousness; and we began to marvel at the cool, confident, almost commonplace way with which the staff was taking the victory. It lacked a few minutes of ten when General von Eichorn said good night to us and went to his room; and after he had gone we heard something about him, that his home was in Frankfort, that his record in maneuvers was one of unbroken success, that the outbreak of war had found him ill, and that this was his first campaign. And then at a hint from Rittmeister Tzschirner, I begged to be excused.

"These officers," he whispered, "have had much to tire them to-day and must be up very early."

I nodded. As we rose the officers did also, and the soldier cook came in to smile a good-by, and the soldier waiters passed platters in which each officer dropped a few coins.

"How much?" I asked Tzschirner.

"One mark eighty pfennigs. But you are not to pay."

And so was celebrated the battle of Augustowo Wald, one of the greatest victories of modern history, with a dinner that cost one mark eighty pfennigs a cover, or about forty cents.

The Strategy of the Battle

The battle of Augustowo Wald, which resulted in the annihilation of an entire Russian army on February 21, actually began on February 7, when Field Marshal Hindenburg secretly transported troops from Poland to East Prussia and new troops, young soldiers who were to get their baptism of fire were brought up from inner garrisons. The total reinforcements were five corps. Concentrating around Gumbinnen, the Tenth German army, under the command of Excellence von Eichorn, awaited the command to advance simultaneously with General von Buelow's army, which was making its preparations behind Lyck. Like a country fence, the Russian line zigzagged across East Prussia, south of the Memel, east of Ragnit, to Gumbinnen, wedging forward along the line of the Angerapp and back through the Masuren lakes to Lyck. Since mid-November the Russians had held this line, a third of the rich East Prussian farmland behind their crooked fence. And the fence must be smashed.

It was on the ninth of February that General von Lowenstein's troops of General von Eichorn's army began the battle by making forced marches in the snow from Gumbinnen toward Pillkallen and Stallupönen. All that night snow fell and

THE BATTLE OF AUGUSTOWO WALD

confident the Germans would not attack because they could not bring up their artillery, the Russians fell back on Eydtkuhnen (East Prussia) and Kibarty and Wirballen, just across the frontier. Here they ate from their field kitchens—something they had been unable to do in twenty-four hours, turned in for a good sleep and left the road without outposts. Why bother with outposts? The snow was sufficient; the Germans could never bring up their cannon on those roads. Apparently since the days of Napoleon, Russia had believed too foolishly that winter is always on its side.

Not being able to advance with their cannon, the Germans came up without it. Unsupported by a single gun, forcing their way through the downpour of snow, the German infantry, young soldiers in their first battle, swept down on Eydtkuhnen. On the road stood two batteries, totaling twelve howitzers and a large number of ammunition wagons. Up to within fifty meters of the Russian batteries the Germans were able to advance before being discovered. In a panic the Russians tried with carbine fire to cover the retreat of their guns, but storming the position the Germans shot down the horses in the traces and piling the dead and the living, blocked the road of escape. Supported now by the captured cannon, the Germans rushed on and there followed a night battle in the streets of Eydtkuhnen, back across the frontier to Russian Kibarty, where ten thousand prisoners were made. By midnight another division of Von Eichorn's army, which broke through at Pillkallen, had driven the Russians down into Wirballen, where the Russians, again surprised by similar forced marches through the snowstorm, fought desperately in the streets and surrendered.

Three hospital trains, one the Czarina's, another Prince Lievin's, were captured in Kibarty, and in them General von Lowenstein's staff found unexpectedly comfortable quarters for the night, and stores of delicacies like preserves and chocolate. Captured cars filled with boots and fur lined vests made the soldiers more comfortable, and when they found one hundred and ten Russian field kitchens filled with warm food, the joy of the young German regiments was complete. For two days they had been living on knapsack rations.

Now while this movement was turning the Russian flank backward on Wilkowiszky, and at the same time General Lieutenant Boulgakew's 20th Army Corps—its communications with the 10th corps cut—was retreating pell mell from Goldap to Suwalki, two other German movements were developing. From north of Ragnit as far as the Baltic and east of the line of the Memel, the Russians were being driven back across the frontier. This important operation protected Von Eichorn's flank and allowed him to sweep down from the north, enfielding the Russians on Suwalki. And with this General von Buelow's 8th army had rolled up the Russians at Lyck, driving them back on a terrific frontal attack to the strongly entrenched line of the Bobr. So they battled from February 10th to the 21st, the crumbling Russian right, composed of the entire Army of East Prussia, under Russky's command, was hurled down from the north against the victorious troops of Von Buelow on the south. The flying Russians pouring out of East Prussia, plunged headlong across the snowy open plains, into Suwalki, where they attempted to make a stand at Suwalki. Fighting as they ran down the road to Augustowo, they were met by Von Eichorn's army, which had marched from Augustowo 120 kilometers through snow in two days. Then Von Buelow, coming across from Lyck, made a junction with Von Eichorn, and pursued them into the forests and frozen swamps—an army of 240,000 men utterly annihilated, its few remaining corps still bravely fighting for seven days in the Augustowo Wald until on the day we saw them, the day the rout was completed, their scattered, hungry remnants laid down their arms—sixty thousand men.

The most important engagement of the war since Tannenberg,—the battle of Augustowo Wald will be written in history beside the charnel fields of other wars. A terrific blow for Russia, for while she can lose thousands of those sullen conscripts, she cannot stand the loss of 350 cannon and countless machine guns, rifles and stores. One hundred and twenty thousand Russians dead and wounded lay in the snows, while a hundred thousand of their comrades shuffled back to Germany under armed guard. Whether one looks at it with the cold eyes of the strategist or appalled at its horror, one can only think of Augustowo in terms of Waterloo, Gettysburg or Sedan.

CHAPTER XII
THE WAR ON THE RUSSIAN FRONTIER

In the East, the war is different. With Hindenburg's army against the Russians, I saw a kind of warfare utterly different from the solid lines of the West. To portray to the most minute detail what is daily transpiring there, I wrote down all the impressions gained in a single day and night. It was near Tauroggen, a stricken village across the Russian frontier that I saw this war of the East; it was at Tauroggen that Prince Joachim, the youngest of the Emperor's sons, led the Germans in the storm.

The diary follows:

11:50 A. M., Tilsit — We have slept late, for we came to Tilsit in the small hours, a weary ride across the snow swept plains from Suwalki. Back there in the pine woods of Augustowo, Von Eichorn's young troops are hammering away at the new army that the Grand Duke has rushed to brace the crumbling front. But we have seen the fighting there, and this morning Rittmeister Tzschirner has promised to show me the war in the north, where the Memel line is protecting Von Eichorn's northern flank.

"We shall journey to one of our outposts in Russia," proposes Tzschirner, and his eyes light hopefully. "There may be fighting there."

Our motor goes barking through the pretty streets of Tilsit, which, by two hours' fighting in the fall, the German soldiers saved from the Russian torch. We cross the winding Memel, where a century ago Napoleon and the Czar met on a canopied pontoon to sign the Peace of Tilsit, while the hills behind us at Engelsberg bristled with the cannon of France; we cross vast river-plains shimmering with snow and mount to the pine fringed hills beyond, where now are strewn the soldiers of another Czar, who thought to march the road to Berlin; and chugging along a wayside strewn with their smashed entanglements, we come to Piculponen. Across the silent stretches of snow there comes the clear scattering cracks of carbines.

"A Russian patrol!" remarks Tzschirner, and he unbuttons his holster, while our red haired mechanician removes the caps from the rifles. "One can never tell," continues Tzschirner, "down which road their patrols may ride."

This puzzles me. "But how can they get through the German lines?" I asked him.

"There is no line, as in the West. We have driven the Russians from East Prussia, but there are many roads down which their patrols can sneak from a frontier village and run back to the troops."

"Could they come down this road?" I asked.

"We hold it to Tauroggen, where we must go, but we have no trenches from Tauroggen to Woynuta, and between these points are cross roads by which they could raid this highway. But if those shots we heard were Cossacks, I do not think they will come here. They are not brave, the Cossacks."

We see that beyond, to the left, an old brick church hides among the pines.

"We shall go there," suggests the Rittmeister. "Do you wish?"

I am wondering why we should waste time on a church when Russian patrols are shooting up the countryside, when Tzschirner says:

"This church is where Queen Louise of Prussia took refuge from Napoleon in 1807."

With the dutiful air that one assumes upon examining an historical landmark, we scramble up the bank toward the church.

"Walk slowly," the Rittmeister said, as we picked our way through a snow covered graveyard, "or you may not see and kick a *grenat*. They explode very easily."

At once we cease thinking of the church of Piculponen as Queen Louise's retreat. We are walking amid a charnel patch of opened graves and tombs that are the gaping craters of shells.

"The Russians tried to hold a position here," remarks Tzschirner.

We turn the corner of the church and see the Russian trenches dug between the graves. We see the great windowed walls shattered with shrapnel and shell. We gaze down into an awful hole where a *grenat* has plunged into a grave. The fragments of the casket are blown into the black mud, and there are other fragments too, fragments a chalky white, for the grave is old; and fragments of brown Russian coats. Nearby stands a white marble cross. "*Ruhig sanft*," it says, "Rest in Peace." The plains of the Memel, as we leave the churchyard, brooding in the white peace of the snow and under the Engelsberg lies Tilsit, vaguely as in a mirage, its slender steepled churches, the spires of a dream.

1:08 P. M. We are climbing a long brown slope of road that has been dug from out of the drifting snow. A kilometer from Piculponen we turn out to pass a clanking column of gray transports, plodding on toward the front. Noticing a wagon loaded with barbed wire, I said to Tzschirner: "What will you do, make this position at Tauroggen permanent? The entanglements are going up."

"Ah, yes, for a time. It is best always to be prepared," and he smiles.

In this clear, cold air our exhaust is barking in loud exaggeration, but as we crest the hill near the huddled houses of Kamstpauriken, we hear a foreign sound. Somewhere across the snows rifles are firing.

"The Russian patrols are very active this morning," Tzschirner is saying.

"How far off is that shooting?" I ask.

"About a mile. On a road which is parallel to this."

"How many in a patrol?" I was thinking that we were five—Gelbricke, who must drive the car; Seyring, the red-haired mechanician, who could use a carbine; Tzschirner, with his Browning automatic; Corey, with a fountain pen, and I with a camera.

"They are very many, the Russians," Tzschirner was saying. "They never ride a patrol under twenty men. It is dangerous," continues Tzschirner with the air of one doing his duty by saying that, although I knew he was spoiling for a scrap.

"We may be surrounded; but I do not think. *Naturlich*, there is the chance. You wish?"

"Rittmeister, these Russians would have to use the road and we could see them coming in time."

"Oh, no," Tzschirner says quickly. "They often ride over the fields; it is very good for patrol, the country here."

"What grand little comforter," I murmur.

Tzschirner looks around and grins. "I will protect you."

I feel he has been quietly laughing at me, until from behind a distant snow capped ridge I see a black belch of smoke.

"They have burned a village," exclaims Tzschirner.

Together we run through the snow in the direction of the smoke, until a hillock gives us a vantage point of the surrounding country. We can see the flames now, streaking through the smoke and above the snowy hills, black clouds stain the cold blue sky.

"Remain here," calls Tzschirner, who is fumbling with his map. "It is little more than a kilometer from here to the village." And while he studies his map I watch the flames through my binoculars.

"That is the village of Robkojen," he presently announces. "See," and he points to it on the Staff map, where even the little summit upon which we stand is marked.

The glasses bring to me a huddle of cottages in flames. It reminds me of a moving picture I have seen—a Western picture with tiny horsemen on a distant ribbon of road. I can see the Russians; their uniforms are different from the brown coated droves I have seen. They are dark uniforms and the horsemen wear tall dark hats. Tzschirner has put his glasses on them. "Cossacks," he mutters. "Soon our men will be there."

Taking the hint, I swing the glasses down the road, that twists like a black swing through the snow to Robkojen. And even then I can discern a tiny movement. It grows to a rush of horses. "They are coming!"

The finish of a Derby has not this thrill. Can the Germans come up fast enough?

Through the smoke I can see a sudden panic. Between two flaming cottages a horse is pivoting; one seems to be rearing. The Germans are drawing nearer. "They are Uhlans!" And then as in a stampede there breaks from behind the smoking village a line of horses that go galloping in black silhouette across the snow. The Uhlans are taking up the pursuit.

Tzschirner's air is one of intense disgust.

"I say, you the Cossacks would not fight. They ended their fighting when they burned the village. They always sneak across the frontier, burn the homes of a few poor people, terrify old men, women and their children by killing a few, and then running like dogs."

"Do they always run, Rittmeister?"

"*Immer*, unless they are greater than our cavalry by six to one," with a sneer, he adds. "I think Russia needs them best for murdering the Jews."

Behind us the dried cottages are flaming like tinder and across the fields from Robkojen a woman, her arms filled with bundles, and leading a child, sinks almost to her knees in the snow. It seems as if she has fled a hell of fire to gain an empty world.

1:45 P. M. "Only a few days ago the Russians ran down this road, taking their dead with them."

We have caught up with the awful refuse of battle. Near Szillutten we see that which no longer horrifies—the slain dead; and then the bloody road of retreat, where German shells split the Russian ranks, and lumped the road with things in brown that only the wheels of the heavy guns can flatten down; a furrowing of frozen ruts, shining with the pounding of transports, the packed snow broken, here and there, to reveal stiff objects, bits of brown cloth matted with flesh.

Burned Laugszargen shows its black walls, and as we cross the frontier we see the red and black striped white posts lying shattered in a ditch beside. And it seems a symbol of these days when frontiers seem but things to be smashed. We are passing through Posheruni, the silent houses echoing back our motor in a hollow, dismal sound.

We enter a woods, the tall pines crowding close to the road; and it seems as though the road has been the path of a storm, as if lightning has struck one upon another of the trees here, for torn white they seem to have fallen into each other's branches, leaning like stricken things, while finding those whom they sought, the shells have daubed them red and flung up bits of torn cloth into their shattered boughs, there to hang, perhaps, as a signal that the black winged birds might see. And passing through the forest of death, we come upon a German battery, hidden behind mounds of clay that are covered with evergreen. The soldiers are fussing about the long, gray barrels. And we have not gone half a kilometer further, when we smile at the guile of this German army; for there in a field to the right of the road is a dummy battery. We count four black logs lying between four sets of farm cartwheels, and each with its little circular shield of earth—a shield deliberately built low, though, so that from afar the Russian observer would not fail to see what seemed to be a gun; and signaling his batteries waste thereafter the ammunition. The road slopes down toward the sunken stream of the Eserina. The burned bridge lifts its skeleton posts in a warning. We get out and see that the German engineers have bent the road to the right, leading it down over a bed of wire-lashed saplings, across a string of planks, and thence up over more dirt-covered saplings to the main road again.

"It is better," suggests Tzschirner, "that we leave the auto." And as the motor bounces over the lashed saplings and takes the bridge, a company hurrying to Tauroggen comes swinging on its heels; for we are getting into Russia now, and near the line of battle, and there can be no delay. We hurry after the car.

"Please, that bridge," and Tzschirner indicates the charred piles; "it saved the Russians. By burning it, they delayed our advance an hour."

"Your engineers changed the course of the road, bending it around that burning bridge, in one hour?"

"Oh, yes," and Tzschirner is almost apologetic; "our pioneers would have finished the work in much less than an hour, but the Russians fired on them with shrapnel," and then as if remarking the weather, he added, "Fifteen were killed."

The car chugs on. A great blue bulbed cupola shows above the trees and we rattle across the Jura.

"The Russians tried to destroy this bridge, too," Tzschirner is explaining, "but we came too fast for them and drove them up into Tauroggen, where they endeavored to stand." ... Our motor is panting up the hill past the Russian church and turns into the village of Tauroggen.

"We put the artillery on them," continues Tzschirner, and we pass rows of narrow, squalid houses, chipped with shrapnel, "and they took Tauroggen by storm. There was street fighting and then, picking up their dead, they ran with them through the village, across the field to the woods," and Tzschirner waves his hand down the road toward a patch of pines, "and they're in the woods now."

We turn into a muddy street where the fighting must have been hot, for the way is littered with cartridge belts and guns and on a pale blue picket fence Russian accouterments dangle like unclean things hung out in the sun.

"If you will excuse me," says the Rittmeister, "I shall speak with Ober-Lieutenant Hoffman."

We find Ober-Lieutenant Hoffman quartered in a clean looking hut, distinguished by a shingle, hand-lettered with that official looking KOMMANDO. After he has conversed with the Ober-Lieutenant, Tzschirner brings him into the motor and we drive through Tauroggen in the direction the Russians have fled. We have put the last outlying house behind us and at a suggestion from Ober-Lieutenant Hoffman the motor is stopped. "It is better," explains Tzschirner, "that the auto remain here. It gives too large a target."

With a strange feeling, almost of superiority, for not thirty feet ahead, what appears to be a first line trench is filled with soldiers, we walk towards them down the road. Over there, a quarter of a mile, across the barren field where the Russians dragged their dead, are the woods, and skulking there are the Russians—the soldiers maintain a nervous vigil. Not a sound breaks the strain, only the clatter of axes, as far to the right the soldiers are clearing a zone for the enfilading fire of the machine guns. And as we walk past the trench and approach the last outpost this tension is communicated to us. We walk through the barricade—a ladder tangled with wire, that slides between two broken carts on either side of the road. We scarcely notice the two sentries who walk twenty paces from the barricade toward the woods, wheel and return. We are watching the woods—that great green semicircle across the field where the Russians are hiding.

Apparently that thought never occurs to Tzschirner. Being a good soldier, he does not indulge his imagination when he is in uniform. He and Ober-Lieutenant Hoffman are walking along, chatting easily as they might on some fine February day along the Linden. As the sentries stride by I catch the words, "*Wagner ist mehr wichtig,*" and a little excited, the sentry with the beard cries: "*Quatch! Strauss ist wunderbar!*" Apparently to decide the merits of Wagner and Strauss is more absorbing than the Russians.

A little bewildered, I walk on. Down where the road divides the woods into a limitless vista of green, I think I see something move. It is about 600 meters away and I focus my glass. Four Russian soldiers sitting on a log, a little fire, and in the middle of the road something that, while indistinguishable, suggests a menace. And even as I watch I see a tree sway and I can *hear* it fall as it crashes across the road, falling like a barricade.

"Look! Look! The Russians!"

And the Rittmeister turns with an amused smile. How commonplace are the Russians, anyway! How incidental to those officers who have seen so many dead that even the living are not to be feared.

"In the middle of the road," I announced, "there is a machine gun. It is pointed this way."

Tzschirner and Ober-Lieutenant Hoffman are discussing some military problem. Tzschirner begins to trace in the road with his sword some formation that is beyond my pen.

"Those Russians," I am saying without putting down the glasses, "appear to be leaving their seats on the log. I think they are showing sudden interest in the gun."

Demonstrating his problem in the mud, Tzschirner turns to me.

"This is the road to Riga. Follow it and we reach that fortress. As we are now midway between the German and Russian lines, I do not think it wise that we go further. Of course, if you would care to storm the Russians in the woods, we shall go on. Do you wish?"

I do *not* wish. Nervy little Tzschirner, one of the gamest men to straddle a horse in this war, has taken us quite far enough. We begin our walk back to the German lines, turning our backs with difficulty upon those silent woods.

"If the Russians should fire," Tzschirner says seriously, "throw yourself at once on the road. The balls will pass over you."

A simple remedy, indeed!

"Strauss," the passing sentry is objecting, "is all chaos."

"Why not?" his bearded comrade defends. "Salome is the music of destruction."

Glancing back toward the woods, I see a flock of black birds fly leisurely across the field, and alighting, wait. Wait for what? Had the Ober-Lieutenant told them that darkness would bring the Russian attack?

"And now, if you like, we shall go to my quarters," says the Ober-Lieutenant, to whom Tzschirner has delivered me. "I am sorry you will not find them very comfortable."

It is as ever, the diffidence of these Prussian officers, putting you a little ill at ease. Self-consciously assuring the Ober-Lieutenant that to be comfortable is my last desire, we walk down a lane of the bluish walled cottages, turning in at the frame structure which is denoted headquarters. As we enter a rather barren room, three orderlies, who appear to be transcribing reports, briefly stiffen in their chairs and go on writing. The gray, iron-bound officers' chest by the window makes a good seat and the Ober-Lieutenant in telling me that having had conscience, many of the natives of Tauroggen fled with the coming of the Germans, leaving their loot behind.

"Loot!" I interrupted. "I do not understand."

"Pardon me, but I forgot," and the Ober-Lieutenant called an orderly. "Here in Tauroggen," he said after consulting the report, "we recovered household belonging to the German frontier villages of Laugszargen, Meddiglauken and Augswilken."

"No matter how fast his flight," I observe, "the Russian soldier still has time to transport his loot."

The Ober-Lieutenant smiles. "But in this time it was not the soldiers. We have learned that the civilians of Tauroggen followed the Russian soldiers across the frontier, stealing from houses, and then sneaking back with their booty to Tauroggen."

Clicking his heels in a salute a young lieutenant comes in. He and the Ober-Lieutenant begin speaking; such hurried German is too much for me. I note the monocle the young lieutenant is wearing. What affectation on the firing line! Clicking his heels to the Lieutenant, bowing to me, the young lieutenant hurries out. The Ober-Lieutenant is drumming his fingers on the table top.

"Ober-Lieutenant," I remark with a smile, "will that young lieutenant wear his monocle if there's a battle?"

The Ober-Lieutenant's gravity dispels a jest. "I imagine he will always wear that monocle," he says. "The Lieutenant had his eye shot out in Belgium." He reaches for a map. "Please pardon me," he smiles. Quite distinctly now I can hear the shots.

"I had hoped," says the Ober-Lieutenant, studying the greenish black dotted patch that means on his map, the woods, "that there would be no engagement here until to-morrow. I wanted to finish our entanglements to-day."

I wonder if our going past the outposts has brought forth the Russians' nervous fire. That seems also to have occurred to the Ober-Lieutenant.

"They might have thought that we were reconnoitering for a night attack," and then abruptly, "Let us go out."

As we pass between the houses a bullet goes snaggering off a roof. It would seem to be a last wild shot for as we turn up the road to the outpost, everything is still. In the little cemetery to the left of the barricade, I see soldiers, squatting behind the tombstones; the great wooden cross suggests an incongruous peace. Calling the sentries who but a time ago, we heard discussing Wagner and Strauss, the Ober-Lieutenant taxes them with questions. They salute and hurry behind the cart, which they have turned blocking the road. "Any wounded?" calls the Ober-Lieutenant down the trench.

"*Nur Russlanders!*" The soldiers laugh and slip fresh clips into their guns.

"*Alles ruhig,*" the Ober-Lieutenant is saying as we walk along the line, apparently scornful of the Russians that the pines will not let him see. "Only nervousness, that shooting."

"You do not believe there will be an attack?"

He shakes his head. "I think not."

But across the belt to the woods, I see the black winged birds, slowly flying and waddling over the ground.

7:30 P. M. During dinner the Ober-Lieutenant has avoided all shop talk. No such food as in the West, here—just a stew of white beans and beef and thick bread, carved off a big black loaf. The thoughtful looking Colonel produces a flask of cognac, and we are finishing with cigarettes, when an under officer reports.

"Both lights are in position," I heard the Colonel say and dismissing the under officer, he seems absorbed in the end of his cigarette. In this barren room, where the candles are scattering strange shadows on the unpainted walls you become conscious of an unspoken army. The Ober-Lieutenant who is talking Nietzsche with me; seems not to have his mind upon it; when appealed to, the Colonel joins in with monosyllables. The orderlies who this afternoon were making reports, are gone but in the corner by the window, a soldier sits with a field telephone in his lap; slowly he writes upon a pad.

"In America," the Ober-Lieutenant is saying, "you have taken too seriously our academic thinkers. Will you believe it, that until we heard about the book from England, not a thousand of my countrymen had read Bernhardi. Suppose we were to judge America by some of the things published there?"

I can see his point. A mad buzz from the telephone jerks us up with a start. With the air, of something expected, fulfilled, the Colonel rubs the fire off his cigarettes.

"What is it?" he calls.

The soldier's manner is decisive. "Patrols report men massing from the woods in the road."

Gulping down the cognac, the Colonel gives a detailed order; the soldier telephones it to some one at the outpost. The Ober-Lieutenant looks inquiring. "You would like to see?" he asks. As we hurry out of the room, a soldier with a rifle, runs down the street. It is dark. The low roofed houses are smothered in a thickening loom of woods and sky. In a window a candle burns but to the end of the street it is dark. The door of the last house is open and I hear a mumbling monotone of prayer. The flash of a pocket torch shows an ancient Hebrew kneeling in the open door. From his shoulders hang a brown vestment of prayer and caught full, his patriarchal, wrinkled face seems almost divine in the halo of the torch. On the heavy air a rifle cracks.

We are running forward. From the woods come a scattered sound, as of monstrous frogs croaking in the night; a bullet sucks in a whistle as it passes by. To the left of the road, behind the little cemetery, is a hut where we will be reasonably safe. Leaving the road and running along the edge of the trees, so as to keep the hut between us and the direct fire we press on. I never knew the sound of bullets could so aid one's speed....

The firing has become general now and as we peer around the edges of the hut ahead and to our right, I can hear the soldiers moving in the trench. It is too dark to see much. Nearby I can discern crouched shadows running through the night and above the place of graves, the great brown cross makes its stiff gesture of peace.

Where are the Russians? Way down among the trees, I see the occasional flashes of their fire. But this is only an exchange of shots. The Germans are not bothering to reply, only with spasmodic shots, I think of the black winged birds; has the noise frightened them away?

Still there is a tension that seems to be tightening. Down in the trench I see the flash of an officer's lamp; it is like a firefly. Other fireflies, glimmer toward the right of the line, flashing and going out. Somewhere in the darkness a young voice laughs nervously.

Where are the Russians? They may be crossing the open field for from the woods the shots no longer come. Everything is silent, everything but the orders that are being given in hushed but distinct tones—almost you think, as though the damp wind might pick up some secret and bear it to the Russian hordes. Where are they? This silence seems interminable.

And then one hears the faint scuffling of their feet; and out of the silence of the night comes a roar as of animals let loose, and across the fields we can see a vague moving mass. They are firing now but they are making as much noise with their voices as with their guns. To hoarse throaty yells they storm up the road. It occurs to me that they are like the Chinese whose idea of war is making a noise. Their bullets are raining through the pines and falling like hail on the houses beyond.

"Why don't your men open fire?"

"It is too soon," whispers the Ober-Lieutenant. Why did he have to whisper?

And then I see the Russians. I see them in the great blinding flash of dusty light. I see them revealed as pausing, blinking things, to whom the searchlights point with fingers of pitiless white. I see them—while all about me becomes the clamor of guns—stumble and fall; they stagger and crawl as if the long dusty flashes were lightning, striking them down; and wherever the white fingers point, there death comes; and their hoarse throaty shouts, become the wails of death; and that open belt between the pines becomes lumpy with men, while the night grows horrid with the rattle of rifles and the quick croaking beat of the guns.

They are being slaughtered out there; they are as bewildered as animals, blinking, then dying, in the glare of the lights that they knew not could come. And now the lights are throwing their dusty glimmer on the distant trees.

"They are retreating!" The Ober-Lieutenant still talks in a whisper.

And, as sweeping this way and that, making their monstrous gestures over the moaning field, the searchlights hold up as targets the scattering Russian retreat; as one after another shadowy form I see cross a beam of light only to fall, and the crash of the rifles seems to have become an unceasing din and in the sweeping flashes of white I see the piles upon the field.

The Ober-Lieutenant gives his opinion of it. "Very fine," he says. "There are many dead." And then, as if after all, this were the important thing, he adds: "To-morrow, I think we can build our entanglements."

7:00 A. M. I have slept little. All night I thought I heard groans from afar. Toward dawn I imagine I hear a screech, but of course it cannot be that.... When we take coffee in the candlelight, the Colonel seems to have lost the distraction he showed at dinner. He laughs and jokes.... It is rapidly growing light when I climb up on the transport that is to take me to Tilsit.... Down over the pines, the black winged birds are flying—a screech? One wonders.

CHAPTER XIII
THE HERO OF ALL GERMANY

Field Marshal von Hindenburg

To the accompaniment of heels clicking in salute we passed the Saxonian sentries and hurrying through the darkened gateway were met by an orderly. Field Marshal von Hindenburg was expecting us. Down the corridors of the castle into a great hall into which opened many doors ever opening and closing to the passage of hurrying soldier clerks; here a telegraph was chattering, there a telephone buzzing, messengers coming and going, staff officers gliding from one room to another, the warm stuffy air vitalized with magic import—this was my first impression of the headquarters of the commander in chief of the German armies of the East.

I was looking at a placard written with a pen and fastened to one of the unpretentious doors, opening into little ante rooms from the great hall, which read—"Commander in Chief." On the other side of that door was the sixty-eight-year-old warrior who has become the national hero of Germany. To name the town where this took place would be a breach of military etiquette. I am, however, permitted to say that the Field Marshal has had his headquarters at Posen, Allenstein, Insterburg, and another place south of Insterburg about one hundred and fifty kilometers which the officers of General von Eichorn's Tenth Army spoke of as "a place unnamed." The reason for this secrecy was reflected in "the town." Plunged in total darkness, save for a few lanterns, it was impossible to locate from the sky. Russian aviators could not steal over it by night and drop bombs to kill the man who is so utterly a master of the armies that the Czar sends against Germany.

There came Captain Cammerer, first adjutant of Hindenburg, a Prussian officer of artillery, who said that the Field Marshal would soon receive us. One gleaned that although the Captain appreciated the distinction, he longed for the battlefield; one heard him talk eagerly of Tannenberg where he had made some Russian prisoners. "But now my fingers are covered with corns," and Cammerer smiled in a melancholy way. "I have to write much." And then the door that bore the sign, "Commander in Chief," opened, and the officer bowed us in. Field Marshal von Hindenburg had risen to meet us.

My first impression was that Von Hindenburg's pictures have done him an injustice. There is no denying that his photographs create the impression of a tremendously strong face ruthless almost to the point of cruelty. But the camera fails utterly to catch the real Hindenburg. His is a face tremendously strong, with a chin that is like a buttress and a forehead of the width that means power and there is a firmness to his little blue eyes; all these things the camera shows. It does not show the twinkle in these eyes; nor does it show the kindness that lurks in the wrinkles of his warty weather-beaten skin. It fails utterly to depict the pleasant smile that his small sharply cut mouth can show. Sixty-eight years you are thinking in amazement. This man does not look more than fifty. All his faculties seem at their zenith. His nose is the nose of the eagle and it impresses you with wonderful alertness. There is much color in his mustache, a tawny shade, a large curving but rather peaceful looking mustache that has not the aggressive angle of the Emperor's. So massive are his shoulders that I thought at first that his close cropped gray head was perhaps a little small. But it is a typically round German head of the strong mold that you see in the pictures of Durer and Holbein.

Von Hindenburg impressed me as being a big man, physically and mentally big, the embodiment of what the conqueror of the Russian armies should be, though I had heard of his suffering with the gout and every known ill; that he was a decrepid invalid who was called from a sick bed to save East Prussia. But simply dressed in field gray, wearing only the order Pour le Merite bestowed upon him by the Emperor for his marvelous skill in the Russian drive, Paul von Beneokendorff und Von Hindenburg has the directness and simplicity of men of real greatness. He is wholly without ostentation, and easier to engage in conversation than many a younger officer who only sports the second class of the Iron Cross.

He eats simply and he works hard. Dinner at Von Hindenburg's headquarters consists of soup and one course around an undecorated table with ten officers. He likes a good wine; when he is drinking a toast he takes his glass of champagne at one gulp to the despair of some of his younger officers. The dinner hour showed him to be very lively. He likes stories where the wit is keen; also he is not a Puritan. He avoids talking military matters and seems at dinner to have thrown off all responsibilities. This light inconsequential converse sounds almost incongruous when you can hear the ta ta of the horns of military automobiles outside. Indeed it is with difficulty that Von Hindenburg can be induced to say anything about the war. His very able assistants, the silent Ludendorff, Chief of Generality, and the lively gesturing brilliant Hoffman, also avoid talking shop. After he has agreed with you that the French are fighting bravely, better than one expected them to, and that everybody in Germany is sorry for them; after he has urged with exaggerated seriousness that the Austrian officers are efficient; after he has uttered his contempt of Belgium and echoed the curse of the German nation for England, he will discuss the Russians.

"The Russians are good soldiers," he says. "They are well disciplined. But there is a difference between their discipline and ours. The discipline of the German army is the result of education and moral. In the Russian army it is the dumb obedience of an animal. The Russian soldier stands because he is told to; but he stands like one transfixed. Napoleon was right when he said 'it does not do to kill a Russian; he must also be thrown down.' The Russians have learned a good deal since the Japanese war. They are very strong in fortifying their positions on the battlefield and understand excellently how to dig trenches and holes. As soon as they have chosen their position they disappear under the ground like moles. Our soldiers had to learn how to do that too. Our soldiers did not like it. They like to fight in the open, to storm and have it over with. But I had to make them wait in position until I was ready. We are not afraid of the Russian superiority of numbers. Russia is vast, but not as dangerous as it looks. The modern war is not decided by numbers. In East Prussia we have broken two Russian invasions. Each time they are outnumbered as three to one. An army is not a horde of uniformed men. An army must have good guns, ammunition, and brains."

The lively Hoffman, a wonderful strategist, adds, "We have absolute confidence in our superiority to the Russians. We have to win and therefore we will win. It is very simple."

And the silent Lieutenant General Ludendorff, a hero of Liége, says shortly, "We will manage it."

When the dinner is over and it is drawing near to eleven o'clock, you get ready to go, for you have heard that around midnight Von Hindenburg generally has "something to do." It is said that he works hardest at that hour. And as you leave the quiet house, it dawns upon you that the little threads of wires leading out from the windows connect with different army corps headquarters and that somewhere to the east under the Russian night gigantic armies are advancing and that the officers with whom you have been talking so peacefully, are the leaders of these armies and that the thing they are making is called The History of the World.

I have seen the likeness of Hindenburg a thousand times. In Houthem, which is a little shell torn village where the Bavarians come to from the firing line in front of Ypres and get a few days' rest, I saw Von Hindenburg's photograph pasted on the window of the canteen. I have seen it in every big city in Germany; I dare say, it is in most houses. I was in the Winter Garden one night when a Berlin crowd went mad over an impersonation of the Field Marshal by one of the actors. The crowd thumped its beer steins on the backs of chairs and got up and cheered.

An American "movie man" finally induced Von Hindenburg to stand before a camera. He did it in a way that made you think of the old J. P. Morgan who wanted to smash every camera he saw. For only a few seconds did Hindenburg walk in front of the movie machine but when that picture was shown in a Berlin theater the audience broke into wild applause. Von Hindenburg is the big man in Germany to-day. As a popular idol he rivals the Kaiser. The Germans have a new war poem that you hear recited in the music halls. It tells of different German generals, heroes of the war, and it ends "but there is only one Hindenburg."

Idol of the people, colossus of the battlefield, Von Hindenburg goes quietly about his work, unconcerned with any of the popular clamor. It is said that one of his staff officers was in great indignation because a high order of war had been conferred upon a general who had not done any actual fighting or big battle-direction in the West. The loyal officer mentioned this to Hindenburg and the old warrior said, "I don't care how many orders they give out, so long as they let me alone out here."

His task is to keep Russia from invading Germany. It is obviously a huge undertaking. It is a bigger job than is held by the head of the great corporation in the world. As with all popular figures, writers have romanced about Hindenburg. When the correspondents in Berlin couldn't get out to the front in the early part of this war, they made copy out of the first idea in sight. So they made a Cincinnatus out of Hindenburg. It pleased them to imagine him ill at his home, with the gout, when there came a special telegram from the Emperor ordering him to take charge of the army of East Prussia. They pictured him getting up from a sick bed, limping on a cane to an automobile and saving Germany. When you mention this to Hindenburg, he gets so red in the face that you think the blood vessels are going to burst and when he can speak, he roars, "Do I look like a sick man?"

Graduated from a military academy at sixteen, appointed to the infantry as a lieutenant before 1866, he fought in the war against Austria. He first came to the attention of the eyes of the German army at the Battle of Königgrätz when with fifty of his men he charged an Austrian battery. A grape shot grazed his skull and he fell stunned. Lifting himself up, he saw that his men had gone on and had captured two of the Austrian guns. The other three field pieces were being dragged away by the Austrians. Staggering to his feet, young Von Hindenburg, his face streaming with blood, rallied his men and with a wave of his sword charged after the fleeing Austrians. On their heels for more than a mile, he finally attacked them, although outnumbered three to one, and captured them. For this he was decorated with the Red Eagle Order.

There came the Franco Prussian war. Von Hindenburg was now an Ober-Lieutenant. He came through the battles of Gravelotte and Sedan; he was in the siege of Paris and when LeBourget was stormed, the young officer led a charge—and they gave him the Iron Cross. From that time on his rise was rapid. A captain on the General Staff, then Major, so up through the grades of the Chief of Staff of the Eighth Army Corps to the Commander of the Fourth Army Corps to a General of Infantry, which high office he held until 1911.

During the period of his retirement which came in 1911, he began to study the farm lands of East Prussia socketed with the lakes and swamps. This was to be the battleground of an inevitable war with Russia. He began to study the region until he knew every square mile by heart from Königsberg on the Baltic down through the network of lakes south of Tannenberg. On paper he fought there a thousand different campaigns. It is said that he became almost fanatical on the subject. In his classes at the War Academy where he was an instructor he became known as The Old Man of the Swamps. He used to go round Berlin with a folder of maps, and any officer whom he could buttonhole, he drew him aside and talked of the Masurian lakes. He became so obsessed with this subject that officers fled at his approach. They began to call him Swampy Hindenburg. But as he rose in rank and as he commanded troops during the maneuvers in East Prussia, the General Staff realized that Hindenburg knew the country.

There came a day when Von Hindenburg was appointed umpire of a big maneuver in East Prussia. The Army of the Red—so the story runs—was commanded by the German Emperor, opposing him was the Army of the Blue. The sham battle ended rather undecisively. The Emperor and all the lesser generals met in

THE HERO OF ALL GERMANY

the center of the field at the Grosse Kritic to hear the criticisms of umpire Von Hindenburg. Hindenburg was unmerciful. He tore the reputation of the General of the Blues to tatters. He demonstrated that this officer had made the grossest blunders. For half an hour in unsparing language Hindenburg, who had his own ideas about how every battle in East Prussia should be fought, criticized the General. It occurred to the Emperor that Von Hindenburg was concentrating his criticism upon the Army of the Blue and that he had said nothing whatever about the Army of the Red, which the Kaiser himself commanded. The Kaiser asked Von Hindenburg about this, remarking that it was noticeable that nothing had been said about his army and adding that for the benefit of all the officers the Army of the Red should also be criticized. Von Hindenburg continued to say nothing about it. Again the Emperor asked him.

"Your Majesty," Von Hindenburg said bluntly, "I deliberately refrained from criticizing your army. That is why I took the leader of the Blues so severely to task. For if I had been he, with his opportunities, I would have driven Your Majesty's troops into the Baltic Sea."

The Emperor concealed his displeasure. Presently Von Hindenburg was retired. Though retired, Von Hindenburg managed to obtain a detachment of grumbling troops from Königsberg and led them down into the Masurian swamp region to work out his problems. He would insist upon the cannon being pulled through the muddiest parts of the lake district and when they became mired fast it always seemed to please him. After several days he would bring the exhausted soldiers and horses and muddy guns back to Königsberg where the officers would tell each other that the "old man" was quite mad.

In those few years Von Hindenburg got the reputation for being a bore. All he would talk about was the swamps. They even say in Berlin that he would pour the blackest of beer on a table top to indicate swamp water, and then would work out a military problem during his dinner. Absurd exaggerations obviously, but still there must have been some basis for it. One day one of those members of the Reichstag who believe that all a country has to do is to make money, proposed that the Masurian lakes be filled in, and that the ground be given over to intensive farming. Von Hindenburg read the news that night in Posen and caught a train for Berlin. He was in a rage. Fill in his pet lakes and swamps! *Unglaublich!* Not to be thought of! They say he went to see the Emperor about it, that he brought with him all his maps and battlelines.

They say that he told the Emperor that if Masurenland was filled in it would be the greatest military crime in the history of the German nation. He did not go away until the Emperor promised that the swamps should remain.

Then came the war. The Russians were mobilized. They were on the frontier. The Old Man of the Swamps offered his services to the Emperor. He was a retired general, though. The Emperor had his regular generals to the army of East Prussia. There was General von Prittwitz, for instance. The Russians got into East Prussia. General von Prittwitz was soon deposed. Everybody in military Germany knows that through the blunders of certain high officers the small army that the Germans had in the field against Russia early in August was very nearly annihilated. I personally know of one atrocious blunder when a single unsupported cavalry division was sent from Insterburg to rescue a Landwehr division that was outnumbered eight to one by the Russians. The cavalry knew that there was so few that they could do nothing. Still the orders were to go and they had to go. Such was the campaign of East Prussia.

The Emperor went to Moltke, then his Chief of Staff. The Emperor said that the German troops in East Prussia were not being handled properly. He demanded another general. Moltke named one man after another and the Emperor shook his head. Moltke was at the end of his list. "Is there no one else you can recommend?" asked the Emperor.

"There is one man, Your Majesty, but, knowing your feelings in the matter, I have purposely refrained from mentioning his name."

"Who is he?" asked the Emperor quickly.

"Von Hindenburg," replied Moltke.

"It is not to be thought of," declared the Emperor.

But the Emperor went away to think it over. Like a vast tidal wave the Russians were breaking over his beloved East Prussia. The Emperor turned it over in his mind. There could be no delay. He sent a laconic message to Moltke. "Appoint Von Hindenburg."

So they took Cincinnatus away from the plow.

"I was not sick in bed," says Von Hindenburg in telling about the summons. "I was just sitting at the table having coffee when this important telegram came. Ludendorff my Chief of Generality had been summoned from Belgium and he came by special train."

And then began the ride to the East Prussian front traveling all the night in one of the high powered army automobiles discussing as he went the position of the troops. Von Hindenburg and Ludendorff arrived at the place that had been chosen as headquarters and he took command of the Army of the East. You know what happened, you know how the Russian invasion poured in across East Prussia, past the Masurian lakes in a semi-circle from Tilsit southwards.

You know that Hindenburg elected to give battle on a field that was four times as large as Sedan. Back of the German line Hindenburg and his staff were watching the big maps. Like a great pair of tongs his soldiers were closing in from north and south. When they had surrounded the Russians, Von Hindenburg would order the battle begun, not before. Field telephones buzzed, the telegraph clicked, the staff officers were ever changing the positions on the big maps, the black lines, signifying the German soldiers were ever drawing closer together. Soon the Russians would be surrounded. And then an aeroplane with black iron crosses painted under its wings dropped down out of the clouds and landed in front of Hindenburg's headquarters. And its observer dashed up to report, "The enemy is surrounded!"

"Begin the battle," ordered Hindenburg.

THE HERO OF ALL GERMANY

And over the field telephones went the commands and the awful slaughter of Tannenberg began—that battle of which historians will write as one of the great conflicts of the world. Back into the lakes and swamps that he knew so well, that he had fought so hard to save from the Reichstag, Von Hindenburg drove the Russians. Whole regiments slowly sank in the ooze and disappeared from sight. By regiments the soldiers of the Czar were driven into the soft bottomed lakes and shifting sands of Masurenland. And behind the line, Hindenburg, who knew every square mile of that country and knowing the topography almost to every tree, could tell the German troops exactly what to do. And from his headquarters the command would go by telephone to the General in the field.

I think it will not be until after this war is over that the world will know in detail what happened at Tannenberg. Von Hindenburg's strategy has jealously been hidden by the German General Staff. Not a single military attaché of a neutral country has been able to learn it. All one knows is that the Old Man of the Swamps drove the Russians into the swamps and that they perished by the thousands.

All I know of the battle of Tannenberg is this. I learned it while at dinner with an officer of Von Eichorn's staff.

"Oh, yes," he said quickly, "I was in the battle of Tannenberg. Some of our officers went insane. You see we drove the Russians back into the swamps and as they felt themselves sinking they threw away their guns and put up their hands, clutching at the air in their death throes. We were coming up to make them prisoners when some of them fired on us. So we turned the machine guns on them," he paused. "I guess it is better that we did. For they were in the swamps and slowly sinking to their death. All night you could hear their cries and the horses made worse screams than the men. It was terrible. Four of my brother officers went out of their minds simply from hearing the shrieks."

An intolerant old warrior who cares not what the newspapers say in his praise, who is bored with the thousands of letters and presents that are being sent him from all parts of Germany, who when this war is over has not the slightest desire to become Minister of War—Field Marshal von Hindenburg is a military genius with a kind German heart in spite of his grim exterior, fond of a glass of good wine and a good story, but accomplishing both work and play in the fascination of strategical study.

But what amazed me more than anything else about Von Hindenburg is the way he is regarded by official military circles in Germany. I knew that to the mass of people and soldiers he is a hero; they think him a military genius of almost divine inspiration. I mentioned this fact one night to a captain in the Great General Staff.

"Oh, yes," he said, "Von Hindenburg is a great general. He has had his opportunity. If he were killed to-morrow there is another general ready to step in and carry on the same work. And if that general were to be killed there is still another. I could mention five or six. You see Von Hindenburg, great man that he is, is simply a cog in a machine. A very great cog, to be sure, but then, don't you see, it is not a single individual that counts but the whole machine. If we lose a part of the machine it is replaced. It is very simple. I know General von Hindenburg and I know that all this talk about him, all this fuss, this idea of asking him, a super man, is very distasteful to him."

Von Hindenburg, only the part of a system! The real hero of Germany then must be the composite of a myriad of remarkably efficient units of which Von Hindenburg is a single element in the war machine of such consummate ability that he seems to stand alone.

CHAPTER XIV
WITH THE AMERICAN RED CROSS ON THE RUSSIAN FRONTIER

A gray morning crept up somewhere beyond the Russian plains and in the half light, the church tower and housetops of Gleiwitz loomed forbiddingly against the dreary sky. A butcher was opening his store as our droschky clattered down the cobbled streets of the old Silesian town. The horses' hoofs echoed loudly; only a few stragglers were on the streets. Coming to a square, massive building of yellowish brick—you instantly had the impression that Gleiwitz had grown up around it. We saw a blue coated soldier standing on the steps.

"Where is the American Hospital?" we asked him.

He stared at us in a puzzled way and, using that German expression which seems to fit any situation: "*Ein Augenblick*" (in a minute), he proceeded to give our driver elaborate instructions. Off we rattled, down another vista of gray cobbles and squat gray houses, and presently we stopped before a clean-looking house of stucco, before which paced a soldier in the long dark gray coat of the *Landsturm*.

"Where is the American Hospital?" we asked.

It was too much for the soldier; he called for help. Help came in the person of a stout, florid-faced officer with flowing gray mustache. To him we put the same question, and his face lighted.

"You want Doctor Sanders, *Gut, Gut!*"

And climbing into our droschky, his sword hanging over the side, close to the wheel, he told us all about the part Gleiwitz was playing in this war, while the cobbled streets rang to the beat of the horses' hoofs. We learned that we were way down in the southeastern corner of Germany, not far from that frontier point where three empires touch; we learned that every night if the wind was good they could hear in Gleiwitz the distant rumble of cannon.

And he was telling us those things when we saw coming down the sidewalk, a familiar color. It was the olive drab of the United States army, and under a brown, broad-brimmed campaign hat, we saw a round, serious face.

"That looks like our man," Poole said to me. A few nights ago Dr. Sanders had been described to Poole and me, and we had come here to see what he and his American outfit were doing down close to the Russian frontier. It was indeed our man, and when he saw us, the serious face broke into a broad grin.

"They telegraphed me you were coming—mighty glad to see you." And Charles Haddon Sanders, whom, if you went to Georgetown University, you knew as "Sandy," climbed into the droschky.

"Gosh, it's good to see an American. What news have you got?" And Dr. Sanders' merry eyes twinkled. "How about it—come on, loosen up! You must have left the States a month after I did." A look of concern clouded his chubby face, and I wondered what worrisome thing was on his mind. "Say," he said, "you're a baseball fan, aren't you?" When I told him I was, he seemed relieved. "Tell me," he begged then, "Walter Johnson didn't sign up with the Feds, did he? I have a hospital in Washington, you know, and whenever Griff's boys are home, I am out there at the park, pulling hard."

And this was the first thing one heard in a city of war! The puffy, mustached sanitation officer bid us good day; the droschky moved on. All the way down the old cobbled streets of dreary Gleiwitz, Dr. Sanders kept talking baseball; not once did the subject of the war come up. I wondered if he were avoiding it as long as possible; later when you learned what he had seen, you could not blame him. Presently our droschky drew up in front of a rather shady-looking café. It had all the appearance of being the Maxim's of Gleiwitz, a sordid place, reflecting all the sordid dreariness of the town. Wondering why the doctor was getting out here—he had not seemed that sort—he said that this was as far as we went. I looked again at the place. It was a gray-stoned building, on the corner of a café, then a hotel entrance, then a gateway. I followed him through this gateway and we came into a cobbled inner court facing a wing of the building that appeared to be a theater; at least the sign over the door read, "Victoria Theater." By now I had begun to guess it, and when a blue-coated German *Landwehr* opened the theater door, I was quite sure.

"Doctor, I suppose you have your office here," I remarked.

He laughed outright. "Office," he said, "this is my hospital."

And I thought of the place, the café, the hotel, the entire building of which this was a part. He must have known what was passing through my mind.

"I know," he remarked, "I felt the same way when I first saw it. It seemed funny, putting a hospital next to a rough house like that. But it was the only place they had left. By the time we got here, every school and public building in the town was filled with the wounded."

As we entered the lobby of the theater I saw that it had been transformed into a corridor for convalescents. The stench of iodoform assailed you. Four German soldiers, their arms or legs bandaged, were sitting at a rough board table drinking beer, which you perceived, as a waiter appeared with a tray full of steins, came by way of a connecting passageway from the café next door.

"Better that they drink the beer here than water," remarked the doctor. "We've had some typhoid and cholera cases in Gleiwitz." Now the utterance of that word cholera has a magical effect. In the war zone it can completely spoil your day; no doubt Dr. Sanders must have noticed my uneasiness, for he hastened to add:

AMERICAN RED CROSS ON THE RUSSIAN FRONTIER

"There's no danger; we've got all those patients isolated outside this building, and if you haven't had an injection of cholera toxin, I'll give you one."

Reassured, I ventured further into the building, and pushing back a swinging door, I saw opened up before me a strange picture. Imagine a theater, its walls washed white, its orchestra stripped of chairs and in their places row after row of hospital cots; a curtain of fireproofed steel, hid the stage, from it hanging the white flag with the red cross, and beside it the stars and stripes and the red, white and black; imagine the boxes filled with rough, hastily made wooden tables where nurses sat making out their reports, a theater where instead of an overture, you heard groans and sometimes a shriek from one of the white cots.

"The soldier is only having a nightmare," Dr. Sanders explained. "They come in here sometimes not having slept for three days and they go off asleep for hours and hours—you wonder how long you can put off dressing their wounds to let them sleep—getting these nightmares every once in a while, and yelling out that the Russians are after them. Nearly every soldier who has a nightmare yells that same thing, queer, because none of them fear the Russians at all."

Suggesting that we would come back to see the ward more thoroughly, Dr. Sanders led us through the lobby and into what appeared to be a cloakroom. Only now the coat racks were half concealed by huge packing cases marked "American Red Cross," and leaning against the wall you saw two brown stretchers of the United States army; and on the floor army sterilizer chests, while all around shelves had been built holding supplies and medical books. You noticed an operating table in the center of the room and in a corner a little stand for anesthetics.

"This is our operating room," smiled the doctor; "you never saw one like it before, did you? Neither did I. But for our purposes it fills the bill."

In the lobby we met two boyish surgeons, one, Spearmin, tall, angular and competent-looking; the other, Stem, a University of Maryland man who was preparing for a surgeonship in the United States army when he got the chance to go to the war zone, and, boy-like, went. Spearmin and Stem handle the wounded. Sanders does the executive work.

"We get plenty of work to do," Doctor Spearmin told me, "and you want to do everything for those fellows that you can. They are the pluckiest lot of men I ever saw. They stand pain better than most of the average hospital cases that I had in Baltimore."

Later we were to learn more of those men stretched their length on the white cots, and the way they stood pain, but Dr. Sanders had a dressing to make upstairs, in a cloakroom once used for the patrons of the balcony. Now it was Antechamber of Death. As we climbed the stairs, the doctor explained: "We keep our most serious cases up here. Whenever we feel we have to put a man in this room, he generally dies. We've only lost six men, though, and we've had five hundred cases, some of them shockingly wounded."

You caught the undernote of pride in the doctor's voice, a sensing of which you had felt at the hospital's very door. Pride seemed to be in the air; you read it in the faces of the nurses; the younger doctors, Stem and Spearmin, showed it, pride because they had turned the one notorious resort of Gleiwitz into an American hospital. And, it is significant—and it was a German officer who told me this—into a hospital of such efficiency that the German Sanitary Authorities always ordered that the worst cases be sent to Dr. Sanders and his assistants; this with thirteen other military hospitals in Gleiwitz.

But I was wondering if the other patients, the men in the orchestra, had come to know what the little room upstairs meant, and if they had heard the cry from that Austrian's bed, and if so, what their thoughts were, if they had all thanked the Almighty for their lesser plights. You felt they had.

"Come on, now," suggested the doctor, "we'll go and talk to some of the patients. Sister Anna can speak German."

Sister Anna you discovered to be a resourceful-looking woman of middle age, dressed in Red Cross gray. She was sitting at a table reading "Alice in Wonderland," and she said she had spent the last ten years in New York at the Lying-in-hospital. Her capable manner impressed you, and when Dr. Sanders whispered: "She was the best supervisor on the Red Cross boat that brought us all over, and I was mighty lucky to get her," you agreed with him. She was walking on ahead between the rows of blue gingham-covered cots and presently she stopped before one at the end of the line. It is a part of the German hospital system to have a metal sign-board on a post behind each hospital bed, and upon this we saw printed the soldier's name, a private, Kaiser, of the 148th Infantry. His wife was sitting beside his bed, a rosy-cheeked woman who recalled one of our middle Western farm girls. Quiet and calm, satisfied that her husband was in the best of hands, she smiled thankfully at Sister Anna and the doctor. Her husband was wounded in both the arm and leg and oddly enough by the same bullet, which, with a little smile, he picked up from a bed table to show us.

"It entered his arm above the elbow," explained the doctor, "went clean through, hit an electric torch in his pocket, glanced off that and went into his thigh. It was an interesting case. On the other side of his thigh, I found the wound of exit. Imagine my surprise when in a few days I discovered that the bullet was still in his leg, and that the exit wound had been made by a piece of bone breaking through."

It seemed that Private Kaiser could understand a little English, and he nodded eagerly. We asked him some questions, and it developed he had been a school teacher in Hamburg.

"I was wounded near Brounsberg in East Prussia," he told us. "It was towards evening, almost dark, and not thinking the Russians could see us, we got up to dig a trench. I was alone, way off at the end of the line when I was shot. It did not hurt me much when the bullet hit me. It took me off my feet, though I spun around twice before I fell. No one saw me and I lay on the ground for ten minutes. Then I was able to get up, and I walked away to the hospital. How I did it I can't tell you, but all at once my strength seemed to come back."

"Probably nervous shock made him helpless," explained the doctor in an undertone, "and when that passed he was able to help himself a bit."

We were going down the line of beds, talking to another patient, when the doctor said it was time for lunch, and that we might visit the patients again in the afternoon. Two of the nurses—there are fourteen American girls at Gleiwitz—walked back with us. I asked one of them, a young Boston girl, why she had come to the war.

"I don't know," she said. "I had made my application for a Red Cross nurse, and I was ready to go to Mexico. Then I got word that they wanted nurses in Europe, so I packed up and came along on twenty-four hours' notice.

"What I've seen of the war here, though," she said, "is not half so terrible as it was in the English Channel. We were on the coast of France one morning when I happened to see a big round thing in the water. I thought it was a mine, and I guess I screamed. Then I thought it was a dummy, but it wasn't that, it was a body, and there were six other bodies, all sailors from those English ships that the submarine blew up. Isn't there some way I could go back home without going through the English Channel? I can't bear thinking of seeing anything like that again."

I told her she could probably take a steamer at Naples or Copenhagen, and she seemed greatly relieved—she who had seen mangled men without a flicker of her nerves. Presently she left us to cross what was evidently the aristocratic street of the town.

"They are going over to a little club—the city club," explained the doctor; "that's where we take our meals. We'll go to my room first, though, if you like, before dinner."

Modestly the doctor spoke of his room, but to our surprise he stopped in front of one of the few imposing-looking houses in Gleiwitz. It was one of those venerable places which makes you think that the man who lives there must about own the other inhabitants body and soul. Occupying about four hundred feet, corner frontage, towering amid symmetrical lawns and flower beds, guarded by a ten-foot iron fence, the old-fashioned house stood back like a castle.

"Nothing like it," said the doctor with a smile. "It belongs to one of the richest men in Silesia. He's at the front, in France. He's a captain, by the way, just won the Iron Cross. His wife is in Berlin for the winter, so we're here, Spearmin, Stem and myself, with ten servants to wait on us, and the best of everything for the asking. Not bad, eh?"

While we were listening to a baseball story of the doctor's, we took in the luxurious appointments of his room. Then you thought of the makeshift hospital and how topsy-turvy war turns everything. From his valise, the doctor produced a Russian bayonet, hat and cartridge belt.

"They cost me two marks," he said, "for the whole outfit. I bought them from the driver of an Austrian ammunition wagon. Have a cartridge?" and he passed the belt as one might pass a box of candy. They were ugly-looking bullets, not as pointed as the Germans'. The bayonet also was uglier, curved like an old-fashioned saber.

"It's no good alongside the German bayonet, though," explained Dr. Sanders;

"that's longer and straighter. You ought to hear how some of the wounded over at the hospital talk about their bayonets. One fellow was telling me the other day that he had ripped it through the stomachs of three Russians." And even the doctor, hardened to such things, made a grimace.

After a luncheon, where, like the father of a large family, the doctor sat at the head of a long table with his nurses and assistants around him, everybody asking if the Christmas mail from the States had come, we returned to the hospital. We found great excitement. Two officers had been there, the orderly explaining that one was the sanitation commander of all hospitals at Gleiwitz, and that the other was Captain Hoffman of the garrison. What did they want? The orderly didn't know, but it must have been something very important, for they had told him to say to Dr. Sanders that they would return in half an hour, and for him please to be there, whereupon the orderly, to my amazement, looked at me a little suspiciously; indeed, his eyes followed me into the lobby.

"What's the matter with that chap?" I asked the doctor.

"Oh, he's spy crazy," replied Dr. Sanders; "you see, they caught two Russians here the other day, and the captain he speaks of presided at the trial. They put the spies up against the wall of that old barn over there. We could hear the shooting."

The doctor's tone was so casual that you concluded spy-killing to be commonplace at Gleiwitz.

"Come down here a second," continued the doctor. "I want you to take a look at a couple of patients."

As you walked between the cots you were conscious of the gaze of the wounded turned hopefully on this business-like American. Of the peasant class nearly all the soldiers seemed to regain hope at the sight of him. So it was with the two boys off in a corner by themselves. They were rather slender fellows, amazingly young, with mischievous faces. "They live next door to each other," said the doctor, "in a little village in Schleswig-Holstein. The one on the left had a bullet in his brain, the other had his arm fractured by a piece of shrapnel."

"How old are they?"

"The boy who had the bullet in his brain," said the doctor, "is not yet seventeen; the other is a few months older."

They met you with a bold smile, fun darting from their mischievous eyes, like American boys might smile at a foreigner. You saw that they wore the clean, light blue jackets that mark every patient of the American Red Cross, but you thought of the dirty, gray-green uniforms and how long these boys had lain before they were picked up. And then, like many youngsters you see in the first classes of a high school, they became self-conscious, giggling like girls at a first party, and you thought of them at war; and a shuddery sensation came over you.

"You think it's terrible, don't you?" he said. "Wait a minute."

He beckoned Sister Anna, and she joined us.

"Sister Anna," he said, "ask that boy with the brain wound to tell the story that he told me the other day."

Sister Anna's manner was reluctant, and you doubt that she wanted to hear that story again. But she put the request in German, and instantly the eyes of the little fellow grew bright.

"We were near Iwangorod," he began. "Max and I were on outpost duty and got cut off from our regiment. Night came and we started back to find them. We were passing through a little village, just five or six houses, when somebody shot at us." He paused, turning, as if for confirmation, to the other bed, where Max, half sitting up, nodded eagerly. "We'll fix them, Max," I said, "and we ran behind a house, so they couldn't shoot again. Then all lights in the windows went out—every light in the village. I was glad there was no moon. We got some wood, a lot of it. We fixed it in piles beside every house. We broke into a cellar and stole some oil. We emptied the oil on the wood, then we lit it, and ran to the next house, and lit it there." His eyes were burning feverishly. "Pretty soon we had the whole village on fire, didn't we, Max?"

"Ja! Ja!" cried Max, from the other bed.

And you realized that they were suddenly boys no longer, that their faces had reddened in a hectic way, and that into their young minds had come the frightful insanity of war. With a sickening feeling you turned from them, and going away, thought that only last July, back in that Holstein village, they doubtless had been playing the games that German boys play; then you heard Max cry out:

"And when we get better, Doctor, we're going back and each kill a hundred Russians!" And with his white hands you saw the boy lunge as though already he could hear the ripping steel.... What if you were his father?

"There are many like that—eager to get out of bed and back to the front," said the doctor. "Not so young, of course, but they all want another chance at the game; that is, all but the older men. You ought to have been here the other day. Count Talleyrand-Perigord was here. He's the nephew of the great diplomat, French descent of course. The Count has an estate near here. He's a young chap. He's been simply splendid to us. I guess he never did very much work before; you can imagine how a young man of his position spends his time. When the war broke out he volunteered for the Red Cross, and they made him a sort of a personal escort for me, to see that everything goes right over here. He spends his entire time with us. He watches all the operations, is intensely interested, asks all sorts of questions about them, and goes with me from bed to bed, asking the men what they want, doing everything he can for them. I tell you it quite surprised me, a young man of his position, in the French nobility, bucking right down to things. Count Szechenyi, you know, who married Gladys Vanderbilt; he's stationed over just across the Austrian border. He came up the other day to see Count Talleyrand and they dropped in here in the afternoon to visit the patients. I had expected something different from Count Szechenyi. You know what that Austrian count is. But he was just as democratic as if he had been a private in the ranks."

While talking, the doctor had been crossing the theater until he came to a side wall exit door that opened out on what appeared to be a promenade. It was glassed in, like a sun parlor and looked out on what had been a cheap beer-garden. Along one wall we saw a row of muddy brown and black boots. On the floor were piles of uniforms, German, Russian and Austrian, and knapsacks, drilled and nicked with bullets. Kicking over a filthy bundle of field gray, I saw that it was slashed.

"We had to cut most of the uniforms off the wounded," explained the doctor. "Most of them we have thrown out—we had to. If you could only have seen what those men looked like when they were brought in! We get them from the field hospital. This is the first hospital behind the lines, and when they are well enough to be moved, they are sent on to better quarters, further into Germany, but the way those fellows looked. Think of it, some of them had not had their uniforms off for three months. When we took off one man's boot, we found a blood clot two inches thick on the sole of his foot. It had run down from a wound on his leg. Why, some of those men were five days on the battlefield before they were found. One or two were out of their minds. You cannot conceive the horror of it! Later, I'm going to get one of those fellows to tell you his story."

The time had swiftly passed and as we came back into the theater, we saw two gray-cloaked German officers, and at their heels the orderly. They seemed very much excited, and I was sure now that they were going to ask the doctor if he was positive that I was not an English spy. It was something more exciting, though. They conversed in German, and I caught the words, "*Eisener Kreuz*."

"What a piece of luck!" the doctor exclaimed; "one of my patients has been awarded the Iron Cross, and Captain Hoffman of the Gleiwitz garrison has come to make the presentation."

We walked then to the bedside of a mild-looking man, who, you learned, was *Landwehr*, private Grabbe of the second Stralsund. A bulkiness to his leg under the covers showed where he had been wounded, and when he saw the gray-coated officers, a question leaped in his quiet eyes. You wondered if he knew and how many days he had lain there doubting and dreaming if ever they would come. The Captain strode towards him, held out his hand, and said, "I congratulate you." You followed the soldier's eyes as they watched the Captain's hands reach into his coat pocket and draw from it the band of black and white ribbon from which dangled the coveted cross. Without a word the Captain fastened it to the second button of the man's hospital jacket and stepping back, saluted him. You saw the soldier pick up the cross in both hands, stare at it a moment, while his eyes filled a little, and then his mild face turning wonderfully happy, he awkwardly expressed his thanks. As the last stammered word was spoken there burst from all the wounded a huzza. The nurses applauded and, overwrought, the soldier tried to sit upright in bed and bow his thanks. He had half succeeded when we saw him wince, and Dr. Sanders made him lie down. The congratulations over, we left him calling for pencil and paper, for at once he must write home about it. And you wondered how much you would have given could that one minute of this soldier's life be included in your own.

"Wait till I tell you what the fellow did," said the doctor, after the officers had bowed themselves away, "It is one of the duties of the *Landwehr*, you know, to guard the railroads. Late in October, when the Germans were retreating from their lines outside Warsaw, they had to hold the railroads to the last. This man's commander was ordered to hold back the Russians from a little railroad depot. Private Grabbe was given ten men and a machine gun and posted by a little house near the station. He had to keep back an overwhelming number of Russians until an entire battalion was on the train, and then with the little detail make a run for it, Well, as the Russians came in great force, his comrades retreated and left him there alone.

"As I told you, men get crazy in battle. Grabbe did not know that he was alone. He stuck by that machine gun, wounded and alone, mowing down the Russians until the whole German battalion—twelve hundred men—had withdrawn. Still he stuck to that machine gun, slaughtering them so, that by George! the Russians retreated. Grabbe's commander came up presently and asked him where the other men were. Grabbe said he didn't know and then the Commander saw that he was wounded."

Outside a violin began to play, and Dr. Sanders explained that often the local talent dropped in to entertain the wounded. The music continued and we went from bed to bed hearing the different stories; then the music stopped, and in a clear, though childishly quavering voice, a girl began a recitation in the lobby outside. Before he came to Gleiwitz, Dr. Sanders didn't know two German words. Now, as he told me, he knows three. Consequently, as the girl spoke on and the faces of all the wounded suddenly became grim, the doctor wondered why. Then here and there a man began repeating the girl's words, others, too weak to speak, following her words with moving lips. Higher and higher quavered her voice; and suddenly I recognized what she was saying. Before I could tell the doctor, though, she swept into a climax, to fierce "*Jawohls*" from the lips of the wounded.

"I don't know what you're saying," shouted Dr. Sanders, rushing into the lobby, "but stop it. It excites these patients."

He saw that I was grinning, and asked what the joke was. "It's on me, what was that girl speaking?"

"A new poem," I told him. "The name is: 'Murderous England.'"

"So that's it, eh?" And he went up to the girl, whose hair was braided down her back and whose cheap, bright pattern dress came barely below her knees.

"Now, little girl," he said, "when you want to come round to the hospital to entertain the prisoners, you learn how to speak 'Mary Had a Little Lamb' or something. Get Sister Anna to teach it to you!" And patting the child on the head, Dr. Sanders gave her a ten-pfennig piece, and asked her who had taught her the poem.

"*Meine Mutter*," replied the child.

We then sat in the lobby for two hours, buying beer for the convalescents and listening to their stories. One man told us how, with two hundred soldiers, he had hid in a Russian barn, and that a shrapnel shell flying through the window had exploded, killing and wounding nearly every one in his company. Another told how he had been on outpost duty with seven other men, and that the Russians had begun machine gun fire at night. All his comrades were either killed or wounded, and he said that although he was only wounded in the arm, he did not dare to get up because the Russians maintained a steady fire for four hours, and that all he could do was to hug the ground with the bullets whizzing over him, knowing that he was growing weaker and weaker every moment. Another had a most interesting experience. While in a shallow trench, he had been hit in the arm and in the leg. The hospital corps got him. The stretcher bearers were taking him back, when suddenly it got too hot for them, and they had to drop him and run for cover. The firing ceased, and, seeing he was alone, the soldier crawled over to a dead German and picked up his rifle. He was half sitting with this in his lap, when he saw some Russians coming. He raised the gun and they ran, and then he discovered they were hospital men. He was cursing his luck, when one of his comrades, a little fellow, who had come back to find him, discovered him. They traveled back to the German lines at intervals of ten minutes, the little fellow having to put him down to rest every so often. Then the doctor began to tell me something about the wounds he had seen as the result of this war.

"What I marvel at is," said Dr. Sanders, "that a man can go into the battleline and come out alive. The amount of lead and steel that is sent flying through the air is appalling. Of course we will not have any statistics on it until after the war is over, but everything I can learn from the wounded, and from the nature of their wounds—and I have men here hit five times—they must be using far, far more ammunition, proportionately of course, than in any war in the world's history. By the way, judging from my patients, the Russians cannot be using dum-dums. I have yet to find one in a man. For every three rifle ball wounds, we get two caused by shrapnel and about one quarter by fragments of bursting shells. We had a man who was hit by a piece of shell—and those fragments are terribly hot. It cut his throat to his ear, but it just stopped at the sheath of the artery. His life was saved by the minute distance. The Germans have the greatest confidence in us here. We have one man here who might have been sent on to another hospital five weeks ago. We didn't send him, though. It was almost a form of paranoia and honestly I dreaded sending that man away. I feared the nervous shock. Doctors who come from the front tell me that they have actually seen cases of men being killed, who only had a bullet wound in their hand. It was the nervous shock that killed them.

"You see those two Russians," and the doctor pointed towards two heavy-faced patients. "Well, they were in mortal terror that we were making them well so as to have more fun by killing them later. It took two weeks to convince them that they would not be put to death. They are pets here now."

The doctor was called away a moment, and as I watched him stride off, his sturdy figure carrying well the olive-drab of the United States army, I noticed again that the heads of the wounded turned, following him with thankful eyes, and it was not difficult longer to understand how these few Americans were able to come into the midst of strange Silesia, and transform that theater, where at night if they forget to shut the door, they can hear the ribald clamor from the cheap cabaret next door; it was not difficult to understand how they, all of them having their first experience with war, had developed an efficiency which the Germans had complimented by sending them the worst cases from the firing line. That sturdy, wide-shouldered man in army olive-drab personified something that made you thrill at the thought that you were an American.

But Dr. Sanders was not the last impression that I had of Gleiwitz, although he waved good-by to me at the train.

As I look back at Gleiwitz now, I can see the flat-floored theater with the gray nurses lighting lamps. The early twilight is coming through the windows. It is all quiet. In two hours the wounded will have supper, and here and there you can hear the deep breathing of sleep. In the lingering light the steel curtain has turned a vague gray and of the three flags, only our own is sharply defined. I see Sister Anna walking softly between the rows of gingham-spread cots, her kind, almost saintly face hallowed by the lamp in her hands. She is beckoning. She raises the lamp so that its pale reflection falls upon a bed. And there I see the boy from the Schleswig-Holstein village, who, with his chum, burned a Russian village, and whose ambition is to kill a hundred men; and the boy's face is buried in the pillow, his arm circling round it, like a baby asleep.

CHAPTER XV
THE SECRET BOOKS OF ENGLAND'S GENERAL STAFF

Of course Germany was prepared. Russia and France were prepared, not so sufficiently, of course, as Germany; yet with their reorganized armies both were judged powerful on land. England though was unprepared. Everybody knew that. The newspapers said so. Statesmen said so, Parliament admitted it. To be sure the British Navy for years was prepared. Winston Churchill announced that. But the empire was not ready for its army was not ready. It was a small army, a quarter of a million men, twice as large as the United States army. It was useful in the colonies. Everybody knew Tommy Atkins. Kipling did that. But for fighting on the continent of Europe was like venturing into a strange land for these soldiers of England's colonial domain. They were not ready. Any Englishman will tell you that. But the most amazing part of it all is that the British army was wonderfully prepared.

This will be merely a document of military wonders; diplomatic considerations will have no part in it. I promise you to abstain from the use of that tiresome word—neutrality.

The English army was ready to go to war. It was ready to go to war in Belgium. Its officers knew everything there was to be known about Belgium. They knew every square mile of Belgium's terrain. They knew what districts were best suited to strategical purposes. They knew what roads best to use for their artillery, what roads best could stand the heavy guns, what roads best could not. They knew every body of water in Belgium. They knew what water was fit to drink and what was not. They knew the current of every stream and the number of boats on it. They knew the number of houses in every Belgian village and the number of soldiers that could be billeted in those houses. They knew the location of every church steeple in Belgium, and whether or not to recommend it as an observation post. They knew what roads their troops could march on without being seen by the aviators of the enemy—what roads were hidden from the sky by the interlacing branches of the big trees. They even knew the best places for their own aviators to land. Every conceivable thing that a modern army should know about a future battleground the British army knew.... How do I know this?

Photographs obtained by Mr. Fox from the originals in the German War Office.

Pages and cover of the English staff books captured at the battle of Mons.

At the battle of Mons in northern France where something happened—the English say it was the French supports; the French blame it on the English—those wonderful soldiers of Great Britain, the professional soldiers, were cut to pieces. The Germans made many prisoners. In the kits of the captured British officers they found some interesting documents. They were books of a size that would fit in a coat pocket. They were about a quarter of an inch to an inch thick. They were printed on white paper and the covers were a light brown. They were finger-marked and muddy. They contained the most amazing collection of military information that any nation ever possessed for its army. Some books were marked *Confidential*; others bore the designation property of His Britannic Majesty's Government; all were prepared by the General Staff, of the English War Office.

All the books were dated 1914, brought right up to the minute. At the Great General Staff in Berlin I saw these books. I sat in Major von Herwarth's room one night and copied their contents until I was overwhelmed with their wonderful detail. I had wanted to take the books to my hotel. It was impossible. They were regarded by the Germans as being so valuable that they could not be taken from this officer's room. I induced the Staff to let me make photographs of the books, of their covers, pages and maps. And when I was finished the officer said to me, "We were very glad to get these books. We were very thankful. Because they are so much better than any information that our General Staff had about Belgium. In fact they are so good, these English books, that we at once had whole pages copied for the use of our officers in Belgium."

The Germans admitting English superiority on a military point! Germany, whom everybody thought was the best prepared nation in Europe, beaten at its own game. So valuable are these books regarded by the General Staff that they are locked in a safe.

As I digested the contents of these English books, I decided that if I had military power behind me, and these books in my pocket, that I could walk, ride, even fly in Belgium—without ever having been there before. I could always know precisely where I was at, where I could best be housed. I saw that each book begins with "roads," and reports the widths, surfacing and nature of the ground on either side of these roads. Every conceivable bit of information about the railroads in Belgium is between the covers, even down to the station masters at small places and the language each one speaks. Rivers, canals, bridges, dikes, have all been tested by the unprepared Englishmen. I thought now English cavalrymen were interested in learning that, "in the village of Eppeghen there are three forges." On another page I learned that "a kindly feeling exists for England because of a school for English children." In Tamines, "a large number of Germans are employed in the electrical work." On page 17 of Volume Two, I read "the farms ... are large solidly built structures, the barns usually being lofty with high eaves. The two storied dwelling houses enclose a barnyard. The Howitzer is the weapon of attack against them and the folds in the ground facilitates its use." Under "Monetary Contributions"; I read, "It may be necessary under certain conditions in an enemy's country to replace supply requisitions in kind by contributions in money."

And the English blame the Germans for their levies in captured cities. In the upper right hand corner of Volume Three, I saw what seemed to be a serial number—349. The other volumes also bore this number. Volume III declares itself to be a report on road, river and billeting conditions in Belgium; it gives information for the country between the river Meuse and the German frontier, going as far south as certain designated military lines. Glancing over this book, I saw on page 20 that the district near the German frontier was particularly suitable for billeting soldiers, that three or four men could be housed with every inhabitant except in Seraing and Liége where only two soldiers could be put up. On page 232 I learned that the billeting report had been reconnoitered every year from 1907 to 1913. This means that in the district covered by this book every dwelling place with a roof over it had been checked up every year for seven years. Thus were proper living accommodations for English soldiers in Belgium verified by the skilled War Office of London.

In Volume IV which gave all military routes for Belgium north and east of the line Brussels, Nivels, Namur, Liége, Vise, I read on page 13 that the reference maps dealing with the section "Brussels-Louvain" were those of the Belgian General Staff of a scale 1/40,000 but that sheets 31 and 31 of the English War Office were also available. Those English sheets were based on a reconnoiter of the entire district made in 1913 by the English. But more significant is it that English officers were referred to the 1/40,000 scale maps of the Belgian staff, which England obviously must at that time have had—as an asset of preparedness.

In the German General Staff I had a number of these English maps photographed. They were drawn by the British War Office and photo-etched by the Ordnance Survey office at Southampton 1912. As you may see from the accompanying illustration their detail is marvelous. Even orchards, ruins and wind mills are designated.

A Staff Officer in possession of one of these books would not have to reconnoiter Belgium. Referring to Volume IV, which devotes a good deal of space to the movement of troops, he would learn that delays in marching might be caused by "a steep ascent for half a mile out of Brussels on the road to Louvain." He would be comforted to know, though, that "there is a good field of fire and fine view from the roadway except between Cortenberg and Louvain where the view is reduced to one half mile. Troops could operate easily anywhere except in the hilly wooded country about Cortenberg to the south." If he wanted an observation post he would learn that at Cortenberg there was a good church steeple. A footnote reassures him that the roadway has been lined with trees which would afford in summer cover from aerial scouts.

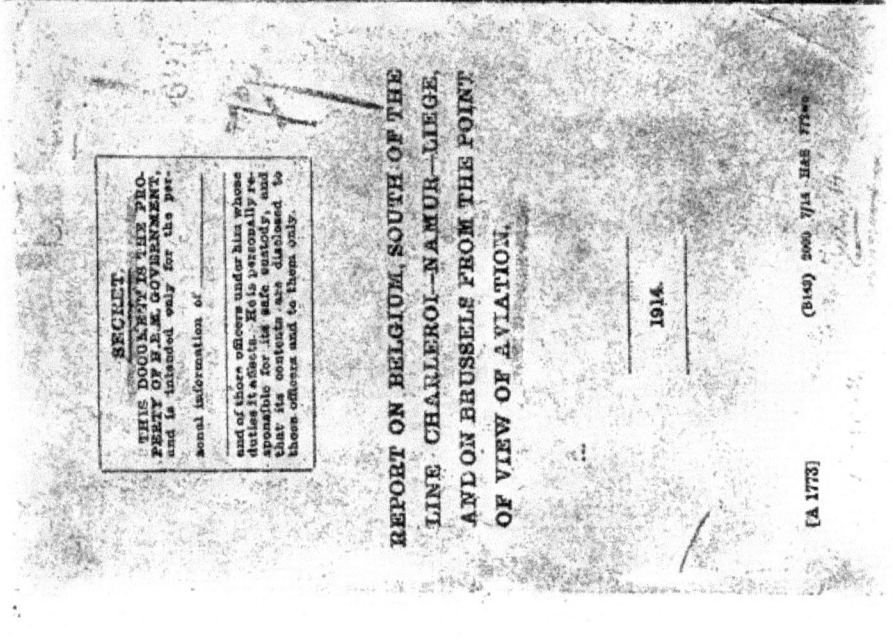

20

Between St. Leger and Ethe there appeared to be no good landing places.

For Ethe and Virton, *see* IV.

To the south and south-west of Arlon, and between Arlon and Marbehan, the country looked open, and no difficulty should be experienced in finding landing places.

VI.—LIÉGE—AYWAILLE—HOUFFALIZE—BASTOGNE.

Liége.

89. The country to the north of Liége is level and open, and that to the south is hilly and much wooded.

The most convenient landing place to the north is 2½ miles out, and on the east side of the Liège—Tongres road, where there is a large expanse of level, cultivated ground. It can be easily recognised from the air by the large cemetery, which lies close to its south-west corner. Wire communication, and a steam tram run along the Tongres road from Liège.

90. On the south there is a possible landing place on level cultivation just south-east of the old La Chartreuse Fort.

91. Five miles out on the east of the Aywaille road, and just north of the Fort d'Embourg, a very good covered landing place on grass could be prepared by the removal of some wire fences. It is completely covered from the south by the fort.

92. To the south-west towards Neuville and Rotheux the country is very broken and wooded. There is a good level cultivated landing place, however, about 1,500 yards south of the Fort de Boncelles; it is covered from the south by trees.

It could be improved by the removal of some wire fences. Wire communication with Liège exists.

93. About a mile south-east of Rotheux is a cultivated and fairly level field sheltered by trees. Landing might be difficult in northerly winds.

There are many workshops and factories in and around Liège, but there appeared to be none situated anywhere near a possible landing place.

Photographs obtained by Mr. Fox from the originals in the German War Office.

Cover and page of book taken from the pocket of British aviator brought down by Germans.

These books throw an interesting light upon the question of shelled churches. The Allies have accused the Germans and the Germans have accused the Allies of using church steeples for observation posts. Both armies have used them, both have shelled them. I make this statement because I saw the cathedral of Malines gaping with a hole that could only have come from a German gun—so did the lines run—and because at Houtem, I climbed the steeple of the church of the Annunciation of Mary the Virgin to a German post, and I make this statement because on page 176 of Volume III of these English books on Belgium, I read under "observation points" the names of no less than five churches for a single small district. I photographed this page; you may read the church for yourself.

Page 70 of Volume III assures an English officer that "a few infantry with sandbags could from the parapet of the barrage near the Belgium line hold the approach to Jalhay up to the valley." On page 91, reconnoitered in 1913, he learns that "the best way to attack Terwagne appears to be from the southwest where there is a good deal of dead ground and artillery co-operation could be obtained from Liveliet." On page 122 he learns that "an advance up the Liffe-Thynes valley supported by guns on the Sorraine ridge appears to be the best way of dealing with (two tactical situations which are called) A and B."

Perhaps some of the most interesting bits of military information are contained in the 1914 issue of secret Field Notes which is numbered A 1775. Using this book an English cavalry commander upon turning to page 32 and looking at (a) reads:

"Classes of persons in Belgium who might be useful as guides."

He sees that *Gardes champetres* are credited with knowing the rural districts well. They should be able to give the English army information about conditions of water, forage, horses, live stock and vehicles. The *gardes forestiers* know in detail the woods in their own districts. "Rural postmen, many who own bicycles and cycle repairers, especially the official repairers to the touring club of Belgium would be invaluable as guides." The English officers are advised to get hold of the drivers of tradesmen carts as they supply most of the villages from the towns, and would therefore know local roads well.

But to me the climax was reached when I read in this book of English field notes a description of the code in use by the Belgium army for writing orders. I shall quote in part exactly what was written. "The names of units are generally replaced by their initials; the numbers of regiments are written in large arabic figures; those of battalions, squadrons or artillery groups in Roman figures; those of company troops (pelotons) of cavalry and batteries in small arabic figures."

They give an example.

$$\frac{\text{EM }^2/_{\text{III}}}{10.}$$

They explain that this means in code, regimental headquarters and the second company of the third battalion of the Tenth Belgian Infantry of the line. Thus in code EM = Infantry headquarters; 2 = 2nd company; III = 3rd battalion; 10 = 10th infantry.

They give

$$\frac{2\text{ C.M.S.S}}{5\text{ D.A.}}$$

They explain that this means the second mechanical motor artillery ammunition column of the Fifth Division. Thus, in code, 2 C.M.S.S. = headquarters 2nd mechanical ammunition column; 5 D.A. = 5th Division, artillery.

And these are code orders of the Belgium army and the English General Staff knew about them before war was declared! And England was unprepared! These books tell me that England was beating the Germans at their own game.

Opening one book I saw a table that ran across two entire pages. This table was filled in the most intimate details regarding a single village.

In one of the road and river reports I read these words, "Data given by the Belgium government railroad cabinet on January 1st, 1912." Thus was the English officer assured of its accuracy. These are the figures that were given for the use of British troops in Belgium.

Locomotives	4,233
Coaches	8,001
Baggage cars	2,714
Goods wagons	86,562
Special wagons, (for oil, etc.)	2,418

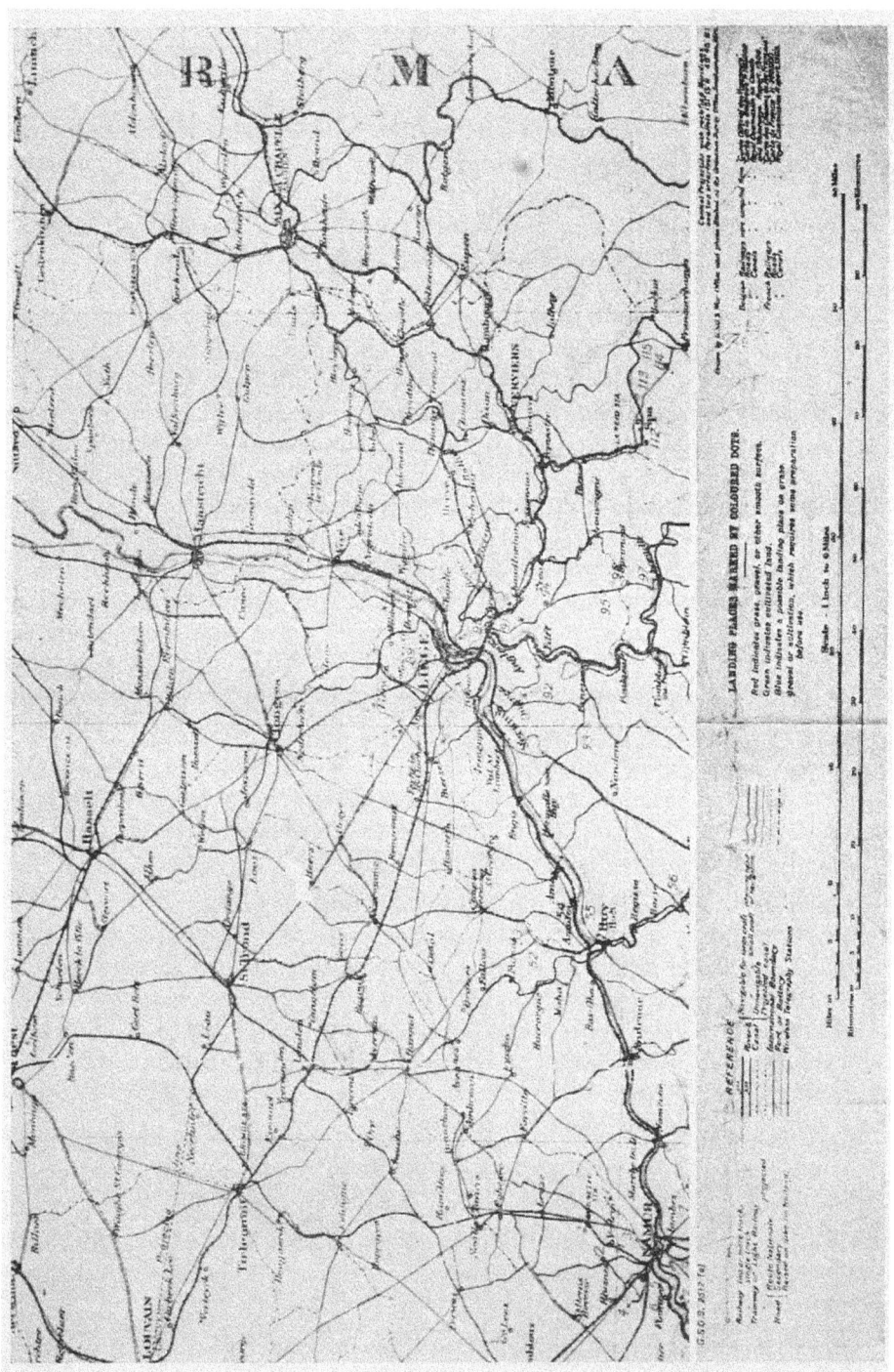

AVIATOR'S KEY MAP

Aviator's key map prepared by English war office.

Photographs obtained by Mr. Fox from the originals in the German War Office.

I think I have quoted enough material from these wonderful books to show the thoroughness with which the British soldiers were ready to fight in Belgium. Now the Germans have shot down many British aviators and on one of these men they found a book. It had the same brown paper cover as the road and river reports. It was of the same convenient pocket size. It had the same serial letter A for army, and it was numbered 1775. I saw this book in the General Staff. It is "A report on Belgium south of the line Charleroi, Namur, Liége and Brussels for aviators." I photographed pages 3, 6 and 20 of this book. Page 3 which began the information gave some interesting generalizations on the whole district. On page 6, dealing with Namur, I read that English aviators were told that the glaces of Fort d'Emine provided unlimited open cultivated ground suitable for landing purposes. In other words they were advised by the English War Office that it would be safe to land under the very guns of this Belgian fort. If they were flying in the Liége district they would read on page 20 that five miles out on the east of the Aywaille road they could prepare a very good landing place on grass by the simple removal of some wire fences. They were assured that from the south they would be completely covered by the Belgian guns of Fort d'Emibourg. In other words the British War Office was so well prepared, knew so exactly what it was doing that in July of 1914 it issued a book advising its aviators how to land in places where they would be covered by Belgian forts.

A map accompanied this aviation book. Let us see how this map was used. Examine this map around Liége. You will see numbers running from 89 to 94. An aviator flying over Liége consulting his map knows that each of these numbers has to do with a landing place. Let us suppose he selects 92.

Opening his book, until he finds the index number 92 he reads that "To the southwest towards Neuville and Rotheux the country is very broken and wooded. There is a good level cultivated landing place, however, about 1500 yards south of the Fort de Boucelles.... Where communication with Liége exists." To use this map a British aviator flying over the section south of the line Charleroi, Namur, Liége and Brussels, would see what point he was over and would then look it up by the index number on the map and in the book he would read whether it was wise to make a landing there and just what conditions he would meet.

Here are some bits verbatim from the book.

"In many cases the woods are so stunted and straggling that during winter, aerial observation of troops actually in them would probably be possible.... Somewhat soft after rain. Difficult for a landing.... The spa race course on the Francorchamps road is useless."

In this and other ways were the British aviators cautioned about using their aeroplanes in Belgium.

For the last few years we have all been hearing about the wonderful maps and information that Germany had of all the countries in Europe. No one, however, has ever seen any of these books; and no one has ever publicly quoted any of their contents. I believe they exist. I think, however, that the photographs printed here are the first permanent public records of the most confidential books in use by the army of a world power. I think they have a certain historical significance. At any rate, that England should possess them is amazing—England whom everybody but Germany thought was the least prepared of all.

CHAPTER XVI
THE FUTURE—PEACE OR WAR

Impressions gained during my talk with the 1914 choice for the Nobel Peace Prize—Professor Ludwig Stein

In The Hague the Temple of Peace is empty; all over the world ordnance factories are full. Since the day of that first convention in Geneva educated men have organized and pushed the international movement, which is called world peace. Is it a success or a failure?

At his home in Berlin, early in February, I talked with one of the leading men of this movement concerning these things. I asked Professor Ludwig Stein,—whose activities for world peace are well known in America, he having been chosen for the Nobel Peace prize of 1914 which was never awarded, he being formerly one of the three permanent members of the Bern Bureau for International Peace, he having been selected to present the famous declaration of peace to the late Edward the Seventh, whom the peace people called Edward the Peacemaker, he having worked side by side with Andrew Carnegie for the "ideal"—I asked him, could peace soon be made in this war? A deliberate man is Professor Stein, and he thought so long without replying that his personality impressed itself upon you before he had uttered a word—a strange combination of the dreamer and the man of to-day, a contrast of gentle eyes and grim jaw.

"At this time," he said, tapping his finger on the copper-topped smoking table in his study, "peace is impossible. President Wilson's endeavors are futile. Before a decisive result has been reached, peace cannot be thought of. Once Warsaw is captured, it is likely that Russia will make peace; or if not Warsaw, if a large really decisive battle is fought."

It seemed significant that such an apostle of peace as Professor Stein should have so completely given up all faith in the immediate efficacy of his movement. I asked him therefore if he considered it a failure.

"The peace movement," he said, "is like a fire department. If a few houses burn, or the conflagration spreads even over a number of blocks, the fire fighters are effective, but if a whole city burns, like the big Chicago fire, the fire department can do nothing. And if the whole world burns, what can the workers for peace do? Our movement is not strong enough; it is not big enough. For the Balkan war, the firemen were effective, they could confine the burning within that limited area, but when all Europe sprang up in flames, we failed." I mentioned to the Professor that

THE FUTURE—PEACE OR WAR

this was a new conception to the peace movement in America, the first admission from a peace-man that the power of the movement was to-day limited. I asked Professor Stein then if we were to think of the movement as being a limited success or was there any chance of it ever attaining something bigger?

"The task of the nineteenth century," he replied, "was to let national feeling grow subconsciously. In Prussia, Fichte, the first rector of the new Berlin University, made his famous 'Speeches for the German Nation.' Jahn preached 'German Unity.' Achim von Arnim collected German songs and war songs of German warriors. Even Schiller wrote in his later years of Germany as the heart and center of Europe, and began to feel more national than Goethe ever did. The idea grew and produced united Italy and united Germany. But this process of attaining national consciousness is not yet achieved. In America it is not nearly finished. It is a sociological, unconsciously pedagogical process. The time will come when nationalism will be thoroughly saturated in each country. When it does and not until then, states will see that it is impossible to produce and consume everything. That will be the beginning of international consciousness. Then the national spirit will become secondary to conscious internationalism. When that time comes, world peace will be possible."

I was going to ask Professor Stein how far off that day was but thought it best first to take up his point, the thorough establishment of the national idea being the beginning of world peace.

"As the national feeling grows," I asked him, "will not the goal for peace become always more remote? It seems to me that international consciousness is dependent upon the people of one country knowing the people of another. How can, for instance, the Russian peasant ever understand the customs and personality of say, the poor man in England? Because of geographical reasons they can never get into touch with one another; how then are the masses of the states of the world ever going to understand each other, and how without this understanding can there ever be world peace?"

Professor Stein believes that this barrier can be overcome.

"Modern science and fast steamers," he replied, "the wireless, and better international trade understanding are constantly bringing together all states. Through journalists, merchants, diplomats and extensive traveling on the part of the people of all countries, the inhabitants of all different parts of the world begin to know each other. A hundred years ago the Roumanian peasant did not know possibly that there was an Argentine. To-day, though, the Roumanian knows that the price he gets for his wheat depends upon what the Argentine farmers get for theirs. I believe that as science progresses and culture spreads over the world, that the geographical barrier to peace can be broken down. Consider Switzerland, it is the ideal. Three races, French, German and Italian, live within its walls, but they are held together by culture."

I pointed out that Switzerland was so small that the French, Germans and Italians had a chance to know and understand their different customs and personalities, and asked Professor Stein if culture was also holding together Austria-Hungary?

"Austria," he said, "is an exception. Politically it is necessary to have the monarchial symbol there, because only in a military state would it be possible for so many different races to live at peace with themselves. Austria is different from Switzerland because it is a crazy quilt of many different, uncultured, mostly illiterate, to some extent nomadic races."

The Professor, who is a great admirer of Herbert Spencer and whom Spencer said understood him better than any Continental thinker, thereupon mentioned the point that the famous Englishman had made.

"Spencer," he said, "wrote that instead of war, a competition in traffic and industry would take place between nations."

"But, Professor," I asked, "does not traffic and industry breed war; what caused this war? Was not commercial jealousy between England and Germany one of the vital causes of the war?"

He admitted that it was, and went on to say:

"After this war, the Englishman will look at his books, he will take his pencil in his hand and he will begin figuring. He will get up a balance sheet, and he will find that war does not pay. England is rational to excess. For years she has been the political clearing house of the world. She could in this way rule five hundred million people as long as these people were not striving for nationalism. But Germany attains its conscious nationalism, and asks herself, Why should I allow the thirty-eight million people of Great Britain, through their political clearing house, to have such a dominate influence on the affairs of the world? Wherefore in the last analysis, this war was caused by the thorough gaining of national consciousness that English diplomacy has no longer been able to retard. And under the industrial system of to-day, things are not done with papers passing through a clearing house, but with blood.

"I regard this war as an expression of the solidarity of the world on the minus side. It is an underground solidarity, but is having, for the moment, a negative influence because commerce is stopped. The United States is feeling it, it is holding up your country. It is holding up China which cannot get money for necessary improvements. But all this is working towards the conscious solidarity of the future, which will be expressed in a positive war; when fighting will be done not with cannons but with contracts; when not blood but ink will be wasted."

"You believe then, Professor," I asked, "that the day will come when there will be no war, when fighting actually will be done with ink? Suppose that day comes, will it be a good thing? Do you consider international peace a friend or an enemy to robust normal manhood? Do you think that war cleans out degenerate tendencies of peaceful civilization?"

Deciding that this was a metaphysical question, Professor Stein preferred not to answer it. He did though say this:

"In the Bible it says that the holy fire must be kept burning on the altar. It is a good thing for the world that there are idealists to keep the fire going. Men like

THE FUTURE—PEACE OR WAR

Carnegie, Rockefeller, and the puritan and quaker elements, they do their service to the world in this way. The world must have ideals. International peace is an ideal. It is like the point of a compass, the north star that the mariner sees, or the star of the desert. It points the way for those who want to go toward a certain goal. I say, that as an ideal, it is impossible of achievement, because the very way to it shows the people where they really want to go."

"But, Professor," I suggested, "if a nation has only ideals, it is going to get into trouble. I have heard it expressed that the peace movement has done the United States more harm than good. Will you, as one of its hardest workers, give some message to the people of America, on the status of international peace to-day and in the future?"

"Your country," he said, "has not yet attained its nationalism, but it is most wonderful, because it is not formed like Austria, of half civilized, uncultured races held together by the monarchical system, but because it is welding itself together from material, a large part of which was composed of the scum of Europe. I wonder that it has been able to make the strides towards nationalism, that it already has. No state in the world has progressed so far by comparison towards national consciousness as has America in so short a time. Up to now, America has been the student of Europe, but from now on, America will be the teacher. To-day doubly so; with the Panama Canal you are the forepost of the white race against the yellow. The geographical and moral position that your country holds, imposes upon it a great duty. It is to hold back the East. Your country cannot step aside from the yellow races. You must be prepared to cope with them."

"What, Professor! You are suggesting armament for the United States. Why! that is against every teaching of the peace propagandist in our country."

"If the people of the United States," stated Professor Stein deliberately, "believe that the peace movement is bound to save them from war, they have either totally misconstrued it, or they have been grossly misinformed. A nation must be prepared for war. If the rulers of a nation leave their country unprepared, they are guilty of criminal neglect. In China its four hundred millions of people are unprepared, and are therefore at the mercy of a few million Japanese who are prepared. That is because in this generation might is right, and all that we workers for peace can do, without injuring our states, is to face the facts of this generation, be prepared for war, if war there is to be, and keep on working for our ideal. Anything else is a dream."

"But, Professor," I remarked, "that is not the peace idea as it has been spread broadcast in America. Those who believe in the movement, think that the peace societies of our country can keep us out of war. What you have just said disagrees with Andrew Carnegie's peace utterances in the United States. Would you mind telling me the difference between your viewpoint and Mr. Carnegie's?"

"I shall be glad to do so," replied Professor Stein. "Mr. Carnegie looks at the peace movement from a puritanical viewpoint. He has interpreted the biblical text of turning the sword into a plow-share literally as applying to the present day. I believe that swords will be turned into plow shares, but not in our generation.

That will come to pass, not because it is in the Bible, but because the imminent logic of history will bring it about. Eventually the imminent logic of history will create international peace. The puritanical workers for peace believe that because it is written in the Bible that all men are born equal, they should try to equalize mankind to-day. It will take about a hundred years to educate and solidify the white race alone. It will take about ten thousand years, let us say, to educate all the races of the world and achieve a world brotherhood. The great mistake that is made is in thinking that the ideals of the Bible are possible to-day. They are utterly impossible."

I then asked Professor Stein to summarize his opinions for me. "I have read your paper," I said, "written before the war, on Cosmopolitism, National, State and International Compromise. There is one point I want to ask you about. You wrote—these are not your exact words, Professor—'What poets and philosophers have dreamed of, and what the Catholic Church has in some respects already realized: One shepherd and one herd! that will be the state of Europe in times coming'—What did you mean, Professor, by that phrase 'One shepherd and one herd'? Did you mean to convey that one state powerfully armed would be a sort of international policeman, strong enough to keep the peace among other nations? Did you have in mind a Germany whose mission would be to shepherd the people of the world?"

"Absolutely not," replied Professor Stein; "by one shepherd I meant the imperialism of the white race. White imperialism will divide the world between the white states. The Western European and American cultural systems will rule. My idea is not the United States of Europe, but the united cultural system of the white race."

"And when will that be possible, Professor?"

"As soon as nationalism has been thoroughly saturated, and conscious internationalism has been achieved, and that will probably be within a hundred years."

"And meanwhile?" I asked.

"ALAS! THE WORLD OF TO-DAY CANNOT BE RULED WITH OIL OF ROSES, BUT ONLY WITH BLOOD."

THE END.

Lector House believes that a society develops through a two-fold approach of continuous learning and adaptation, which is derived from the study of classic literary works spread across the historic timeline of literature records. Therefore, we aim at reviving, repairing and redeveloping all those inaccessible or damaged but historically as well as culturally important literature across subjects so that the future generations may have an opportunity to study and learn from past works to embark upon a journey of creating a better future.

This book is a result of an effort made by Lector House towards making a contribution to the preservation and repair of original ancient works which might hold historical significance to the approach of continuous learning across subjects.

HAPPY READING & LEARNING!

LECTOR HOUSE LLP
E-MAIL: lectorpublishing@gmail.com

Lightning Source UK Ltd.
Milton Keynes UK
UKHW010646090820
367908UK00002B/432